NORTHSTAR

Focus on Reading and Writing

High Intermediate

Andrew K. English

Laura Monahon English

SERIES EDITORS
Frances Boyd
Carol Numrich

LONGMAN

NorthStar: Focus on Reading and Writing, High Intermediate

Pearson Education, 10 Bank Street, White Plains, NY 10606

Editorial director: Allen Ascher
Senior acquisitions editor: Louisa Hellegers
Director of design and production: Rhea Banker
Development editor: Penny Laporte
Production manager: Marie McNamara
Managing editor: Linda Moser
Senior production editor: Lynn Contrucci
Manufacturing supervisor: Edith Pullman
Photo research: Diana Nott
Cover design: Rhea Banker
Cover illustration: Robert Delaunay's *Circular Forms, Sun No. 2,*
    1912-1913. Giraudon/Art Resource, NY. L&M Services B.V.
    Amsterdam 970902
Text design and composition: Delgado Design, Inc.
Text credits: See page xiii
Photo and art credits: See page xiv

Library of Congress Cataloging-in-Publication Data

English, Andrew K.
    NorthStar : Focus on reading and writing, high
intermediate/Andrew K. English, Laura Monahon English
           p.   cm. — (NorthStar)

    ISBN 0-201-84669-1 (pbk.)

    1. English language—Textbooks for foreign speakers. 2. Reading
comprehension—Problems, exercises, etc. 3. Report writing—
Problems, exercises, etc. I. English, Andrew II. Title III. Series.

PE1128.E58 1998   97-43261

428.6'4—dc21   CIP

    5 6 7 8 9 10—RTN—03 02 01 00

For our parents who raised us with books and for our little masterpiece of calipedia, Sam.

Nandy
Bet gorgaci

Re

It Feels so good to win!

There she goes
There it is
Here it is
I'm stuck
It's stuck

Relationship

20 →
80 → 64.000
5c → 40.000

She raised me
I want to save money to special things.
She really does love him
Really

How was it?
I take off My glasses
excuse me
You have the wrong number
which one was that
you're yelling again
I started dating
you're wasting
They didn't charge me
This is Fantastic. Fantastic.
It's a huge problem
It's so cozy
It's started my Period.
May I come in?
let me ask you something
who's making the request
They're Towing my car.
where is that stuff
It's gone
I'd like it
I'd like to return back.
I'd like to return

I washed no luck
I have some calls
to returns
I'm getting old.
I didn't expect to see
will you charge Me?
They didn't charge me.
It's a huge problem
It has started my Period.
who's making the request
It feels so good to win
She raised me
They're Towing my car.
It's stuck
I'm stuck
You have the wrong number.
I really do love him.
She really does love him.
Take off your glasses.
I started dating with him
when I came United States
I tried to break off this
relationship
We'd never had sex
relationship
She put her baby in Trash bag,
I was very emotional.

CONTENTS

election
I'm voting
i governer
We choose evey two year

INTRODUCTION

NorthStar is an innovative four-level, integrated skills series for learners of English as a Second or Foreign Language. The series is divided into two strands: listening/speaking and reading/writing. There are four books in each strand, taking students from the Basic to the Advanced level. The two books at each level explore different aspects of the same contemporary themes, which allows for reinforcement of both vocabulary and grammatical structures. Each strand and each book can also function independently as a skills course built on high-interest thematic content.

NorthStar is designed to work alongside Addison Wesley Longman's *Focus on Grammar* series, and students are referred directly to *Focus on Grammar* for further practice and detailed grammatical explanations.

NorthStar is written for students with academic as well as personal language goals, for those who want to learn English while exploring enjoyable, intellectually challenging themes.

NORTHSTAR'S PURPOSE

The *NorthStar* series grows out of our experience as teachers and curriculum designers, current research in second-language acquisition and pedagogy, as well as our beliefs about language teaching. It is based on five principles.

Principle One: In language learning, making meaning is all-important. The more profoundly students are stimulated intellectually and emotionally by what goes on in class, the more language they will use and retain. One way that classroom teachers can engage students in making meaning is by organizing language study thematically.

We have tried to identify themes that are up-to-date, sophisticated, and varied in tone—some lighter, some more serious—on ideas and issues of wide concern. The forty themes in *NorthStar* provide stimulating topics for the readings and the listening selections, including why people like dangerous sports, the effect of food on mood, an Olympic swimmer's fight against AIDS, experimental punishments for juvenile offenders, people's relationships with their cars, philanthropy, emotional intelligence, privacy in the workplace, and the influence of arts education on brain development.

Each corresponding unit of the integrated skills books explores two distinct topics related to a single theme as the chart below illustrates.

Theme	Listening/Speaking Topic	Reading/Writing Topic
Insects	Offbeat professor fails at breeding pests, then reflects on experience	Extract adapted Kafka's "The Metamorphosis"
Personality	Shyness, a personal and cultural view	Definition of, criteria for, success

Principle Two: Second-language learners, particularly adults, need and want to learn both the form and content of the language. To accomplish this, it is useful to integrate language skills with the study of grammar, vocabulary, and American culture.

In *NorthStar*, we have integrated the skills in two strands: listening/speaking and reading/ writing. Further, each thematic unit integrates the study of a grammatical point with related vocabulary and cultural information. When skills are integrated, language use inside of the classroom more closely mimics language use outside of the classroom. This motivates students. At the same time, the focus can shift back and forth from what is said to how it is said to the relationship between the two. Students are apt to use more of their senses, more of themselves. What goes on in the classroom can also appeal to a greater variety of learning styles. Gradually, the integrated-skills approach narrows the gap between the ideas and feelings students want to express in speaking and writing and their present level of English proficiency.

The link between the listening/speaking and reading/writing strands is close enough to allow students to explore the themes and review grammar and reinforce vocabulary, yet it is distinct enough to sustain their interest. Also, language levels and grammar points in *NorthStar* are keyed to Addison Wesley Longman's *Focus on Grammar* series.

Principle Three: Both teachers and students need to be active learners. Teachers must encourage students to go beyond whatever level they have reached.

With this principle in mind, we have tried to make the exercises creative, active, and varied. Several activities call for considered opinion and critical thinking. Also, the exercises offer students many opportunities for individual reflection, pair- and small-group learning, as well as out-of-class assignments for review and research. An answer key is printed on perfo-

rated pages in the back of each book so the teacher or students can remove it. A teacher's manual, which accompanies each book, features ideas and tips for tailoring the material to individual groups of students, planning the lessons, managing the class, and assessing students' progress.

Principle Four: Feedback is essential for language learners and teachers. If students are to become better able to express themselves in English, they need a response to both what they are expressing and how they are expressing it.

NorthStar's exercises offer multiple opportunities for oral and written feedback from fellow students and from the teacher. A number of open-ended opinion and inference exercises invite students to share and discuss their answers. In information gap, fieldwork, and presentation activities, students must present and solicit information and opinions from their peers as well as members of their communities. Throughout these activities, teachers may offer feedback on the form and content of students' language, sometimes on the spot and sometimes via audio/video recordings or notes.

Principle Five: The quality of relationships among the students and between the students and teacher is important, particularly in a language class where students are asked to express themselves on issues and ideas.

The information and activities in *NorthStar* promote genuine interaction, acceptance of differences, and authentic communication. By building skills and exploring ideas, the exercises help students participate in discussions and write essays of an increasingly more complex and sophisticated nature.

DESIGN OF THE UNITS

For clarity and ease of use, the listening/speaking and reading/writing strands follow the same unit outline given below. Each unit contains from 5 to 8 hours of classroom material. Teachers can customize the units by assigning some exercises for homework and/or skipping others. Exercises in sections 1–4 are essential for comprehension of the topic, while teachers may want to select among the activities in sections 5–7.

1. Approaching the Topic

A warm-up, these activities introduce students to the general context for listening or reading and get them personally connected to the topic. Typically, students might react to a visual image, describe a personal experience, or give an opinion orally or in writing.

2. Preparing to Listen/Preparing to Read

In this section, students are introduced to information and language to help them comprehend the specific tape or text they will study. They might read and react to a paragraph framing the topic, prioritize factors, or take a general-knowledge quiz and share information. In the vocabulary section, students work with words and expressions selected to help them with comprehension.

3. Listening One/Reading One

This sequence of four exercises guides students to listen or read with understanding and enjoyment by practicing the skills of (a) prediction, (b) comprehension of main ideas, (c) comprehension of details, and (d) inference. In activities of increasing detail and complexity, students learn to grasp and interpret meaning. The sequence culminates in an inference exercise that gets students to listen and read between the lines.

4. Listening Two/Reading Two

Here students work with a tape or text that builds on ideas from the first listening/reading. This second tape or text contrasts with the first in viewpoint, genre, and/or tone.

Activities ask students to explicitly relate the two pieces, consider consequences, distinguish and express points of view. In these exercises, students can attain a deeper understanding of the topic.

5. Reviewing Language

These exercises help students explore, review, and play with language from both of the selections. Using the thematic context, students focus on language: pronunciation, word forms, prefixes and suffixes, word domains, idiomatic expressions, analogies. The listening/speaking strand stresses oral exercises, while the reading/writing strand focuses on written responses.

6. Skills for Expression

Here students practice related grammar points across the theme in both topics. The grammar is practiced orally in the listening/speaking strand, and in writing in the reading/writing strand. For additional practice, teachers can turn to Addison Wesley Longman's *Focus on Grammar*, to which *NorthStar* is keyed by level and grammar points. In the Style section, students practice functions (listening/speaking) or rhetorical styles (reading/writing) that prepare them to express ideas on a higher level. Within each unit, students are led from controlled to freer practice of productive skills.

7. On Your Own

These activities ask students to apply the content, language, grammar, and style they have practiced in the unit. The exercises elicit a higher level of speaking or writing than students were capable of at the start of the unit. Speaking topics include role plays, surveys, presentations, and experiments. Writing topics include paragraphs, letters, summaries, and academic essays.

In Fieldwork, the second part of On Your Own, students go outside of the classroom, using their knowledge and skills to gather data from personal interviews, library research, and telephone or Internet research. They report and reflect on the data in oral or written presentations to the class.

AN INVITATION

We think of a good textbook as a musical score or a movie script: It tells you the moves and roughly how quickly and in what sequence to make them. But until you and your students bring it to life, a book is silent and static, a mere possibility. We hope that *NorthStar* orients, guides, and interests you as teachers.

It is our hope that the *NorthStar* series stimulates your students' thinking, which in turn stimulates their language learning, and that they will have many opportunities to reflect on the viewpoints of journalists, commentators, researchers, other students, and people in the community. Further, we hope that *NorthStar* guides them to develop their own viewpoint on the many and varied themes encompassed by this series.

We welcome your comments and questions. Please send them to us at the publisher:

Frances Boyd and Carol Numrich, Editors
NorthStar
Addison Wesley Longman
10 Bank Street
White Plains, NY 10606-1951
or, by e-mail at:
aw/elt@awl.com

ACKNOWLEDGMENTS

Writing a textbook, as with any writing process, is a process filled with peaks, valleys, and roads leading to territories unknown. Fortunately we had wonderful guides throughout this process whose expertise and creativity are woven into every page of this book. To these people we owe great thanks. First, to Allen Ascher for bringing this project to us and having confidence in us. Second, to Carol Numrich, our sage, for her outstanding patience, expertise, and most importantly her unending support and enthusiasm. Words truly cannot express what a joy and privilege it was to work with her. Third, to our editor Penny Laporte for her humor in the late stages of editing (when humor is a requirement) and for her dedication to her craft. We would also like to thank Diana Nott for her enthusiastic support and help researching the artscript in the eleventh hour. Last, but by all means not least, we owe a great deal of thanks to our students at Roxbury Community College and Boston University for their feedback, cooperation, and inspiration during the piloting process.

AKE and LME

Text Credits

For permission to use the selections reprinted in this book, the authors are grateful to the following publishers and copyright holders:

Photo and Art Credits

Page 1, Rueters/Win Mcnamee, Archive Photos. **Page 3**, David Shopper Photography, Inc., Stock Boston. **Page 6**, Dusan Petricic. **Page 26**, Dusan Petricic. **Page 27**, Ron Chironna. **Page 32**, © Barrie Maguire. **Page 33**, reprinted with permission of Macmillan USA, a Simon & Schuster Macmillan Company, from *Macmillan Visual Almanac*, Bruce S. Glassman, Editor. Text by Jenny Tessar. Computer Graphics by David C. Bell. A Blackbirch Press Book. Copyright © 1996 by Blackbirch Press. **Page 38**, © David Woo, Stock Boston. **Page 55**, Micheal Newman/PhotoEdit. **Page 63**, compliments of Wisconsin Center for Film and Theater Reasearch. **Page 77**, Photos courtesy of American Red Cross. **Page 79**, Len Shalansky. **Page 84**, Brown Brothers, Sterling, Pennsyvania. **Page 97**, Photo courtesy of *Recycling Today* magazine. **Page 102**, Dusan Petricic. **Page 106**, A. Stegmeyer Photography. Photo courtesy of Solar Survival Architecture. **Page 123**, Frank Fournier/Contact Press Images. **Page 126**, Len Shalansky. **Page 128**, from *It's Our World Too!* by Phillip Hoose. Copyright © 1993 by Phillip Hoose. Photo reprinted with permission from Little, Brown and Company. **Page 153**, © Pat Clear Photography/PhotoEdit. **Page 162**, © Barrie Maguire. **Page 179**, courtesy of NASA, Lyndon B. Johnson Space Center. **Page 191**, *Newsweek* graphic by Dixon Rohr and Christoph Blumrich. © 1996, Newsweek, Inc. All rights reserved. Reprinted by permission. **Page 207**, (*left*) Gus Bower/Compliments of IMG; (*middle*) printed with permission from Robert Woolmington, photographer; (*right*) distributed by Los Angeles Times Syndicate. Photo courtesy of Farrar, Straus and Giroux. **Page 211**, courtesy of the Statue of Liberty National Monument. **Page 231**, © Bill Layne. **Page 233**, Don Punchatz, first appeared in *Boy's Life* magazine. **Page 235**, Courtesy of Intergraph. **Page 242**, courtesy of the Thoreau Society.

UNTRUTH AND CONSEQUENCES

1 APPROACHING THE TOPIC

high-profile.
court cases

A. PREDICTING

1. Look at the photograph and the title of the unit. Take some notes about the picture. What does it show? What is happening? How do the people in the picture feel? What do you think "Untruth and Consequences" refers to? What do you think this unit will be about?

2. Work in a small group. Discuss the following questions: Where do people learn about news? Who decides what is news and what is not news? What news source do you most frequently use—newspapers, magazines, television, radio? Why?

B. SHARING INFORMATION

Work in a small group. Read the following quotations describing news. What do you think they mean? Circle the most appropriate interpretations for quotes 1 and 2. Then write your own interpretation of quotes 3 and 4. Discuss your answers with the group. Do you agree with any of these quotations? Why or why not?

1. "When a dog bites a man, that is not news; but when a man bites a dog, that is news."   —Leo Rosten, political scientist and author

   a. News is only about exciting or unusual events.

   b. News is only interesting when an animal is involved.

2. "A dog fight in Brooklyn [New York] is bigger than a revolution in China."   —*Brooklyn Eagle* (newspaper)

   a. News about the United States is always more newsworthy than international news.

   b. People are more interested in local news than international news even when the international news is more newsworthy.

3. "Good news isn't news. Bad news is news."

                                        —Henry Luce, founder of *Time Magazine*

   This means:

   _____

4. "What is news? You know what news is? News is what (you) news directors interpret it as. News is what we at CNN interpret it as. The people of this country see the news that we think they oughta[1] see. And quite frankly, a lot of that decision is geared to what's gonna[2] keep them interested, keep them at your station."

                                        —Ted Turner, founder of CNN
                                        (Cable News Network)

   This means:

   _____

   _____

   [1] *oughta:* ought to
   [2] *gonna:* going to

PREPARING TO READ

A. BACKGROUND

1 *Read this information.*

News is everywhere and serves many different functions. The news gives instant coverage of important events. News also provides facts and information. In addition, news is business: a way to make money by selling advertising and/or newspapers and magazines. Sometimes news is propaganda or disinformation: a way to control a population. But whatever news is, it is all around us. You can't escape it. Every day we are bombarded by information: newspapers, magazines, television, and the Internet.

"News" does not always mean something that is unquestionably true. Although the news *seems* to be based on facts, these facts are interpreted and reported the way the media chooses to report them. For example, some information that appears as news is really only speculation or theories formed by the reporters. Furthermore, many journalists and reporters sensationalize or dramatize a news event in order to make a story more interesting. Unfortunately, sensationalism often bends the truth and causes anguish to the people it victimizes. Therefore, as consumers of news we must learn to think critically about the news, the media, and what the truth is.

2 *The news functions in many different ways. In your experience, can you recall the news functioning in any of the following ways? Complete the chart with your own examples. Share your examples in small groups.*

FUNCTION OF NEWS	EXAMPLES
To give instant coverage of important events	
To provide facts	
To make money for the newpaper or radio/television station	
To spread propaganda or disinformation	
To sensationalize events	

avoid →
دور کردن ، حذف ، دار کردن

B. VOCABULARY FOR COMPREHENSION

Work with a partner and guess the meaning of the vocabulary words.
Use your dictionary if necessary. Check (✔) the category or categories
you associate with each word. The first one has been done for you.

newspaper
Internet
magazine
Tv etc.

VOCABULARY WORDS	PRINT MEDIA	TELEVISION	PEOPLE IN THE NEWS
Reporters	✔	✔	
Affiliates local stations		✓	
Anchors		✓	
Celebrities	✓	✓	
Columnists	✓		
Correspondents	✓	✓	
Editors	✓	✓	
Heroes		✓	
High-profile personalities		✓	✓
Journalists	✓		
Magazines	✓		
Movie stars		✓	✓
Networks		✓	
Senators			✓
Tabloids	✓		

glob
people

2) *Appendix A1–A7*
N. spages 11–16
homework
Azar P. 34–44 all
hand in ex. 12:44

3 READING ONE: Peeping Tom[1] Journalism

A. INTRODUCING THE TOPIC

Read the first three paragraphs. Work with a partner to answer and discuss the questions in paragraph 3. Then read the rest of the article.

Peer Reading writing

Peeping Tom Journalism

BY NANCY DAY

(from *Sensational TV—Trash or Journalism*)

1   Reporters constantly struggle with what and how much to tell. Sometimes the facts are clear. Other times, journalists must rely on their own judgment.

2   A retired minister[2] in a small town does not return from a fishing trip. Police find his car parked about halfway to the lake. It is locked and undamaged. In it they find a half-eaten ham sandwich, fishing tackle, a gun with one shell fired, and a copy of *Penthouse*

---

[1] *Peeping Tom*: a person who secretly watches others
[2] *minister*: a person who performs religious functions in a Protestant church

(a magazine that contains pictures of naked women). The minister is missing. You're the reporter and your story is due.

3   What do you report? Suppose the minister just went for a walk? Do you risk embarrassment and mention the magazine? Is the gun important? Should you propose any theories about what might have happened?

4   The reporter who actually faced these decisions decided to mention the gun, the sandwich, the fishing tackle, and the condition of the car, but not the magazine or any speculation. The minister's body was later found. He had been killed by a hitchhiker, who had left the magazine in the minister's car.

5   In the old days, reporters knew politicians (including presidents) who slept around, movie stars who were gay, and public figures who used drugs or abused alcohol. They just kept it to themselves. Now, at least in part because the public seems to have an endless hunger for it, reporters sometimes cover these aspects of celebrities' lives more than any other.

6   Some of the interest can be justified on the basis that character affects how people perform their jobs. But what if the information isn't relevant? For example, does the public need to know that a senator is gay? When a famous person dies, does the public have a right to all the details? Should the public know which public figures are unfaithful to their spouses? Are these things we need to know or just things we want to know?

7   When Gennifer Flowers alleged a twelve-year affair with President Bill Clinton, she first sold the story to the tabloid *Star*. CNN reported the story and so did the networks and the major newspapers and news magazines. Peter Jennings, anchor for ABC's[3] "World News Tonight," was against broadcasting the Flowers story without further reporting by ABC correspondents, but says, "it was made clear to [me] . . . that if you didn't go with the story, every [ABC] affiliate in the country would look up and say, 'What the hell's going on in this place? Don't they know a story when they see it?'"

8   Some stories receive such wide visibility that to ignore them is to "play ostrich man," says Shelby Coffey, editor of *The Los Angeles Times*. "You have to give your readers some perspective on the information they are getting."

9   Scrutiny may be the price one pays for fame. But what about relatives of celebrities? Are they fair game too? And what about the average person?

10   When Sara Jane Moore pointed a gun at President Ford, a man in the crowd knocked her hand, deflecting the shot. The man, Oliver W. Sipple, became an instant hero. He was thirty-three years old and a Marine veteran. What else did the public want or need to know about

---

[3] *ABC:* American Broadcasting Companies, Inc.; a major television network in the United States

him? Initial reports did not mention Sipple's sexual orientation. But when a San Francisco news columnist said that local gay leaders were proud of Sipple's actions, other papers began to report it. Sipple sued the columnist and several newspapers for invading his privacy. He said that he suffered "great mental anguish, embarrassment and humiliation." Lawyers argued that by becoming involved in an event of worldwide importance, Sipple had given up his right to privacy because the public has a legitimate interest in his activity.

11   Rosa Lopez was a maid working quietly and anonymously until she became a key witness in the O. J. Simpson trial.[4] Suddenly, she was the focus of intense scrutiny. Lopez was hounded by cameras and reporters everywhere she went. Her every move was analyzed. She eventually returned to her native country to escape the pressure, only to find that the media followed her there.

12   How many witnesses will come forward in the future, knowing what kind of treatment awaits them? Do people who accidentally find themselves involved in such high-profile cases have rights, or do we deserve to know everything about them?

---

[4] O. J. Simpson is a famous former football player, actor, and sportscaster who was accused of killing his ex-wife and a male friend of hers. His trial was followed closely by the media. He eventually was found not guilty in criminal court but guilty in civil court.

B. READING FOR MAIN IDEAS

"Peeping Tom Journalism" can be divided into four main ideas. What does the reading say about each idea? Circle the letter of the sentence that gives the best summary.

1. Reporting of facts

　a. Journalists sometimes use their own judgment and leave out certain facts when reporting a story.

　b. Journalists usually report all the facts that they know about a story.

2. Reporting about famous people

　a. In the old days, certain facts about celebrities were held back from the public. This is not always the case today.

　b. In the old days, certain facts about celebrities were held back from the public. This is still the case today.

3. Choosing to report all stories

    a. The decision to report or not report a story is based only on the reporter's judgment.

    b. The decision to report or not report a story is influenced by many factors. The reporter's opinion is just one of these factors.

4. Right to privacy

    a. All people agree that the public has a right to know about a famous person's life.

    b. Some people believe that you lose the right to privacy when you are famous. Others disagree.

C. READING FOR DETAILS

Find examples or details the author uses to support each of the four main ideas. Complete the chart with the supporting details. The first one has been done for you.

MAIN IDEA	EXAMPLE GIVEN TO SUPPORT THE MAIN IDEA
1. Reporting of facts	case of the retired minister
2. Reporting about famous people	Politicians
3. Choosing to report all stories	Gennifer Flowers
4. Right to privacy	oliver sipple, Rose lopez

D. READING BETWEEN THE LINES

The reading raises some interesting questions about one's right to privacy. Would the author agree or disagree with each of the following statements? Check (✔) your answer. (Notice that the author addresses each of these issues but does not actually state her opinion. Nevertheless, through careful reading it is possible to infer what her opinion is.)

When you are finished, discuss your answers with a partner. If necessary, refer back to the text to support your reasons for believing the author would agree or disagree with each statement.

1. The public has the right to know about the sexual preferences of politicians.

   writer agrees _____   writer disagrees_____

2. When a famous person dies, the public has a right to know all the details of the person's life and death.

   writer agrees _____   writer disagrees_____

3. The public should know which public figures are unfaithful to their spouses.

   writer agrees _____   writer disagrees_____

4. An average person who suddenly becomes the focus of unwanted media attention has no right to privacy.

   writer agrees _____   writer disagrees _____

5. It was easier to be a reporter in "the old days."

   writer agrees _____   writer disagrees _____

6. The Gennifer Flowers story should not have been covered by CNN and the other major networks.

   writer agrees _____   writer disagrees _____

4 READING TWO: Focus on Bomb Suspect Brings Tears and a Plea

A. EXPANDING THE TOPIC

Before you read "Focus on Bomb Suspect Brings Tears and a Plea," read this background information about the Richard Jewell case. Work in a small group and discuss the questions that follow.

On July 27, 1996, during one of the first evening celebrations held at the Olympics in Atlanta, Georgia, a bomb exploded in Centennial Olympic Park.[1] The bomb killed one person and injured 111 others. Richard Jewell, a security guard at the park who discovered the bomb and helped numerous people to safety, was at first considered a hero of the tragic incident. Later, he was accused of putting the bomb there. The media then surrounded him and scrutinized his every action: past and present. They left nothing about his personal life untouched. He was later cleared of any suspicions, but his life would never be the same.

1. In your opinion, was it legitimate for the reporters to scrutinize and make speculations about Richard Jewell?

2. How should the media have conducted the investigation?

---

[1] *Centennial Olympic Park:* a large park and central meeting place located in Atlanta, Georgia, site of the 1996 Summer Olympic Games

Focus on Bomb Suspect Brings Tears and a Plea

By Rick Bragg (from *The New York Times*)

1   Barbara Jewell stared into the unblinking eyes of the television cameras she has come to despise and spoke in tears today of how life had changed for her son, Richard, since he was named a month ago as a suspect in the bombing in Centennial Olympic Park. "Now my son has no real life," said Mrs. Jewell, a little gray-haired woman, speaking out for the first time since her 33-year-old son was suspected—but never arrested or charged—in the bombing that killed one person and injured 111 others.

2   "He is a prisoner in my home," Mrs. Jewell said at a news conference this afternoon. "He cannot work. He cannot know any type of normal life. He can only sit and wait for this nightmare to end."

3   She begged President Clinton to clear her son's name and asked reporters to spread the word that

her son was innocent of any wrongdoing in the July 27 bombing. After her tearful request, her son's lawyers said they would file civil lawsuits over reporting on the case.

4   Richard A. Jewell, a security guard in Centennial Olympic Park and a former sheriff's deputy,[2] was at first hailed as a hero for discovering the bomb and helping to clear people from the area. Then news accounts, including a special edition of the *Atlanta Journal*,[3] named him as a suspect. Since then, television and news executives have repeatedly debated the intense attention focused on Mr. Jewell, with most deciding that too many people knew he was a suspect for his name to be avoided or suppressed.

5   "Last week, a close family friend of twenty-nine years took seriously ill," Mrs. Jewell said. "While he was on his deathbed, because Richard did not want to subject him to the world attention of the media, he did not go see him. Richard was not able to see his friend before he died." Her son did go to the funeral home after his friend died, she said. "When we returned from the funeral home, for the first time I saw my son sobbing," Mrs. Jewell said, breaking into tears herself as she recounted the story. He said, "Mama, everybody was looking."

6   "I do not think any of you can even begin to imagine what our lives are like. Richard is not a murderer," said Mrs. Jewell, an insurance claims coordinator. But, she said, "He has been convicted in the court of public opinion."

7   Meanwhile, the Jewells continue to be besieged by reporters. "They have taken all privacy from us," Mrs. Jewell said. "They have taken all peace. They have rented an apartment which faces our home in order to keep their cameras trained on us around the clock. They watch and photograph everything we do. We wake up to photographers, we go to sleep with photographers. We cannot look out the windows. We cannot walk our dogs without being followed down the sidewalk."

8   Mrs. Jewell said she was not just saddened and hurt by the ordeal, but was also angry.

---

[2] *sheriff's deputy:* law enforcer
[3] *Atlanta Journal:* newspaper

Complete the right side of the chart showing how Richard Jewell's life changed after he was named a suspect in the bombing.

BEFORE THE BOMBING	AFTER THE BOMBING
1. Worked as a security guard	1. _____
2. Visited friends	2. He can't
3. Went out; walked his dogs	3. He can't
4. Could have a private life	4. No

B. LINKING READINGS ONE AND TWO

Imagine you are Barbara Jewell. Complete the following letter to the Atlanta Journal, *the newspaper that first named your son as a suspect in the Olympic bombing. In the letter express your anger at being named as a suspect and explain how your life has changed because of it. Address the issue of a person's right to privacy. Use people mentioned in Reading One (Rosa Lopez and Oliver Sipple) as examples of others whose lives the media has damaged.*

background information

show how the newspaper report

To the Editor:

Sensationalist reporting is harmful to all people involved and has no place in our society.

_____

_____

_____

_____

_____

_____

_____

_____

_____

As a result of the media's tolerance for irresponsible reporting, my family and I are a few more victims of sensationalism at its worst. On behalf of all victims of sensationalism, we demand a formal apology.

Barbara Jewell

5 REVIEWING LANGUAGE

A. EXPLORING LANGUAGE: Idioms

You know you are reading an idiom when you understand each separate word in an expression, but not the expression as a whole. Work in a small group. Read the sentences that follow and circle the best explanation for each underlined idiom.

1. In the old days reporters <u>kept</u> some information about politicians and movie stars <u>to themselves</u>.

   to keep something to oneself

   ✓ a. to not talk about something

   b. to make a promise

   c. to care for oneself

2. Now, at least in part because the public seems <u>to have an endless hunger for</u> it, reporters sometimes cover these aspects of celebrities' lives more than any other.

   to have an endless hunger for

   a. to need to constantly eat

   b. to have continual need for something

   c. to dislike something immensely

3. Some stories receive such wide visibility that to ignore them is <u>to "play ostrich man,"</u> says Shelby Coffey, editor of *The Los Angeles Times*.

   to play ostrich man

   a. to wear a special bird costume

   b. to try to find the truth in something

   ✓ c. to ignore something that is obvious

4. Scrutiny may be <u>the price one pays</u> for fame.

   to pay the price

   a. to suffer for your actions

   b. to spend what you are not able to afford

   c. to pay the amount you are willing to spend

5. But what about relatives of celebrities? Are they <u>fair game</u> too?

fair game

   a. victims of sensational writing

✓**b.** an approved object of attack

   c. a game that is played at a fair or festival

6. Lopez <u>was hounded</u> by cameras and reporters everywhere she went.

to be hounded

   a. to be found

✓**b.** to be followed

   c. to be treated like a dog

7. She begged President Clinton to clear her son's name and asked reporters to <u>spread the word</u> that her son was innocent of any wrongdoing.

to spread the word

   a. to hide the fact

   b. to stop reporting

✓**c.** to tell everyone

8. Even though Richard Jewell's friend <u>was on his deathbed</u>, Richard didn't visit him.

to be on your deathbed

   a. to be in the bed you have chosen to die in

✓**b.** to be extremely sick, dying

   c. to be in a deep sleep

9. "Richard Jewell is not a murderer," says his mother, but "he has <u>been convicted in the court of public opinion.</u>"

to be convicted in the court of public opinion

✓**a.** to be considered guilty by everyone before going to trial

   b. to be in a special trial in which you are found guilty

   c. to be forced to take part in a trial as a member of the jury

10. Reporters watched the Jewell family <u>around the clock</u>.

around the clock

   a. from sunup to sundown

✓**b.** twenty-four hours a day

   c. during the night

B. WORKING WITH WORDS

Work in a group or with a partner to determine which of the following people could have made the statements listed below. Indicate the appropriate letter in the space next to each statement. In some cases, it is possible that more than one of these people could have made the statement. Refer to the readings to support your answers.

a. Gennifer Flowers, woman alleged to have had an affair with President Clinton

b. Reporter of the minister story

c. Shelby Coffey, editor of *The Los Angeles Times*

d. Peter Jennings, ABC News anchor

e. Rosa Lopez, key witness in the O. J. Simpson trial

f. Richard Jewell, the man accused of the Olympic Park bombing

_c_ **1.** The public seems to have an endless hunger for news, and it is our responsibility to provide information to the readers so they can form their own opinions.

_a_ **2.** I want the public to know about my life; if the President wants to keep his private life to himself, that's his business.

_f_ **3.** The media can ruin your life. Reporters have no right to invade my privacy by hounding me around the clock.

_d_ **4.** Even though there are some stories I would rather not report, I can't play ostrich man all the time.

_b_ **5.** I'm glad I waited to report all the facts, because some of them might have been misinterpreted. I don't want anyone to be convicted wrongly in the court of public opinion.

_e_ **6.** Just because I'm a small part of a news story does not mean that unrelated parts of my life are fair game for reporters to write about.

6 SKILLS FOR EXPRESSION

A. GRAMMAR: Passive Voice

1 *Examine each of the following sets of sentences and answer the questions with a partner.*

Passive Voice	**Active Voice**
◆ The minister had been killed by a hitchhiker.	A hitchhiker had killed the minister.
◆ Rosa Lopez was hounded by cameras and reporters everywhere.	Cameras and reporters hounded Rosa Lopez everywhere.
◆ At first, Richard Jewell was hailed as a hero (by people).	At first, people hailed Richard Jewell as a hero.

a. Each of the sets of sentences has the same meaning but different grammar structure. What is the common grammar structure in the passive sentences? Is this the same structure in the active sentences?

_____

_____

b. List the words in subject position in the passive sentences.

_____   _____   _____

c. List the words in subject position in the active sentences.

_____   _____   _____

d. The change in subject in the active to the passive sentences changes the focus of the sentence. In the active sentences the focus seems to be on *a hitchhiker, cameras and reporters*, and *people*. The subject in these sentences performs the action. What seems to be the focus of the passive sentences? Do the words in the subject position in these sentences perform the action?

_____

_____

Passive Voice

Form of the Passive Voice

To form the **passive voice**, use the correct form of **be** + past participle. At times, the person or thing (the agent) responsible for doing the action is used. In this case, use **by** + the name of the agent:

Subject Position	*Be*	Past Participle	(*By* + Agent)
◆ Rosa Lopez	**is**	**hounded**	**by** cameras and reporters.
◆ Rosa Lopez	**was**	**hounded**	**by** cameras and reporters.
◆ Rosa Lopez	**has been**	**hounded**	**by** cameras and reporters.

- -

Use of the Passive Voice

Active sentences focus on the person or thing that performs an action. **Passive sentences** focus on the person or thing that receives or is the result of an action. The meaning of passive and active sentences is usually similar, but the focus changes.

Use the passive voice when:

1. you don't know who is responsible for an action, or it is not important to know:

   ◆ "The minister's body **was** later **found**."

   (You don't know who found the body; it doesn't matter who found the body. What is important is that someone, anyone, found the body.)

2. the person responsible for the action is understood from the context:

   ◆ "It **was made clear** to Peter Jennings that he had to go with the story."

   (It is understood that a superior, probably his boss, made it clear to him.)

3. you don't want to name the person responsible for the action:

   ◆ "The FBI said the Richard Jewell investigation **was carried out** incorrectly."

   (The FBI does not want to name exactly who in the FBI made mistakes during the investigation.)

4. you want to make the receiver of the action more important than the one who performs the action:

◆ "Lopez **was hounded** by cameras and reporters everywhere she went."

(Lopez is the focus of the sentence. She is more important than the cameras and reporters that hounded her.)

Use the passive voice with an agent (**by** + noun) when the information is necessary to complete the meaning, or when it is new or surprising information.

◆ "The story **was reported by** Peter Jennings."

Use the passive voice *without an agent* when:

the agent is not known or is not important.

the agent is clear from the context.

you want to avoid naming the agent.

❷ *Complete the following sentences. Use the active or passive voice in the past tense. The first one has been done for you.*

1. The news columnist ___reported___ on all aspects of Oliver Sipple's
(report)
life, not only those related to his act of heroism.

2. The Gennifer Flowers story __was broadcasted__ on all the major TV
(broadcast)
networks.

3. Some of the interest in the lives of politicians __was justified__ on
(justify)
the basis that character affects how people perform their jobs.

4. The retired minister __did not return__ from his fishing trip.
(not return)

5. A half-eaten ham sandwich, a gun, fishing tackle, and a magazine
__were found__ in the minister's car.
(find)

6. The reporter who wrote the story about the minister __decided__
(decide)
to mention the gun and the sandwich, but not the magazine.

7. The reporter's story _was read_ by many people, including the
(read)

minister's relatives.

8. Sara Jane Moore _pointed_ (active) a gun at President Ford.
(point)

9. The shot _was deflected_ when Oliver W. Sipple knocked her hand.
(deflect) (passive)

10. Witnesses _were question_ about the shooting by the police.
(question)

11. Rosa Lopez _fleed_ the United States to avoid the intense
(flee)

scrutiny of the media.

3 *Complete the following sentences. Use the passive voice in the past tense. Include the agent only if it is necessary information. The first one has been done for you.*

1. The local police force worked hard. The investigation

_____was completed_____ in less than seventy-two hours.
(complete/police)

2. Richard Jewell _was interviewed by_ FBI about where he saw the
(interview/FBI)

package containing the bomb and why he suspected that it contained a

bomb.

3. They interrupted the news to report that the president
murder
killer → Famous Person
was shot by an assassin
(shot/an assassin)

4. Richard Jewell's mother felt Richard _was convicted by media_
(convict/media)

before he even went to trial.

5. The celebrity _was married by a_ minister today at 5:00 P.M.
(marry/a minister)

6. The newspaper story, which _was written by_ Peter Jennings, talks
(write/Peter Jennings)

about the responsibility of the media in reporting the news.

7. The defendant, a news reporter, _was found guilty_ by a jury of
(find guilty/a jury)

character defamation after a three-week-long jury trial.

It made up

B. STYLE: Topic Sentences

Title

1 *Examine this paragraph from the background reading, and discuss the questions with the class.*

News is everywhere and serves many different functions. The news gives instant coverage of important events. News also provides facts and information. In addition, news is business: a way to make money by selling advertising and/or newspapers and magazines. Sometimes news is propaganda or disinformation: a way to control a population. But whatever news is, it is all around us. You can't escape it. Every day we are bombarded by information—newspapers, magazines, television, and the Internet.

a. What is the topic of this paragraph?

b. The first sentence is the topic sentence. What two ideas are presented in this sentence?

c. How does the content of the rest of the paragraph relate to the topic sentence?

General topic [*News*

Controlling idea

Topics and Topic Sentences

Functions *Where do you find news.*

The topic sentence is an essential part of a well-written paragraph. The **topic sentence** controls the content of the rest of the paragraph: It introduces the topic and states the main ideas. This control helps the writer focus on supporting details in the paragraph that are directly related to the topic sentence.

The first step in writing a topic sentence is to choose a subject and find a point of view or idea about the subject. For example:

Subject		Topic/Point of View
news	→	News is everywhere.
television	→	Television is a bad influence.
reading	→	Reading is good for you.

The next step is to narrow the topic even more by finding a "controlling idea." The controlling idea is the idea you want to explain, illustrate, or describe in the paragraph. For example:

Topic		Controlling Idea (Topic Sentence)
news is everywhere	→	News is everywhere and serves many different functions.
television is bad	→	Television has a violent influence on children.
reading is good	→	Reading helps you expand your mind and broaden your interests.

2 *Each of the following paragraphs is missing a topic sentence. Circle the topic sentence that best fits the paragraph. Discuss your choices with a partner.*

1. For example, you can't pick up a newspaper these days without reading about some outrageous or gruesome crime. The top television news story is usually about a murder or other violent incident. We need to read and hear about the good news stories, too. Otherwise, we will continue sending the message that only violence is worth reporting. And what kind of message is that for our children?

   a. Our society is becoming more and more violent every day.

   b. Television news coverage focuses only on violent news.

   c. All the media has become increasingly negative by focusing only on violence.

2. As a result of live television, people can receive news as it happens. For example, during the Gulf War, CNN viewers around the world could watch the war as it was going on. Because of "live" reporting, people nowadays can feel as though they are participating in history, not just reading or hearing about it afterwards. It has changed the viewer's role completely.

   a. These days there is more live television coverage than ever before.

   b. "Live" television reporting has changed the way we see the news.

   c. CNN changed the way we saw the news during the Gulf War crisis.

3. Experts recommend limiting viewing to one hour per day during the week and up to two hours per day on weekends. The programs should be educational in content and promote discussion between the parent and child. Programs on animal behavior and family values, and programs that teach basic learning skills, are highly recommended.

   a. Watching television is not bad for children.

   b. Watching television is fine for children as long as you limit the hours and monitor the programs.

   c. Programs for children should be educational in content so that the time spent watching TV is not wasted.

4. What we see on the nightly news has been carefully selected by the news department at the television station. Because the station is interested in making money, the news that is selected is not necessarily the most important news but rather the news which will attract the most viewers. As a result, we only see the news that has been chosen for us, which is not always the most informative.

   a. News makes money.

   b. The news director selects the news.

   c. News is not simply what we see, but what the news director at the television station wants us to see.

3 *The topic sentences in the following paragraphs are underlined. They are rather weak. They do not state the main idea. Rewrite each topic sentence, making sure that there is a controlling idea.*

1. <u>Celebrities have jobs</u>. Being a movie star or sports star is their job. It is what they are good at. They should not be under the continual scrutiny of the media just because of their profession. They have a right to a private life just like you and me.

   Rewrite: _Celebrities deserve private lives like any other person._

2. <u>News is different</u>. In the old days, people got their news by word of mouth. As society became more literate and printing costs decreased, newspapers became the medium. Radio then brought a sense of immediacy to the news. Television added the visual impact. Now we have the Internet, which gives up-to-the-second news about any news event any time we want it. Who knows what the news medium of the future will be?

   Rewrite: _we have the different news_

Discuss

3. <u>Politicians are public figures.</u> As a president, one is supposed to represent the qualities of honesty and integrity. Remaining faithful to your husband or wife is the purest example of these qualities. If a president is unfaithful to his or her spouse, how can we trust that he or she is honest in his or her presidential duties? Therefore, the media has the responsibility to inform us when a public figure is unfaithful.

Rewrite: _____

4. <u>Reading is hard.</u> As with any program of exercise, you have to discipline yourself and make reading the newspaper a part of your everyday routine. And just as exercise makes your body stronger, reading makes your mind stronger. It broadens your interests, gives you the ability to think critically about important issues, and enables you to participate in interesting conversations. In conclusion, reading the paper, like any exercise, is time well spent.

Rewrite: _____

7 ON YOUR OWN

A. WRITING TOPICS

Write a paragraph about one of the following topics. Be sure to use some of the vocabulary, grammar, and style that you learned in this unit.

1. Does sensational news ever have a place in our society? If yes, be specific and describe when and in what place. If no, be specific and explain why not.

2. How can the media influence or shape a society's values? Be specific and give examples.

3. Do governments have the right to censor television programs (for nudity and violence, for example)? Be specific and explain why or why not.

4. Does the media reflect society, or does society reflect the media? Be specific and give examples.

B. FIELDWORK

PREPARATION

Work in a small group. Think about news events in the past or present when you felt the media (television or print) sensationalized the reporting of the story and caused anguish to the person(s) involved. Discuss how the media sensationalized the story and how it should have covered the story instead. Take notes below and share your examples with the class.

News story:

How the story was sensationalized:

How the media should have covered the story:

RESEARCH ACTIVITY: Becoming a Critical News Hound

Over the course of a few days, find examples of sensationalized news events from newspapers, magazines, or television news programs. Try to find articles about the same story covered in different newspaper or magazine sources. Compare the information in the different sources. Bring the articles or stories to class and discuss them in groups. Answer the following questions about each story.

1. If you have more than one source that covers the same story, is there any difference in the information presented in each news source? What are the differences? Which source do you feel covered the story best? Why?

2. How was the story sensationalized?

3. Why do you think the media covered this story?

4. What does the media think you want to know about this story?

5. Does the story change the way you feel about the news event or the people involved in the event? If so, how?

3/5 test CH11

2. Azar - do 297-304
           N
3. NS.P. 37-46

CRIME AND PUNISHMENT

The Straits Times

SINGAPORE

JUVENILE CRIME LEADS TO SHARP INCREASE IN ARRESTS

دلين كوُنتَر هووُنان

The number of juvenile delinquents arrested for violent crimes has doubled in the last ten years. A worrisome trend is that more girls are getting arrested. The number of girls arrested went up from 494 to 722 within the past year.

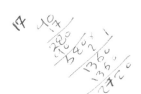

1 APPROACHING THE TOPIC

journalist اوُلنَشَمَىٰ
get arrest

A. PREDICTING

1. Look at the title of this unit, the news headline, and the picture. Discuss these questions with a partner: What is the problem presented here? Who is the person in the picture? Where is she? What has happened to her?
2. Write a list of problems involving juvenile crime in countries you know. Then make a list of solutions those countries have developed in an effort to correct those problems. Share your list with the class. Do you think the solutions are effective?

B. SHARING INFORMATION

curfew → time limit

1 *Read the news summaries. Then work with a partner and answer the questions.*

Russian Press Digest	**The New York Times**	**Paris, Press Service**
BATTLE WITH CRIME The juvenile crime rate increased 6% in the first four months of this year.	**YOUTH CRIME: TOUGHER LAWS?** The rate of violent crime among teenagers is soaring, even as it is decreasing among adults.	**EUROPE: YOUTH DETENTION CENTERS** While general crime figures remain stable, the number of juvenile crimes has risen 15%.

Is the increase in juvenile crime unique to one country? Why do you think juvenile crime is increasing? What type of crime would you expect teenagers to be involved in the most?

2 *Read each of the following statements. If you agree, write **A**. If you disagree, write **D**. Then share your opinions with a partner. When possible, support your opinions with examples from your own experience.*

D 1. Most juvenile offenders continue with a life of crime as adults.

A 2. Societal support (programs in support of juveniles, such as teen centers and jobs for teens) can keep juveniles off the streets and away from a life of crime.

A 3. Most juvenile offenders come from problem homes with alcohol-abusing or drug-abusing parents, physically abusive parents, or absentee parents (parents who are never at home).

A 4. Juveniles should have a curfew; that is, the law should require teenagers to be off the streets and indoors by a certain hour of night.

D 5. Parents of a juvenile offender should also be punished when their child breaks the law.

D 6. Corporal punishment (physical punishment such as beating, striking, or hitting) is an effective way to keep a juvenile offender from committing a crime again.

get connected

2 PREPARING TO READ

A. BACKGROUND

accused =

With the rate of crime by juveniles on the rise, people have been forced to take a careful look at the causes and to try to create effective ways to stop this trend. Below are three solutions some cities have tried in order to control juvenile delinquency. What do you think about them?

Read the information and write your opinion. Begin: "I believe this program would (or would not) work because. . . ." An example has been done for you.

Teen court

1. TEEN COURT

At most teen courts, teenagers who have been accused of minor crimes, ranging from traffic violations to attempted burglary, agree to admit to the crime. A jury made up of their peers—that is, other people their age—decides on the penalty or punishment.

I believe this program would work because teens listen to other teens

more than they listen to adults.

_____

_____

2. CURFEWS

Curfews are time limits that require a certain population of people to be off the streets by a specific time. For example, in some cities, anyone under 18 years of age must be indoors by 8 P.M. on school nights and 11 P.M. on Fridays and Saturdays.

_____

_____

_____

_____

3. PARENTAL PUNISHMENT

Some towns have put a law into effect that makes parents responsible for the behavior of their teenage children. When teens commit a minor crime, the law allows judges to make parents pay up to $1,000 and take "parent effectiveness" classes.

_____

_____

_____

_____

B. VOCABULARY FOR COMPREHENSION

Work with a partner and help each other to guess the meaning of the underlined words. For each sentence, circle the word which has the most similar meaning to the underlined word. Use your dictionary if necessary.

1. In the United States, 40 to 50 percent of teen <u>offenders</u> commit crimes again.

   a. lawbreakers

   b. good citizens

   c. athletes

2. At teen courts, <u>penalties</u> are set by a jury of peers.

   a. rewards

   b. punishments

   c. crimes

3. Many teenagers <u>accused</u> of a minor crime choose to <u>plead guilty</u> rather than plead innocent. In exchange, they receive a reduced punishment and they can avoid going to trial.

   a. ask for forgiveness

   b. admit to the crime

   c. don't admit to the crime

4. Many teen juries <u>hand down</u> harsher penalties than the standard courts do.

   a. receive

   b. reduce

   c. give

5. The laws in some communities allow judges <u>to fine</u> parents up to $1,000 and require them to take "parent effectiveness" classes if their child commits a minor crime.

   a. to punish financially

   b. to discover

   c. to pay

6. Supporters of teen courts say they are an effective way to control <u>delinquent</u> teens before they become serious criminals.

   a. late

   b. law-breaking

   c. attentive

7. After the girl was caught with the lipstick in her pocketbook, she admitted to <u>shoplifting</u> while the clerk was helping another customer.

   a. paying for it

   b. stealing from the store

   c. borrowing it

8. Despite the apparent success of curfews in reducing teen crime, curfews have been criticized by teens. Many <u>law-abiding</u> teens find the curfews unfair.

   a. non-criminal

   b. law-breaking

   c. delinquent

9. While the idea of teen court is very appealing, there is no <u>conclusive</u> <u>evidence</u> that it is really effective in reducing crime.

   a. theory

   b. experiment

   c. proof

10. Sometimes the inexperience of teen juries leads to <u>overzealous verdicts</u>. For example, a convicted teen may be punished by having to stay at home for six months, just for being caught in the street five minutes after curfew.

too harsh √ **a.** severe judgments

b. light judgments

c. religious judgments

READING ONE: Crimebusting: What Works? Methods of Punishing

A. INTRODUCING THE TOPIC

Read the title and the first paragraph of the article. Write three questions that you think the article will answer. Then read the rest of the article.

1. Who? _____

2. What? _____

3. Why? _____

Crimebusting: What Works?
Methods of Punishing

By John M. DiConsiglio, James Anderson, and Patricia Smith (from *Scholastic Update*)

1 Round up every teen on the street after sundown? Send shoplifters to courts where the judge, lawyers, and jury[1] are all teenagers? Punish parents if their kid gets caught with a beer? Cities and towns across the country [the United States] have come up with some unusual solutions to juvenile crime. Here's your chance to pass judgment on three of them.

Teen Court

2 The 16-year-old defendant hasn't got a prayer. It's not a question of whether or not she committed a crime. She's already admitted shoplifting a tube of lipstick from a department-store counter. Slouching in the witness stand, absent-mindedly twirling her hair, she looks as if her day in court is boring her. And in teen court—where the judge, lawyers, and jury are all teenagers— bad attitude is a serious offense.

3 "She didn't show the court any respect," says Philip Dela Rosa, the director of the Family YMCA Teen Court in Houston, Texas. "Here, dissing[2] the jury is a very big mistake."

4 Nationally, however, teen courts are gaining respect and attention, with at least 185 operating in 24 states. At most of these courts, teens charged with misdemeanors— minor crimes ranging from traffic violations to attempted burglary—plead guilty in exchange for having their penalty set by a jury of their peers.

5 Although teen juries usually cannot order fines or jail time, they can sentence offenders to perform community service, offer apologies, write essays, and return to teen court as jurors. Once the sentence is completed the teen's record is wiped clean, as though he or she never committed a crime.

---

[1] *jury:* a group of people who decide if a person is guilty or not guilty in a court of law
[2] *dissing:* insulting; not showing respect

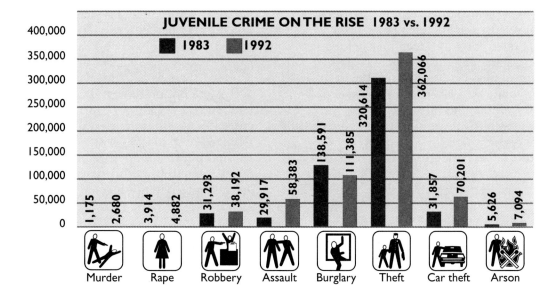

JUVENILE CRIME ON THE RISE 1983 vs. 1992

1983 / 1992

Crime	1983	1992
Murder	1,175	2,680
Rape	3,914	4,882
Robbery	31,293	38,192
Assault	29,917	58,383
Burglary	138,591	111,385
Theft	320,614	362,066
Car theft	31,857	70,201
Arson	5,626	7,094

6   "This is not a mock trial—these are no Mickey Mouse[3] courts," says Dela Rosa, who has helped create more than 50 teen courts around the country. "The teens take this court very seriously. And if they don't, they learn their lesson the hard way."

7   In fact, many teen juries hand down harsher penalties than the standard courts do. The lipstick thief had to perform 48 hours of community service, attend an anti-theft class, write a 1,000-word essay, and serve on a teen-court jury.

8   But do teen courts really help keep kids out of trouble? Supporters say the courts are an effective way to reach delinquent teens before they become serious criminals. The courts help ease the burden on the already overloaded juvenile justice system. And they have a track record of success. Nationally, 40 to 50 percent of teen offenders commit crimes again. But of those who go through teen courts, less than 10 percent get arrested again.

9   Critics say such numbers are deceiving. Since most defendants are first-time offenders charged with minor crimes, few are likely to become repeat offenders anyway. "For the young people involved, teen court is an invaluable learning experience," says Hunter Hurst, director of the National Center for Juvenile Justice in Pittsburgh. "But as for changing behavior, the evidence is not there at all."

10   Legal experts also question whether teen courts are really fair to defendants. Dangling the option of a teen jury before teenagers facing an adult judge may pressure them to plead guilty, even if they're not. And while teen-court jurors receive weeks of training and must pass a law test, critics say even the most highly trained teen is not mature enough for jury duty.

11   Sometimes inexperience leads to overzealous verdicts. Bad attitude, although not a crime, can yield harsh punishment, as the Houston shoplifter found out. A jury in Los Angeles ordered one offender to perform 750 hours of community service. And some teen courts have seen their proceedings disrupted by participants who have dozed off, broken into laughter, or arrived unprepared to try a case.

12   "If young people are sufficiently different from adults to warrant a different legal process, are they capable of running a court?" asks Hurst. "Is that what we want?"

The Law Says: Be Home by 8:00

13   It's a typical night in New Orleans. At the St. Thomas housing project,[4] 14-year-old boys spray gunfire into the night. Across town, in the city's famed French Quarter, a group of teenage girls vomit on the street after a night of heavy drinking.[5] Not far away, police burst into a motel room chock-full of stolen goods, and arrest two 17-year-olds and a 16-year-old.

14   As one of the nation's most violent cities, New Orleans has had its share of youth crime. So last year, the city adopted a curfew to get teenagers off the street. Today, anyone under 18 must be indoors by 8 P.M. on school nights and 11 P.M. Friday and Saturday.

15   New Orleans police say the curfew has produced dramatic results. In the past year, police have rounded up 3,900 kids for violating the curfew. Juvenile murders have fallen by 33 percent, rape by 67 percent, armed robbery by 33 percent, and car theft by 42 percent.

16   Seeing these results, local governments across the nation have found youth curfews hard to resist. Of the 77 largest American cities, 59 now have curfews. The laws vary from place to place. Most allow police to round up teens at night, while others also cover school hours. In some cases, offenders are taken to detention centers;[6] in others,

---

[3] *Mickey Mouse:* pretend; not serious
[4] *housing project:* government-sponsored housing
[5] *heavy drinking:* drinking a large amount of alcohol
[6] *detention center:* a building specifically for juvenile delinquents

they are handed a citation, like a parking ticket, and then escorted home.

17 Despite their apparent success, curfews have drawn a chorus of criticism from teens, parents, and civil liberties advocates. Many law-abiding teens find the restrictions unfair. "It is totally and completely wrong to punish all of the teenagers when only a small percentage are the really guilty ones," says Jessica Levi, 15, of Washington, D.C., where a curfew was adopted this summer.

18 Parents and their kids often complain that curfews get in the way of after-school jobs, social activities, and athletics. And civil liberties groups such as the American Civil Liberties Union charge that curfews violate the First Amendment right to peaceful assembly. Courts have overturned[7] many curfew laws on these grounds.

19 Law enforcement groups, however, say you can't argue with success. In Dallas, where crime dropped 15 percent during curfew hours, police are content with the new law. "We don't look at the curfew as another way to hassle juveniles," says Vicki Hawkins of the police department. "We look at it as another tool to keep kids safe."

Punish the Parents

20 When 15-year-old Jeremiah Beck was caught shoplifting a bottle of cologne, he got off scot-free—but his mother didn't. Though she hadn't set foot near the scene of the crime, Anita Beck went to court for Jeremiah's mistake. The charge? Failing to supervise her son.

21 Faced with a growing number of minor crimes committed by juveniles, the town of Silverton, Oregon, where the Becks live, passed a law holding parents responsible for their kids' wrongdoings. The law allows judges to fine parents up to $1,000 and require them to take "parent effectiveness" classes if their kids commit a minor crime.

22 The law was recently adopted statewide and may become a model for communities around the nation. The reason: It seems to be working. Since the law took effect in January, Silverton's juvenile crime rate has declined by 55 percent, Police Chief Randy Lunsford claims. Before, minor offenders often went unpunished and felt free to try more serious crimes, he says. Now, parents are forced to step in and police their kids before they graduate from petty thievery to armed robbery.

23 "This ordinance was never meant to punish parents; it was meant to get them actively involved in parenting their kids," says Tina Lasater, assistant to Silverton's city manager. "The kids are still held accountable. We're just putting the other element in: getting their parents involved."

24 Not everyone considers the law such a shining model. Many parents claim it's unconstitutional to charge one person for someone else's crime. "This law smacks of totalitarianism," says attorney Jossi Davidson, who represents a group of parents challenging the law. "It's too much government intrusion into families' lives. It absolutely violates due process,[8] under which you can't be punished unless you've done something wrong."

25 Anita Beck was found innocent, but sooner or later, Davidson says, a Silverton parent who is found guilty will appeal.[9] A higher court, he predicts, will judge the law unconstitutional.

26 Meanwhile, other parents are still stuck in court. Sylvia Whitney was cited when her 17-year-old son, Scott, got caught with a beer. While Scott takes a court-ordered alcohol awareness course, his mom is fighting the charge. Scott takes her side. "It should be my fault," he says. "I got in trouble; she didn't. The government's trying to be my dad, and it's not right."

---

[7] *overturn:* reverse a legal decision
[8] *due process:* the legal system that is meant to protect you as a citizen
[9] *appeal:* to ask a higher court of law to change the decision of a lower court of law

B. READING FOR MAIN IDEAS

Put the following main ideas in the order they appear in the article. Number them from 1 to 7. The first one has been done for you.

_____ **a.** Last year, New Orleans adopted a curfew to get teenagers off the street.

_____ **b.** Supporters say the courts are an effective way to reach delinquent teens before they become serious criminals.

_____ **c.** Not everyone considers the parental law such a shining model.

_____ **d.** Silverton, Oregon, passed a law holding parents responsible for their kids' wrongdoings.

_____ **e.** Curfews have drawn a chorus of criticism from teens, parents, and civil liberties advocates.

_____ **f.** Teen courts are becoming more and more popular every year.

__1__ **g.** Cities and towns across the United States have come up with some unusual solutions to teen crime.

C. READING FOR DETAILS

"Crimebusting: What Works? Methods of Punishing" can be divided into three main parts. Each part describes a different type of program.

Work in groups of three to complete the chart on the next page. Each person should complete the chart for a different program. Then share your information with the group so that the chart is complete for all three programs.

TYPE OF PROGRAM	ARGUMENTS IN FAVOR OF THE PROGRAM	ARGUMENTS AGAINST THE PROGRAM
Teen Court		
Teen Curfew		
Parental Laws		

D. READING BETWEEN THE LINES

Read the following scenario. Complete the exercise in a small group.

Your group is the town council for a small town called Little Bend. The town council is an elected group of people who act as the town's government. As a group, you make decisions on education, land development, town resources, and crime.

You have gathered today to discuss solutions to your town's most recent problem: teen crime. Last year, teens committed 51 percent of all crimes. That is up 10 percent from the year before. You have come together to decide on a program to reduce juvenile crime. Three programs have been proposed: teen court, teen curfew, and parental laws.

1. Decide which program would be best for your community. Use the chart in Exercise 3C on page 37 to talk about the pros and cons of each program. Take note of the following community facts:
   - ◆ 10,000 people live in Little Bend
   - ◆ There is a ten-person police department

   You must also take the following issues into consideration:
   - ◆ How easy is the program to set up and maintain?
   - ◆ Is the program fair to all the people involved?
   - ◆ Does the program encourage education for the criminal? How?
   - ◆ Does the program encourage stronger communication and commitment within the family? How?
   - ◆ What does the program focus on: the immediate benefit for society, or the teen criminal?

2. Come to an agreement and write a group paragraph. In the paragraph, give the group's decision and explain why the group came to the decision.

3. Exchange paragraphs with another group. Read the other group's decision and discuss the similarities and differences in the two decisions.

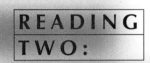

4 READING TWO: Michael Fay's Caning

A. EXPANDING THE TOPIC

Read this background information, answer the questions that follow, and discuss your answers in small groups. Then read the two opinion statements written by American high school students at the time of Michael Fay's caning.

On May 5, 1994, Michael Fay, a 19-year-old American living in Singapore, received a caning (four whippings by a stick on his bare bottom) as punishment for a crime he committed. The crime: spray-painting graffiti on cars. In the United States, news of the lashings received both support and criticism. Many people who were fed up with crime and violence felt the lashings were a good lesson for Fay and other young people involved with crime. Other people felt the lashings were a cruel form of justice and that because Fay was an American, he should have been sent back to the United States to receive punishment.

1. Do you think caning is an appropriate form of punishment? Why or why not?

2. Do you think that foreigners should receive the same form of punishment as nationals? Why or why not?

Spray-painting graffiti on a wall.

Michael Fay's Caning

By Sarah Fenske and Tram Kim Nguyen (from *The Plain Dealer*)

Opinion One

1   Ages ago, Socrates wrote of the implied contract. This is the idea that if one voluntarily chooses to live in a country, one has the duty to obey that country's laws and accept its jurisdiction. If you don't intend to follow through on this contract, you have no business living there.

2   When Fay chose to live in Singapore, he made the unspoken decision to obey its laws and accept its punishments. When Fay blatantly broke the law, he could expect to receive the harsh punishments that Singapore is known for. As a resident, it was clearly his duty to accept it. His very presence in the country indicated his agreement to receive what the government decreed, no matter how unusual.

Sarah Fenske, Lutheran High School

Opinion Two

3   Caning and other methods of corporal punishment do not have a place in our culture, where cruel and unusual punishment is deemed unacceptable. The most evident proof of the failure of violent punishments to deter crime is the death penalty.[1] Death sentences have not mitigated the crises of teeming prisons and a society of victims. Even the phrases *death by electrocution* and *death by injection* sound absurd and incongruous with modern society.

4   Those who propose such violent methods to end teen crime are setting a precedent whereby younger children will learn the twisted idea that violence is acceptable and the ends justify the means.

Tram Kim Nguyen, Newbury High School

[1] *death penalty:* sentencing a criminal to death; 38 of 50 states in the United States have the death penalty

Complete the following statements.

1. Sarah Fenske believes that if you live in a foreign country, you must

_____ .

2. Tram Kim Nguyen believes that "violent" punishments are

_____ .

B. LINKING READINGS ONE AND TWO

You have now read about four different ways of dealing with juvenile crime. Discuss the following questions with your classmates. Then choose one question and develop a well-written answer. Refer to the readings if necessary.

1. Some people believe that you must accept and abide by all the laws and punishments of the country or town in which you live. Others disagree. Do you believe that you always have to agree with the laws and punishments wherever you live? Are the laws always made to protect you? What can people do when they disagree with the laws?

2. The juvenile punishments presented in this unit have both supporters and critics. Which punishments that you have read about in this unit do you find acceptable? Which punishments do you find unacceptable? Why?

5 REVIEWING LANGUAGE

A. EXPLORING LANGUAGE

Work with a partner. Read the numbered sentence and the lettered choices that follow. For each item, circle the lettered choice that is closest in meaning to the numbered sentence.

1. She didn't show the court any respect. Her dissing the jury was a very big mistake.

    a. She was rude and disrespectful to the court.

    b. She kept her distance and remained cool.

2. These are no Mickey Mouse courts.

    a. These courts are very serious.

    b. These courts are not for young people.

3. The teens take this court very seriously. And if they don't, they learn their lessons the hard way.

    a. It is difficult for a teen to learn anything in court.

    b. When teens are not serious about their court appearance, they will be in trouble.

4. Dangling the option of a teen jury before teenagers who would otherwise go before an adult judge may pressure them to plead guilty, even if they're not.

    a. Teenagers who choose a teen jury are usually guilty.

    b. Many teenagers would rather lie and say they are guilty than go before an adult judge.

5. Some teen courts have seen their proceedings disrupted by jurors who have dozed off, broken out in laughter, or arrived unprepared to try a case.

    a. Some teen jurors have been rude, impolite, and unprepared in court.

    b. Some teen jurors laugh and sleep in court, but they always arrive ready to discuss the issues.

6. In the past year, police have rounded up 3,900 teenagers for violating the law.

    a. Almost 4,000 teenagers have been arrested in the last twelve months.

    b. There have been almost 4,000 rapes involving teenagers in the last twelve months.

7. We don't look at the curfew as another way to hassle juveniles.

    a. Curfews have not been established to bother juveniles.

    b. Establishing curfews has not been considered.

8. When 15-year-old Jeremiah Beck was caught shoplifting a bottle of cologne, he got off scot-free.

    a. Jeremiah Beck took a bottle of cologne, but he was not punished because the cologne was free.

✓ **b.** Although Jeremiah Beck stole a bottle of cologne, he was not punished.

9. Now, parents are forced to step in and police their kids before they graduate from petty thievery to armed robbery.

✓**a.** It's the parents' responsibility to not let their kids progress from small to large crimes.

    b. Because of their parents, many teens commit crimes and therefore have contact with the police before they graduate.

10. The government's trying to be my dad, and it's not right.

✓**a.** The government is trying to control areas of my life that do not concern it.

    b. The government wants to arrest my father and put him on trial.

B. WORKING WITH WORDS

Working with a partner, cross out the word that does not belong in each group. Describe the category for the remaining three words. The first one has been done for you.

1. detention center   community work   ~~parent class~~   jail time

   Category: *teen punishments by traditional courts*

2. lethal injection   electrocution   lashing   hanging

   Category: _____

3. traffic violations   shoplifting   murder   underage drinking

   Category: _____

4. go to court   pay a fine   spray graffiti   attend parent class

   Category: _____

5. written apologies   community work   anti-theft class   jail time

Category: _____

6. shoplifting   robbery   rioting   stealing

Category: _____

7. stealing   beating   lashing   caning

Category: _____

6 SKILLS FOR EXPRESSION

A. GRAMMAR: Gerunds and Infinitives

ing form   *to use*

1 *Examine the sentences and answer the questions with a partner.*

  a. <u>Decreasing</u> crime is the goal of teen courts. *S*

  b. The <u>curfew</u> prohibited <u>walking</u> on the street after 8:00 P.M.

  c. He was sent to jail for <u>breaking</u> the law.

  d. He said the government was trying <u>to be</u> his dad.

  e. The court can sentence offenders <u>to perform</u> community service.

  f. Some juvenile offenders felt free <u>to try</u> more serious crimes.

  g. You have a duty <u>to obey</u> the laws of the country you are in.

1. In sentence **a**, what is the subject? *Decreasing crime*
2. In sentence **b**, what is the object of the verb? *on the street*
3. In sentence **c**, what word follows the preposition *for*?
4. Look at the underlined words in **a**, **b**, and **c**. They are gerunds. How are gerunds formed?
5. In sentence **d**, the main verb is *try*. What is the verb that follows it?
6. In sentence **e**, the main verb is *sentence*. What is the object of the main verb? What is the verb that follows it?
7. In sentence **f**, what is the verb that follows the adjective *free*?
8. In sentence **g**, what is the verb that follows the noun *duty*?
9. Look at the underlined words in **d**, **e**, **f**, and **g**. They are infinitives. How are infinitives formed?

FOCUS ON GRAMMAR

See Gerunds and Infinitives in *Focus on Grammar, High Intermediate.*

Gerunds and Infinitives

Gerunds

To form a gerund, add **-*ing*** to the base form of the verb.

Use the gerund:

1. as the subject of a sentence

2. as the object of the sentence after certain verbs (such as: *prohibit, admit, deny*)

3. after a preposition (such as: *for, in, of, about*)

- -

Infinitives

To form an infinitive, use ***to*** and the base form of the verb.

Use the infinitive after:

4. certain verbs

Some verbs are often followed by an infinitive (such as: *try, fail, hope*)

Some verbs are followed by an object and then an infinitive (such as: *sentence, allow*)

Others are followed by an infinitive with or without an object (such as: *want, need*)

5. certain adjectives (such as: *free, hard, wrong*)

6. certain nouns (such as: *duty, decision, method*)

2 *Underline the gerund or infinitive in each sentence below. Work with a partner and decide which of the rules in the above grammar box applies to each sentence. Write the number of the rule in the space next to each lettered sentence. The first one has been done for you.*

__1__ **a.** <u>Seeing</u> the results helped local governments make a decision.

__G__ **b.** Teens plead guilty in exchange for <u>having</u> their penalty set by a jury of their peers.

__4.5__ **c.** Local governments across the nation have found youth curfews hard <u>to resist</u>.

____ **d.** The lipstick thief needed to perform 48 hours of community service.

_____ **e.** A jury in Los Angeles sentenced one offender to perform 750 hours of community service.

2 G **f.** She's already admitted shoplifting a tube of lipstick.

6 n **g.** Some people say it is a citizen's duty to obey all laws even if the law seems unfair.

4 **h.** Some say because Fay did not choose to live in Singapore, he should have been sent home for his punishment.

3 **i.** Are teenagers capable of running a court?

4 **j.** Some people wanted the city to establish a curfew for teenagers.

3 _Read the following information about teen crime. Summarize each situation using a form of the first verb given and the gerund or infinitive form of the second verb. The first one has been done for you._

1. The town set a curfew for teenagers. They had to be off the streets by 8:00 P.M.

   The town **didn't allow** teenagers **to be** on the street

   after 8:00 P.M.

   (not allow/be)

2. The teenager's parents were never at home during the day. They didn't know what he did all day or who his friends were.

   _____

   _____

   (fail/supervise)

3. The grocery store was missing a candy bar. The boy was found with a candy bar in his pocket. He said that he had taken it.

   _____

   _____

   (admit/shoplift)

4. The teenager hadn't committed the crime. There was no evidence implicating him. Nevertheless, he was convicted and sent to a juvenile detention center.

   _____

   _____

   (be wrong/punish)

5. The teenager was convicted. The judge told his parents that they were responsible for the teen's actions. Therefore they had to pay a fine and take a course on "effective parenting."

_____

_____

(sentence/participate)

6. Although the teen admitted that she had committed the crime, she begged the judge not to send her to jail. She thought something bad would happen to her there.

_____

_____

(be afraid of/go)

7. There are many ways that a community can protect its citizens. Curfew, more police, stricter laws, and education are a few of the ways that a community can choose.

_____

_____

(choose/protect)

8. The parent was shocked. She kept shaking her head in disbelief. She couldn't believe that her son had been involved in a crime.

_____

_____

(be surprised/hear)

9. After he was caught with the stolen car, the teen said he was very sorry for what he had done and for the damage he had caused to the car. He realized that he had been very foolish and wanted people to forgive him.

_____

_____

(apologize for/steal)

10. Despite all the evidence, the teenager said that he hadn't written the graffiti on the school wall.

_____

_____

(deny/write)

B. STYLE: The Three-Part Paragraph

① *Work with a partner. Examine the paragraph below and answer the questions that follow.*

There are many problems with implementing a teen curfew in our town. First of all, not all teens are criminals, but if we are treated as criminals, we will begin to believe we are. In addition, many teens have busy lives; the curfew will interfere with our lives. I, for example, work at a movie theater on the weekends and do not get out of work until after midnight. Finally, the law doesn't even make sense because statistics show that teen crime occurs most frequently in the afternoons between 3:00 and 5:00 P.M., not in the late evening. In conclusion, the use of curfews is not only senseless, but it also treats teens as second-class citizens, without the respect and support that we need. It is respect and support that will keep us off the street, not curfews.

1. What is the topic of the paragraph? Underline it.

2. What is the controlling idea? Circle it.

3. What are the supporting sentences? Double-underline them.

4. What is the conclusion? Underline it.

NOTE: For more information on topic sentences and controlling ideas, see Unit 1.

The Paragraph

A **paragraph** is a group of sentences that talks about one main idea. There are usually three parts to a paragraph: **the topic sentence**, **supporting sentences**, and **the concluding sentence**.

- -

The Topic Sentence

The topic sentence introduces the subject you are going to write about and your ideas or opinions about the subject. In this way, it controls what you write in the rest of the paragraph. For example, in the paragraph above, the first sentence is the topic sentence. It introduces the topic, *teen curfews*, and the controlling idea, *many problems*. All the sentences in the paragraph must relate to, describe, or exemplify the topic sentence.

Supporting Sentences

The second part of the paragraph includes details or examples that develop your ideas about the topic. This part of the paragraph is usually the longest, as it discusses and explains the controlling idea. In the paragraph in 6B, page 47, there are three examples of problems with having a teen curfew: *it makes all teens feel like criminals; it interferes with daily life; it doesn't make sense.*

The Concluding Sentence

The last part of the paragraph can do several things. It can summarize the paragraph, offer a solution to the problem, restate the introductory sentence, or offer an opinion. The paragraph in 6B, page 47, concludes with: *In conclusion, the use of curfews is not only senseless, but it also treats teens as second-class citizens.* This paragraph also adds the final comment: *It is respect and support that will keep us off the street, not curfews.*

Transition Words

Transition words are often used in supporting sentences and concluding sentences. They help the reader follow the progression of examples, details, and ideas. Some of these words are listed below.

Use	Transition Words
For the first support	*First, For one thing, First of all*
For additional support	*In addition, Furthermore, Moreover, Also, Another reason*
For examples	*For example, For instance, Specifically*
For final support	*Finally, Last of all*
For the conclusion	*In short, In conclusion, In summary*

NOTE: Transition words and phrases are followed by a comma (,).

2 *Read each topic sentence and cross out the one lettered idea that does not support the topic sentence. The first one has been done for you.*

1. Some people believe that juvenile court is not fair to the defendants.

   a. Reasons why juvenile court isn't fair

   ~~**b.** Definition of juvenile court~~

   c. What the defendants think about juvenile court

2. Laws that punish parents for their children's crimes get parents involved in their children's lives.

   a. Reasons why parents get involved

   b. Examples of how parents become involved

   c. Other ways (besides these laws) parents can become involved with their children

3. Juvenile crime seems to be on the rise all over the world.

   a. Some examples of crime statistics from around the world

   b. What juveniles do in their free time

   c. Reasons why juvenile crime is on the rise

4. When people choose to live overseas, they must obey the laws of that country no matter how harsh they may seem.

   a. Reasons why people choose to live overseas

   b. Reasons why people should obey the laws

   c. Reasons why people should expect to receive punishments

3 *In each of the following paragraphs there is one supporting sentence that does not directly relate to the topic sentence. Cross out this sentence and explain why it is unrelated. The first one has been done for you.*

1. There are a number of reasons why juvenile court is not fair to teen defendants. First, teens may plead guilty just so they can avoid adult court. In addition, many teen jury members are not mature enough to judge their peers reasonably. ~~Finally, many defendants should be tried as adults.~~ Clearly these concerns must be addressed if we want these courts to succeed.

   Explanation:

   This paragraph explains why teen courts are unfair to teens, not why teens should be tried as adults.

2. Making laws that punish parents for their children's crimes is a good way to get parents involved in their childrens' lives. First of all, parents must stop their children from committing crimes if they themselves don't want to go to jail or be fined. Furthermore, in other countries these laws seem to work. Most importantly, it opens communication between the parents and the children because they are all involved.

Explanation: گرفتار / مبهمودن

_____

_____

3. Juvenile crime seems to be on the rise all over the world. For example, in Hamburg, Germany, crimes committed by children increased by 24.7 percent. Also, in Poland juvenile crime increased by 10 percent. Even more shocking, in Russia the juvenile crime rate increased 6 percent in the first four months of this year. Juvenile crime was not an issue when I was growing up. We must make every effort to find the cause of this international trend and try to stop it.

Explanation:

_____

_____

4. When people choose to live overseas, they must obey the laws of that country no matter how harsh they may seem. For one thing, you can't expect the laws to change just because you are a foreigner. Another reason is, by disrespecting the laws of the country you are disrespecting the people and the culture. Finally, as the expression says, "When in Rome, do as the Romans do." We are all citizens of planet Earth and should learn to get along.

Explanation:

_____

_____

4 *For each topic sentence below, write two or three supporting sentences. Use transition words and phrases.*

1. There are some important things parents can do to keep their children away from a life of crime.

_____

_____

_____

_____

2. Sports are a good way to keep teens off the streets.

_____

_____

_____

_____

_____

3. There are many ways people can work together to keep communities safe from crime.

_____

_____

_____

_____

_____

4. Being a teenager is difficult, especially if you move overseas.

_____

_____

_____

_____

_____

5. Punishments for juvenile crime vary from state to state and country to country.

_____

_____

_____

_____

_____

ON YOUR OWN

A. WRITING TOPICS

Write a paragraph about one of the following topics. Be sure to include a topic sentence and to support your ideas with examples and details. Include transition words and a concluding statement.

1. In your own culture, how are juvenile crime offenders treated? Do you agree with the treatment? Why or why not?

2. Do you believe teens should have the same rights and privileges as adults? Why or why not?

3. Do you think teens should be tried and convicted as adults? If yes, why and under what circumstances? If no, why not?

4. Should teenagers under eighteen years of age be sent to their home countries for trial when convicted of crimes overseas?

5. What kinds of programs should cities and towns provide for teens to keep them off the streets and away from lives of crime?

B. FIELDWORK

RESEARCH ACTIVITY

*Research a teen court organization through your local library or on the Internet at keywords **teen court** and/or **juvenile court**. If you do not have access to a library or the Internet, write a letter to an organization requesting information (see references on page 53). Try to find the following information:*

- Program purpose, goals, and objectives
- Methods used
- Sentencing options
- Selection, use, and training of volunteers
- Success rates (statistics)

SHARING YOUR FINDINGS

When you have collected the information, share your findings with your classmates. Compare different programs.

REFERENCES

For general information about teen courts, an excellent resource is:

National Criminal Justice Reference Service
P.O. Box 6000
Rockville, MD 20849
Internet: http://www.ncjrs.org

The following are addresses for individual teen court programs:

Midland Texas Teen Court Program
Midland ISD Administration Building
615 West Missouri #226
Midland, TX 79701
Internet: http://www.basinlink.com

Knox County Teen Court
55 West Tompkins Street
Galesburg, IL 61402
Internet: http://tqd.advanced.org

Division 7
Aurora Municipal Justice Center
15001 E. Aurora Drive
Aurora, CO 80012
Internet: http://www.ci.aurora.co.us/munteen.html

Keywords

Here are some other useful keywords for searching for other resources on the Internet:

> teen court information
> implementing teen courts
> juvenile justice
> problems and juvenile justice
> alternative juvenile justice

2) Finish unit 2 ___ Finish unit 2
hand in answers + ~~end~~ P. 50-51
to ex 4

Azar. P. 304-310

hand in ex. 5.302

1. Tuesday Reading Test
1+2

9. Tuesday -

NSP 63 → p 63-67

3. Azar p 326-330
347. 358

DYING FOR THEIR BELIEFS

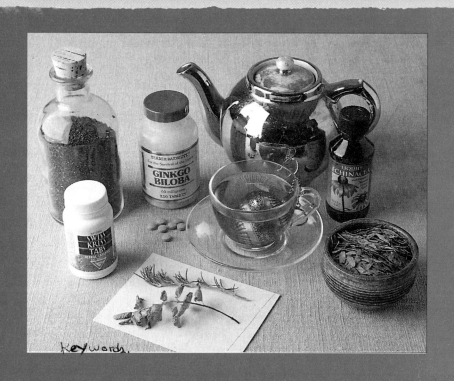

Keywords.

1 APPROACHING THE TOPIC

A. PREDICTING

Look at the title of this unit and the photograph. Then answer these questions with a partner.

1. What do you think are some types of conventional medical treatment?
2. What do you think are some types of nonconventional, or alternative, medical treatment?
3. Which types have you used?
4. Who do you think should be responsible for deciding what or how much medical treatment a person receives? Is this also true in the case of children?

B. SHARING INFORMATION

Read the following statements regarding medicine. Write A if you agree or D if you disagree. Discuss your answers in small groups.

_____ 1. If you are sick, taking drugs (medicine) is the best way to get better.

_____ 2. Praying can cure sickness.

_____ 3. People who have a positive attitude will be cured faster than those who don't have a positive attitude.

_____ 4. Sickness is often only in the mind of the person who is ill.

_____ 5. Medicine could be more effective if we paid more attention to alternative and natural or herbal remedies.

_____ 6. Rest, proper diet, exercise, and fresh air are the best kinds of treatment.

_____ 7. Patients have the right to choose the treatment they believe in, conventional or alternative, even if doctors do not agree.

_____ 8. Parents, rather than doctors or the government, should choose the treatment they believe is best for their children.

PREPARING TO READ

A. BACKGROUND

Read this information and do the exercise that follows on page 57.

Mary Baker Eddy: Founder of the Christian Scientists

Mary Baker Eddy was an American religious leader and the founder of the Christian Science movement. She was born in Bow, New Hampshire (USA), on July 16, 1821. As a child she was not very healthy; as a result she missed a great deal of school. Her education came through home schooling and study of the Bible and scriptures.

She continued to suffer from poor health as an adult and tried many alternative therapies of the times. These included mesmerism (hypnosis), hydrotherapy (water cures), and mental healing. Once, after falling on ice and suffering a severe injury, she asked for her Bible and read a Gospel[1] account of one of Jesus's healings. After reading the New Testament,[2] she was completely cured and felt she had finally found the answer to her medical problems: the scriptures.[3]

Eddy believed that all sickness was mental rather than physical. She began the practice of healing others by reading the Bible and teaching others to be healers as well. In 1875 she published *Science and Health with Key to the Scriptures*. Eddy later published sixteen other books. In 1879 she founded the Church of Christ, Scientist, an organization she oversaw closely until her death.

Her followers, the Christian Scientists, believe that disease, as well as sin and death, do not originate with God and therefore are not real. They see God as the only healer. Instead of medicinal remedies, Christian Scientists pray for the sick person. In addition, a church "practitioner"[4] prays for the sick and a church nurse gives nonmedical physical care.[5] The church, however, does not stop its members from seeing a doctor; it leaves the choice to the individual. The church does permit conventional therapy for "mechanical" problems such as broken bones and dental cavities.

Today there are more than 2,700 Christian Science churches worldwide.

---

[1] *Gospel:* in the Bible, one of the four stories of Christ's life
[2] *New Testament:* part of the Bible that tells about Christ's life and his teachings
[3] *scriptures:* holy books or writings of a religion; the writings of the Bible
[4] *"practitioner":* a person who has been schooled and trained in praying for the sick
[5] *nonmedical physical care:* includes taking care of hygiene and dietary needs as well as caring for wounds and injuries; does not include giving any medication

Not everyone believes in conventional medicine. Some people do not agree that doctors, drugs, or surgery are the best way to treat medical problems. Instead, they seek alternative types of medical care. Mary Baker Eddy created a religious movement whose beliefs supported nonconventional medical care. What do you think? Complete the following sentences individually and then discuss your answers with a partner.

1. Some people try nonconventional methods of healing because _____

_____

2. Many people look to spiritual healing—reading religious scriptures—
to help them get better because _____

_____

3. I agree (or disagree) with Mary Baker Eddy's philosophy that all sickness is mental rather than physical because _____

_____

B. VOCABULARY FOR COMPREHENSION

Reading One examines the role of the legal system in controlling a person's choice of medical treatment. Look at this list of words and put them in one of the two categories in the chart below. Discuss their meaning with a partner. If you are not sure of their meaning, use your dictionary. Some words may be applied to both categories.

Verb phrases
commit (a crime)
convict
go (to court)
heal
judge *l*
shed (weight) m
stand (trial) *l*
suffer m

Nouns
accuser *l*
ailment m
ambulance
attorney *l*
autopsy m
consequence M
diabetes M
felony ∟
manslaughter L
physician M
practitioner M
prosecutor ∟
stomachache M

Adjective phrases
listless M
sunken (eyes) M

LEGAL SYSTEM VOCABULARY		MEDICAL VOCABULARY	
✓			

3 READING ONE: Dying for Their Beliefs

A. INTRODUCING THE TOPIC

Read the first three paragraphs and discuss these questions with a partner.

What is the problem?

What do you think is happening to Amy at home?

Dying for Their Beliefs: Christian Scientist Parents on Trial in Girl's Death

By Jeffrey Good (from *St. Petersburg Times*)

healthy happy

1   Amy Hermanson was a sunny seven-year-old with blond hair and bubbly ways. She liked to serenade adults with her favorite song: Disney's "It's a Small World After All."

2   But Amy's world went awry one Sunday in 1986. An adult friend of her family noticed the child's sunken eyes, her listless manner, the way her clothes hung from her tiny bones. She tried to get the child to sing her favorite song.

3   "She used to come over and sing every verse to me. I couldn't even get her to make a comment on the song, let alone sing it," the friend, Mary Christman, would later tell investigators. She recalled her husband saying, "If the child does not receive medical attention, she will be dead within a week."

4   But Amy's parents are Christian Scientists. They decided to try to heal the child with prayer rather than seek a doctor's aid. Two days after the Christmans saw her, Amy died of diabetes.

5   On Monday, Amy's parents are scheduled to go on trial in the Sarasota County Courthouse on charges of third-degree murder[1] and felony child abuse.[2] Prosecutors say William and Christine Hermanson committed a crime by putting religious principles ahead of protecting their daughter. The Hermansons say their accusers are wrong. If convicted, the couple could face three to seven years in jail.

6   At issue is a legal principle with national ramifications. Since 1967, no Christian Scientist in the United States has stood trial for denying children medical care for religious reasons. Six similar cases are pending, but the Hermansons are the first to go to court.

7   "The children are entitled to protection, and if the parents won't give it to them, they [the parents] will suffer the [legal] consequences," says Mack Futch, an assistant state attorney in Sarasota County.

---

[1] *third-degree murder:* murder without intention
[2] *felony child abuse:* a serious crime involving hurting a child physically or psychologically

8   The Hermansons, however, have maintained that prosecutors want to violate their constitutional right of religious freedom. And in interviews last week, their supporters maintained that the couple treated their daughter with a proven—if unconventional—method of healing.

9   Frederick Hillier, a Christian Science "practitioner" who was ministering to the child when she died, said that Christian Scientists regard prayer as a better treatment than conventional medicine. "A Christian Scientist is doing nothing any different than anyone who has found medical treatment to be effective," said Hillier, who also acts as the spokesman for Florida Christian Science churches. "Why do Christian Scientists rely on spiritual healing when they could go to a physician if they wanted to? In their experience, they found it to be effective."

10   Church members acknowledge that their methods sometimes fail, just as doctors sometimes fail, he said. But that doesn't mean the Christian Scientists deserve criminal charges any more than the doctors do, he said. "We don't claim any more than anyone else claims to be 100 percent effective," Hillier said. "Even Jesus didn't."

11   Amy's third grade report card was her last. It showed A's in reading, English, spelling, mathematics, science, and social studies. "Amy takes a keen interest in all her work," a teacher wrote.

12   But in September 1986, Amy began fourth grade as a different child. Teachers noticed her dozing off in class, shedding weight at an alarming rate, and complaining of stomachaches. At one point, she held her hands over her ears and pleaded, "Stop the noise. Stop the noise," at the sound of a pencil scratching paper.

13   "After the school year began, Amy was often upset. She would cry and say that she did not feel well," said June R. McHugh, director of the private Julie Rohr Academy attended by Amy and her older brother, Eric. McHugh told investigators that about a week before Amy's death, she told Mrs. Hermanson her daughter might be suffering from a physical ailment. McHugh recalled that Mrs. Hermanson said "the situation was being handled."

14   On September 22, one of the practitioners began praying for the child.

15   On September 25, the Hermansons left Amy in a baby-sitter's care and went to Indiana for a Christian Science conference on spiritual healing. They returned on September 29.

16   But at 8:30 A.M. on September 30, 1986, a state social worker in Sarasota took a call from Amy's aunt. The worker's notes sketched a chilling picture: "Over the last two weeks (Amy) has lost 10 pounds, drinks constantly, eats large amounts of food, muscle tone is virtually gone, eyes are sunken and functioning separately. Child can barely walk and has to be carried—All indications point to diabetes but parents refuse to take said child to the doctor as they are Christian Scientists."

17   A court hearing was scheduled for 1:30 P.M. and Amy's father arrived early. At 1:27 P.M., Hermanson took a phone call from home reporting that Amy had taken a turn for the worse and an ambulance was en route. Learning this, the judge ordered that a medical doctor examine Amy.

18   But it was too late. With Christian Science practitioner Hillier nearby, Amy had died in her parents' bed.

Most Important Right

19   After performing an autopsy on the child, Associate Medical Examiner James C. Wilson concluded that medical treatment up to just hours before her death probably could have saved Amy. The Hermansons have acknowledged they never sought such treatment. That does not make them criminals, say their lawyers and supporters.

20   "There isn't anyone who is more loving to their children than Christian Scientists," said Bob Drabik, chairman of the board of directors at Sarasota's First Church, Christian Science, where the Hermansons are members.

21   Florida law says parents can't be judged "abusive or neglectful" because they withhold conventional medical treatment for religious reasons. Similar laws exist in most states. They were enacted under heavy lobbying from the Boston-based church after one of its members, Dorothy Sheridan of Harwich, Massachusetts, was convicted in 1967 of manslaughter in the death of her child. "William and Christine Hermanson, at all times material[3] to the facts in

---

[3] *material:* related

this case, followed the religious teachings of their church and relied upon Christian Science healing in the care and treatment of Amy Hermanson," the court record states.

22   Within the legal community, there is considerable debate over whether that is an adequate defense when a child dies. Harvard law professor Alan Dershowitz says that such trials revolve around two important constitutional rights: parents' freedom of religion, and children's right to grow up healthy.

23   In cases where one right must take priority, Dershowitz says, the choice is clear: "It's not a difficult question. Children have a right to live and be brought up to make their own religious decisions."

24   Hillier, the Christian Science spokesman, said that church members view prayer as the best way to make sick children well. "We don't want the right to do harm to children," he said, "we only want the right to do what is good for children."

Handwritten notes:

8. Why do christian scientists rely on Prayer?
9. What grade was Amy in?
10. What symptoms did Amy show in Sep. 1986?

1. How old is Amy?
2. Who is Mary christman?
3. What religious group do Amy's Parents Follow?
4. Can you describe this religion?
5. Why are Amy's Parents on trial?
6. Who is Mack Futch?
7. Who is Frederick Hilliers?

B. READING FOR MAIN IDEAS

Handwritten:
11. Who is June McHugh?
12. When did Amy die?
13. Who is James Wilson?
14. what two legal issues are being

Handwritten multiplication:
500 ×
850
2500
4000
425,000

Complete the following sentences based on your understanding of the reading.

1. Amy's disease was _____

_____

2. Amy could have been saved if _____

_____

3. Her parents are going on trial because _____

_____

4. Christian Scientists and other supporters defend the Hermansons because _____

_____

5. Some people in the legal community believe that there are two issues:

_____

_____

Handwritten:
Her
(Her Parents)

H

C. READING FOR DETAILS

*Write whether the following sentences are true (**T**) or false (**F**).*

T ___ **1.** If Amy had received medical care just two hours before she died, she probably could have been saved.

F ___ **2.** Some of the symptoms of Amy's disease were: loss of weight, stomachaches, and an intense interest in schoolwork.

F ___ **3.** The Hermansons feel children have the right to make their own religious decisions.

T ___ **4.** Christian Scientists and their supporters believe they want only to do what is good for their children.

T ___ **5.** Christian Scientists believe prayer is better than conventional medicine.

F ___ **6.** In Florida, parents can be judged "abusive or neglectful" if they choose to deny their children conventional medical care for religious reasons.

D. READING BETWEEN THE LINES

Work in groups and decide which of the following people could have made the statements on the next page. In some cases, it is possible that more than one of these people could have made the statement. Write the appropriate letter(s) next to each statement. Refer to the reading to support your answers.

a. Amy Hermanson
   sick child

b. Alan Dershowitz
   Harvard law professor

c. Mack Futch
   assistant state attorney

d. Frederick Hillier
   Christian Science "practitioner" and spokesman

e. Dorothy Sheridan
   Christian Scientist convicted of manslaughter

f. James C. Wilson
   associate medical examiner

_C_ **1.** If parents don't give their children medical protection, the court (government) must then get involved.

_d&e_ **2.** Prayer, although not always effective, is the best treatment available.

_C_ **3.** The Hermansons are responsible for Amy's death.

_E_ **4.** This was a senseless death. Medically, it could have been prevented.

_d&e_ **5.** Our right to religious freedom allows us to decide what is best for our children.

_a_ **6.** Being a good student is easy if you can concentrate on your schoolwork.

_b_ **7.** A child should be able to live long enough to make his/her own religious decisions.

_d&e_ **8.** It's worth being convicted of a crime if what we do is for the benefit of our children.

_d_ **9.** Spiritual healing is just as legitimate a type of medical treatment as drugs.

_b_ **10.** A child's right to live is more important than his or her parents' religious beliefs.

4 | READING TWO: | Norman Cousins's Laugh Therapy

A. EXPANDING THE TOPIC

Charlie Chaplin, comedian

Read this background information about Norman Cousins. Work with a partner and answer the questions that follow. Then read "Norman Cousins's Laugh Therapy."

Norman Cousins was a well-known writer and editor who, when diagnosed with a serious illness, decided to find his own type of alternative therapy. After writing about his recovery, he received mail from all over the world. Many letters came from doctors. They supported his idea. Norman Cousins stressed the importance of a positive attitude in healing.

1. What do you think Norman Cousins meant by "a positive attitude in healing"?

2. What do you think you can do to have a positive attitude?

3. Why do you think Charlie Chaplin (see the photograph on page 63) could be associated with a positive attitude and healing?

Norman Cousins's Laugh Therapy

1   In the summer of 1964, well-known writer and editor Norman Cousins became very ill. His body ached and he felt constantly tired. It was difficult for him to even move around. He consulted his physician, who did many tests. Eventually he was diagnosed as having ankylosing spondylitis, a very serious and destructive form of arthritis.[1] His doctor told him that he would become immobilized[2] and eventually die from the disease. He was told he had only a 1 in 500 chance of survival.

2   Despite the diagnosis,[3] Cousins was determined to overcome the disease and survive. He had always been interested in medicine and had read the work of organic chemist Hans Selye, *The Stress of Life* (1956). This book discussed the idea of how body chemistry and health can be damaged by emotional stress and negative attitudes. Selye's book made Cousins think about the possible benefits of positive attitudes and emotions. He thought, "If negative emotions produce (negative) changes in the body, wouldn't positive emotions produce positive chemical changes? Is it possible that love, hope, faith, laughter, confidence, and the will to live have positive therapeutic value?"

3   He decided to concentrate on positive emotions as a remedy to heal some of the symptoms of his ailment. In addition to his conventional medical treatment, he tried to put himself in situations that would elicit positive emotions. "Laugh therapy" became part of his treatment. He scheduled time each day for watching comedy films, reading humorous books, and doing other activities that would bring about laughter and positive emotions. Within eight days of starting his "laugh therapy" program his pain began to decrease and he was able to sleep more easily. His body chemistry even improved. Doctors were able to see an improvement in his condition! He was able to return to work in a few months' time and actually reached complete recovery after a few years.

4   Skeptical readers may question the doctor's preliminary diagnosis, but Cousins believes his recovery is the result of a mysterious mind-body interaction. His "laugh therapy" is a good example of one of the many alternative, or nonconventional, medical treatments people look to today.

---

[1] *arthritis:* a disease that causes pain and swelling of the joints of the body
[2] *immobilized:* not able to move
[3] *diagnosis:* identification of the cause or nature of an illness

Write short answers to the following questions.

كى الفول
ر ، ب   react

1. What was Norman Cousins's original diagnosis?

A very serious form of arthritis.

باانحرا   كى الفل الجهارت والنشئ ب   riakt

2. How did he react, or respond, to his diagnosis?   جرم

He wanted to fight the ~~deasea~~ diseaa.

3. What is the connection between mind and body in laugh therapy?

If negative emotions bring negative
Positive emotions ~~bring~~ should bring Positive
laughter has a positive

4. What are some examples of laugh therapy?

Watching funny movies and reading funny books.

5. What was the result of Cousins's laugh therapy?

He was able to overcome his diseas.
↓
Verysick
or cancer

B. LINKING READINGS ONE AND TWO on

Work in a small group. Discuss the following questions. Then choose one of the questions and write your own response.

1. What are the similarities and differences between Norman Cousins's laugh therapy and the Christian Scientists' therapy through prayer and the Bible?

2. Norman Cousins decided to take responsibility for his own health care; he applied laugh therapy. In other words, he used an alternative form of treatment to help cure his arthritis—and he is convinced this therapy saved his life. He used his right as an adult to choose the treatment he believed was best for him. Does this right also extend to parents' choice of treatment they believe is best for their child? Why or why not?

5 REVIEWING LANGUAGE

A. EXPLORING LANGUAGE

Work with a partner. Indicate whether the following pairs of words are similar (S) or different (D) in meaning. The first one has been done for you.

1. doze	sleep	S *sim*
2. symptom	ailment	D *def*
3. persuade	convince	S *sim*
4. skeptic	follower	D
5. conventional	alternative	D
6. principles	beliefs	S
7. accuse	defend	D
8. attorney	lawyer	S
9. acknowledge	admit	S
10. shedding	losing	S
11. debate	agreement	D

B. WORKING WITH WORDS: Analogies

An **analogy** is a comparison between two words that seem similar or are related in some way. In the word sets below, the two words in the second set relate to each other in the same way that the two words in the first set relate to each other. For example, in set 1 *arthritis* is a type of *diagnosis*; in the same way, *achiness* is a type of *symptom*.

Working with a partner, discuss the relationship between the words. Underline the word that best completes each analogy. The first one has been done for you.

1. *arthritis* is to *diagnosis*

   as *achiness* is to _____

   a. *disease*   b. *symptom*   c. *cure*

2. *therapy* is to *cure*

   as *treatment* is to _____

   a. *heal*   b. *regimen*   c. *practitioner*

3. *lawyer* is to *attorney*

   as *doctor* is to _____

   a. *nurse*   b. *patient*   c. *physician*

4. *typical* is to *common*

   as *unconventional* is to _____

   a. *conventional*   b. *mainstream*   c. *alternative*

5. *judge* is to *verdict*

   as *doctor* is to _____

   a. *symptom*   b. *diagnosis*   c. *disease*

6. *medicine* is to *physician*

   as *law* is to _____

   a. *prosecutor*   b. *accuser*   c. *attorney*

7. *evidence* is to *crime*

   as *symptom* is to _____

   a. *jury*   b. *ailment*   c. *treatment*

6 SKILLS FOR EXPRESSION

A. GRAMMAR: Past Unreal Conditionals

1 *Work with a partner. Examine the sample sentences below. Write whether the statements following these sentences are true (**T**) or false (**F**).*

a. If Amy <u>hadn't died</u>, the medical examiner <u>wouldn't have examined</u> her.

b. If Amy's parents <u>had seen</u> a conventional doctor, Amy <u>could have taken</u> medicine to control her diabetes.

c. If Amy <u>had sung</u> her favorite song, Mrs. Christman <u>might not have noticed</u> she was sick.

In **a:** Amy died. _____

      The medical examiner didn't examine her body. _____

In **b:** Amy's parents didn't see a conventional doctor. _____

      Amy didn't take medicine to control her diabetes. _____

In **c:** Amy didn't sing her favorite song. _____

      Mrs. Christman didn't notice she was sick. _____

FOCUS ON GRAMMAR

See Unreal Conditionals: Past in *Focus on Grammar, High Intermediate.*

Past Unreal Conditional

Form of the Past Unreal Conditional

A **past unreal conditional** sentence has two clauses: the **if clause**, which states the condition, and the **result clause**, which states the result. The sentence can begin with either the *if* clause or the result clause and the meaning is the same. Notice the use of the comma (**,**) when the *if* clause comes at the beginning of the sentence. Notice also the verb forms used in each clause.

If Clause	Result Clause
If + subject + past perfect,	subject + *would (not) have* + past participle
	could (not) have
	might (not) have

◆ **If** Amy **hadn't died,** he **would not have examined** her.

Result Clause	*If* Clause
Subject + *would (not) have* + past participle *could (not) have* *might (not) have*	*if* + subject + past participle

◆ Amy **could have taken** medicine **if** her parents **had brought** her to a doctor.

- -

Meaning of the Past Unreal Conditional

The past unreal conditional talks about past unreal, untrue (contrary to fact), or imagined conditions and their results. Both parts of the sentence describe events that are the opposite of what really happened.

Conditional statement:	Mrs. Christman might not have noticed if Amy had sung.
What really happened:	Mrs. Christman noticed. Amy didn't sing.

The past unreal conditional is often used to express regret about what really happened. To express possibility or uncertainty about the result clause, use **might have** or **could have** in the result clause.

2 *Read the conditional sentences. Decide if the statements that follow each conditional are true or false. Write **T** or **F**. The first one has been done for you.*

1. If Mary Baker Eddy hadn't slipped on the ice, she wouldn't have broken her ankle.

   __T__ She slipped on the ice.

   __F__ She didn't break her ankle.

2. If Norman Cousins had been healthy, he wouldn't have had to try laugh therapy.

   _____ Norman Cousins was healthy.

   _____ He didn't have to try laugh therapy.

3. According to the medical examiner, Amy Hermanson might have lived if she had been given medication.

_____ Amy died.

_____ Amy wasn't given medication.

4. If Amy had stayed awake in class, her teacher might not have noticed that something was wrong.

_____ Amy slept in class.

_____ Her teacher noticed that something was wrong.

5. If Mary Baker Eddy hadn't been so religious, she might not have turned to prayer to cure herself.

_____ Mary Baker Eddy was religious.

_____ She turned to prayer to cure herself.

6. If Amy's parents hadn't been Christian Scientists, they might have gotten conventional medical help for Amy.

_____ Amy's parents are not Christian Scientists.

_____ Amy's parents didn't get her conventional medical help.

7. Amy's parents wouldn't have gone on trial for third-degree murder if she had not died.

_____ Amy's parents didn't go on trial for third-degree murder.

_____ Amy died.

8. If Norman Cousins hadn't believed in a mind-body interaction, laugh therapy might not have worked for him.

_____ Norman Cousins didn't believe in a mind-body interaction.

_____ Laugh therapy didn't work for him.

3 *Write a sentence about each of the following situations. Use the past unreal conditional. An example has been done for you.*

1. Mary Christman had a headache. She took some aspirin. She soon felt better.

If she hadn't taken aspirin, she might not have felt better.

2. James C. Wilson had a problem with his allergies. He didn't go to a homeopathic doctor. He continued to have problems.

_____

_____

3. Norman Cousins read extensively about alternative medicine. When he was diagnosed with ankylosing spondylitis, he already had some ideas about alternative treatments.

_____

_____

4. Norman Cousins was sick. He tried to cure himself by using laugh therapy. He soon got better.

_____

_____

5. Mack Futch was not a Christian Scientist. He believed in conventional Western medicine. He gave his daughter drugs when she was sick.

_____

_____

6. Amy began dozing off in class. Her teacher noticed that something was wrong. She called Amy's parents.

_____

_____

7. Norman Cousins didn't like his doctor's treatment plan. He developed his own laugh therapy treatment.

_____

_____

B. STYLE: Opinion Essays

They did it   doe

William and Christine Hermanson were found guilty in the death of their child, Amy. They received a four-year suspended sentence and were placed on probation for fifteen years. The sentence created a great deal of discussion both in favor of and against the verdict. Many people wrote to newspapers expressing their opinion.

Work with a partner. Examine the opinion essay on page 72 and answer the questions that follow.

49

The sentencing of the Hermansons is a shock and disappointment to me. That any such loving and devoted parents could be convicted of negligence in the death of their children is a mystery. First let me say that I am a loving and devoted parent. I am president of our local parent-teacher association. I am a Harvard graduate and a lawyer. I am a Christian Scientist also. I know that spiritual healing can be an effective treatment and I would like to share my positive experiences with you.

When I was born, I had a blood problem. The doctor gave me two hours to live. At the time, blood transfusions were not available for this problem. My mother, a Christian Scientist, brought in a practitioner and through their prayer I was healed. I believe that if my mother hadn't been a Christian Scientist, I would probably not have lived. With my own children there have been numerous occasions where conventional medicine would have prescribed antibiotics for ear infections, colds, etc. With the power of prayer, my children have been healed without these medicines.

In the end, I believe that the type of medical treatment chosen should be left up to the individual. Not only is this my opinion, but, in fact, it is a right guaranteed by our constitution. Choosing the treatment you feel is most effective is a right that cannot be taken away. Children die under medical treatment too, and no one accuses the parents of negligence or brings them to court.

opinion

a. What is the writer's opinion?

b. How does she use her background to support her opinion?

c. What details and examples does she use to support her opinion?

d. What is her conclusion? How does she support her conclusion?

Opinion Essays

An **essay** includes several paragraphs which are written about the same subject. An **opinion essay** is written to persuade or convince the reader that your opinion is "the right way to think about things."

- -

Organization

The simplest opinion essay includes three parts:

◆ An introductory paragraph that clearly states the opinion of the writer

◆ The body of the essay (one or two paragraphs) that gives examples, details, and facts to support the opinion

◆ The concluding paragraph that summarizes the arguments in the essay and reinforces the opinion.

Audience

When writing an opinion essay, you must think about your audience —your readers—and any opinions or knowledge they already have. If your readers have no opinion on the subject, persuading them to agree with you may not be difficult. However, if the audience has an opinion contrary or opposite to yours, persuading them may be more challenging. In that case, you must try to convince the readers that at the very least, your opinion is justifiable and worth considering. In order to do this you must present your arguments clearly and support your opinion with evidence: examples, facts, or personal experience.

Supporting Evidence

If you are trying to convince the readers to accept your opinion, you need to give evidence to support your opinion. You also need to give reasons which explain why the evidence supports your opinion. You need to explain why you feel your opinion is correct and the readers' opinions are incorrect.

NOTE: See Units 1 and 2 for information on paragraph writing.

2year.

june

Tha July
August
Sepey
oct
Novey
December

2 *What is your opinion on the court's judgment of the Hermansons? Prepare to write an opinion essay (do not actually write it).*

1. Begin by taking a position. Do you support the decision? Why or why not?

2. Complete the chart on page 74 with notes to introduce, support, and conclude your essay. Use information from the readings and from personal experience.

3. Discuss your outline with a classmate. Is your opinion clearly stated? Do your supporting details really support your position?

THREE MAIN PARTS

I. The introduction: Clearly state your position/ identify your position	Introduction: _____ _____ _____ _____
II. The body: Give details and examples to support your position	Body: _____ _____ _____ _____
III. The conclusion: Summarize and reinforce your position	Conclusion: _____ _____ _____ _____

7 ON YOUR OWN

A. WRITING TOPICS

Write a short opinion essay on one of the following topics. Be sure to include the three parts of an essay. Try to use the past unreal conditional and any ideas or language you have learned in this unit.

1. Write an essay giving your opinion on the court's decision regarding the Hermansons. Use the above chart to guide you as you write.

2. Different cultures define nonconventional medicine in different ways. What do you think nonconventional medicine is? How do you feel about the use of nonconventional medicine? Write about your ideas and opinions.

3. What do you think of Norman Cousins's laugh therapy? Do you think there is any truth to the idea of a mind-body interaction? Have you ever had a medical experience where your mind was stronger than your body? Write an essay expressing your opinion. If possible, include personal experiences.

B. FIELDWORK

Take a survey of your classmates. What do you and your classmates do for the following ailments? Do you think the treatments your classmates use are conventional or nonconventional? Enter your findings on the chart. Then discuss the questions on page 76 with your class.

AILMENT	CONVENTIONAL	NONCONVENTIONAL
Cold		
Cough		
Headache		
Backache		
Stomachache (nausea)		

1. Which remedies are most commonly used by your classmates?

2. Which remedies do you personally use most often?

3. Are there any remedies your classmates use that you would like to try? Explain your answer.

4. Do you and your classmates have the same ideas about what is conventional and nonconventional medical treatment? If not, discuss the differences.

RESEARCH ACTIVITY

Work in small groups. What treatment would you like to know more about? Brainstorm places where you can get information about this treatment (such as a library or a drugstore). Research the treatment. Share your research with your group. Then write a brief report and present it to the class. Answer the following questions in your report.

1. What is the name of the treatment?

2. What does the treatment cure?

3. Where can you find this treatment (for example, in a drugstore, a health food store, in another country, in nature)?

4. Is this treatment commonly used?

5. Do you need a prescription (written permission from a doctor) to buy it?

6. Where does it come from (for example, a plant, a tree, an animal, man-made products)?

7. How do you take it (for example, a pill, a drink, a compress)?

8. How does it make you feel (for example, tired, happy, dizzy)?

THE CALM AFTER THE STORM

Tornado

Severe storm (hurricane)

Earthquake

Forest fire

1 APPROACHING THE TOPIC

A. PREDICTING

Look at the photographs and the title of this unit. Take some notes about each of the natural disasters you see pictured. Describe what has happened. What do you think "The Calm after the Storm" refers to?

77

B. SHARING INFORMATION

1 *Work with a partner. Look at the photographs on page 77 and your notes. What happens in a natural disaster? Match the pictures with some of the common consequences (listed below) of each of the natural disasters shown. Some of these consequences may occur after more than one type of disaster.*

ashes falling like rain
flames pouring down
collapsed and smashed buildings
flooded streets and homes
ships lost at sea

water main breaks
debris in the streets
fallen walls
disruptions of telephone service
earth moving and shaking

2 *Discuss one or more of the following topics with a partner.*

- ◆ Describe a time when you felt the most panicked in your life.

- ◆ Describe a time when you felt the most alone in your life.

- ◆ Discuss a time when patience and the passage of time were the only solutions to a predicament.

PREPARING TO READ

A. BACKGROUND

Work with a partner. Look at the two pictures on the next page and answer the following questions.

1. In which picture does the man appear to be in the safest position, protected from the water and sea creatures? Why?

2. What do you think has happened to this man?

3. How do you think he feels?

Gunwale

Life raft

Basket   **Gu**

B. VOCABULARY FOR COMPREHENSION

Work in a small group. Circle the word which does not belong in each set of words. Use a dictionary if necessary. Discuss how the remaining three words are related. The first one has been done for you.

1. sun	(horizon)	moon	stars
2. desperation	(torture)	patience	hopelessness
3. alone	solitude	loneliness	hope
4. abandoned	deserted	thick	empty
5. red	dark	yellow	violet
6. dense	thick	packed	glowing
7. quiet	straight	silent	tranquil
8. look	scrutinize	divert	watch
9. immense	endless	inevitable	infinite
10. search	throw	fling	toss
11. blink	whip	hit	slap

bright

I got slap

3

My First Night Alone in the Caribbean

A. INTRODUCING THE TOPIC

During a severe storm in February 1955, several crew members of a Colombian destroyer were thrown over the side of the ship and disappeared. Ten days later one of the crew was found, half-dead, on a deserted beach in northern Colombia. At that time, novelist Gabriel García Marquez was working for a newspaper in Colombia. The book entitled *The Story of a Shipwrecked Sailor* is his account of that sailor's story. The excerpt below, a passage from the book, describes the sailor's first night alone in the Caribbean.

Before you begin reading the excerpt, make a list of the dangers you think this sailor may have faced. Compare your list with a partner's.

My First Night Alone in the Caribbean

BY GABRIEL GARCÍA MARQUEZ
(from *The Story of a Shipwrecked Sailor*)

1   At first it seemed impossible that I had been alone at sea for three hours. But at five o'clock, after five hours had passed, it seemed I might have to wait yet another hour. The sun was setting. It got very big and red in the west, and I began to orient[1] myself. Now I knew where the planes would appear: with the sun to my left, I stared straight ahead, not moving, not daring to blink, not diverting my sight for an instant from the direction in which, by my bearings,[2] Cartagena[3] lay. By six o'clock my eyes hurt. But I kept watching. Even after it began to get dark, I watched with stubborn patience. I knew I wouldn't be able to see the planes, but I would spot their red and green lights heading toward me before I heard the noise of the engines. I wanted to see the lights, forgetting that, in the darkness, no one in the planes would see me. Soon the sky turned red, and I continued to search the horizon. Then it turned a deep violet as I kept watching. To one side of the life raft like a yellow diamond in a wine colored sky,

---

[1] *orient:* to locate
[2] *bearing:* direction or relative position
[3] *Cartagena:* large city in Colombia on the Caribbean coast

the first star appeared, immobile and perfect. It was like a signal: immediately afterward, night fell.

2   The first thing I felt, plunged into darkness so thick I could no longer see the palm of my hand, was that I wouldn't be able to overcome the terror. From the slapping of the waves against the sides, I knew the raft was moving, slowly but inexorably. Sunk into darkness, I realized I hadn't felt so alone in the daytime. I was more alone in the dark, in a raft that I could no longer see but could feel beneath me, gliding silently over a dense sea filled with strange creatures. To make myself less lonely, I looked at the dial of my watch. It was ten minutes to seven. Much later—it seemed as if two or three hours had passed— it was five minutes to seven. When the minute hand reached twelve, it was exactly seven o'clock and the sky was packed with stars. But to me it seemed that so much time had passed, it should now be nearly dawn. Desperately I went on thinking about the planes.

3   I started to feel cold. In a life raft it's impossible to stay dry even for a minute. Even if you are seated on the gunwale, half your body is underwater because the bottom of the raft is shaped like a basket, extending more than half a meter below the surface. By eight o'clock the water was not as cold as the air. I knew that at the bottom of the raft I was safe from sea creatures because the rope mesh that protected the bottom prevented them from coming too close. But that's what you learn in school, and that's what you believe in school, when the instructor puts on a demonstration with a scale model of the life raft and you're seated on a bench among forty classmates at two o'clock in the afternoon. When you're alone at sea at eight o'clock at night, and without hope, the instructor's words make no sense at all. I knew that half of my body was in a realm that didn't belong to men but to the creatures of the sea, and that despite the icy wind whipping my shirt, I didn't dare move from the gunwale. According to the instructor, that was the least safe part of the raft. But all things considered, it was only there that I felt far enough away from the creatures: those immense unknown beasts I could hear passing the raft.

4   My first night at sea seemed very long because absolutely nothing happened. It is impossible to describe a night on a life raft, when nothing happens and you're scared of unseen creatures and you've got a watch with a glowing dial that you can't stop checking even for a minute. The night of February 28—my first night at sea—I looked at my watch every minute. It was torture. In desperation, I swore I would stop doing it and I'd stow[4] the watch in my pocket, so as not to be so dependent on the time. I was able to resist until twenty to nine. I still wasn't hungry or thirsty, and I was sure I could hold out until the following day, when the planes would arrive. But I thought the watch would drive me crazy. A prisoner of anxiety, I took it off my wrist to

---

[4] *stow:* to put away, to store

stuff it in my pocket, but as I held it in my hand it occurred to me that it would be better to fling[5] it into the sea. I hesitated a moment. Then I was terrified: I thought I would feel even more alone without the watch. I put it back on my wrist and began to look at it again, minute by minute, as I had in the afternoon when I searched the horizon for airplanes until my eyes began to hurt.

5   After midnight I wanted to cry. I hadn't slept for a moment, but I hadn't even wanted to. With the same hope I had felt in the afternoon as I waited for airplanes, that night I looked for the lights of ships. For hours I scrutinized the sea, a tranquil sea, immense and silent, but I didn't see a single light other than the stars.

6   The cold was more intense in the early hours of morning, and it seemed as if my body were glowing, with all the sun of the afternoon embedded under my skin. With the cold, it burned more intensely. From midnight on, my right knee began to hurt and I felt as though the water had penetrated my bones. But these feelings were remote: I thought about my body less than about the lights of the ships. It seemed to me, in the midst[6] of that infinite solitude, in the midst of the sea's dark murmur, that if I spotted the light of only a single ship, I would let out a yell that could be heard at any distance.

---

[5] *fling:* to throw
[6] *midst:* middle

dist.

B. READING FOR MAIN IDEAS

Complete the chart. Summarize the sailor's physical and emotional state from the first afternoon at sea through the following morning. An example has been done for you.

TIME	PHYSICAL STATE	EMOTIONAL STATE
During the first afternoon	okay so far, doesn't seem cold yet	patient, hopeful, able to see the beauty in the sunset
After dark		
Early the following morning (after midnight)		

C. READING FOR DETAILS

Write short answers to the following.

1. Why was the sailor afraid to blink during the first afternoon?

2. Why did he feel so much terror in the dark?

3. What had he learned in school about being in a raft?

4. Why didn't he want to move away from the gunwale and into the life raft?

5. How did he try to overcome his loneliness?

6. Why did his watch begin to drive him crazy?

7. From midnight on, what was his main concern?

D. READING BETWEEN THE LINES

Imagine that you are the sailor in the story. You have just found an empty bottle in the sea, and you want to write a note to put in the bottle. Complete the note on the right. Describe what happened to you, how you have been feeling, and any other information you think is important. Think about the following feelings as you write your note: patience, terror, loneliness, anxiety, and hopelessness.

Hello!
I hope someone finds this soon and can help rescue me. I was swept off the deck of a ship on February 27, 1955. By my calculations, I believe I am near the northeast coast of Colombia.

4 READING TWO: The Story of an Eyewitness

A. EXPANDING THE TOPIC

In 1906, San Francisco was hit by one of the biggest and deadliest earthquakes in U.S. history. Jack London, an American novelist, was working as a reporter at the time.

Work in groups. Make a list of damages an earthquake causes to a large city. Then read the article.

By Jack London (from *Colliers*)

The Story of an Eyewitness

earthquake. earthquake.

1   On Wednesday morning at a quarter past five came the earthquake. A minute later the flames were leaping upward. In a dozen different quarters south of Market Street, in the working-class ghetto, and in the factories, fires started. There was no organization, no communication. All the cunning[1] adjustments of a twentieth-century city had been smashed by the earthquake. The streets were humped into ridges and depressions, and piled with the debris of fallen walls. The steel rails[2] were twisted into perpendicular and horizontal angles. The telephone and telegraph systems were disrupted. And the great water mains had burst. All the shrewd contrivances and safeguards of man had been thrown out of gear[3] by thirty seconds' twitching of the earth-crust.

2   By Wednesday afternoon, inside of twelve hours, half the heart of the city was gone. At that time I watched the vast conflagration[4] from out on the bay. It was dead calm. Not a flicker of wind stirred. Yet from every side wind was pouring in upon the city. East, west, north, and south strong winds were blowing upon the doomed city. The

---

[1] *cunning*: clever, smart
[2] *steel rails*: railroad track
[3] *thrown out of gear*: disrupted
[4] *conflagration*: large fire that destroys property

heated air rising made an enormous suck.[5] Thus did the fire of itself build its own colossal chimney through the atmosphere. Day and night this dead calm continued, and yet, near to the flames, the wind was often half a gale,[6] so mighty was the suck.

3   Remarkable as it may seem, Wednesday night, while the whole city crashed and roared into ruin, was a quiet night. There were no crowds. There was no shouting and yelling. There was no hysteria, no disorder. I passed Wednesday night in the path of the advancing flames, and in all those terrible hours I saw not one woman who wept, not one man who was excited, not one person who was in the slightest degree panic-stricken.

4   At nine o'clock Wednesday evening I walked down through the heart of the city. I walked through miles and miles of magnificent buildings and towering skyscrapers. Here was no fire. All was in perfect order. The police patrolled the streets. Every building had its watchman at the door. And yet it was doomed, all of it. There was no water. And at right angles two different conflagrations were sweeping down upon it.

5   At one o'clock in the morning I walked down through the same section. Everything still stood intact. There was no fire. And yet there was a change. A rain of ashes was falling. The watchmen at the doors were gone. The police had been withdrawn. There were no firemen, no fire-engines, no men fighting with dynamite. The district had been absolutely abandoned. I stood at the corner of Kearney and Market, in the very innermost heart of San Francisco. Kearney Street was deserted.

6   It was at Union Square that I saw a man offering a thousand dollars for a team of horses. He was in charge of a truck piled high with trunks from some hotel. It had been hauled here into what was considered safety, and the horses had been taken out. The flames were on three sides of the Square, and there were no horses.

7   Also, at this time, standing beside the truck, I urged a man to seek safety in flight. He was all but hemmed in by several conflagrations. He was an old man and he was on crutches. Said he: "Today is my birthday. Last night I was worth thirty thousand dollars. I bought five bottles of wine, some delicate fish, and other things for my birthday dinner. I have no dinner, and all I own are these crutches."

8   On Thursday morning, at a quarter past five, just twenty-four hours after the earthquake, I sat on the steps of a small residence on Nob Hill. . . .

9   I went inside with the owner of the house on the steps of which I sat. He was cool and cheerful and hospitable. "Yesterday morning," he said, "I was worth six hundred thousand dollars. This morning this house is all I have left. It will go in fifteen minutes." He pointed to a large cabinet. "That is my wife's collection of china. This rug upon which we stand is a present. It cost fifteen hundred dollars. Try that piano. Listen to its tone. There are few like it. There are no horses. The flames will be here in fifteen minutes."

---

[5] *suck:* air current, vacuum
[6] *half a gale:* 15 to 30 mile per hour winds

Write short answers to the following questions.

1. Parts of San Francisco were devastated by the earthquake. What were some of the damages? Are these damages similar to what you predicted in your group before you read the article?

2. By the night after the earthquake, all was seemingly quiet. How does Jack London describe the people and city at that time?

B. LINKING READINGS ONE AND TWO

The authors of the two readings address some similar themes (underlined in the questions below) relating to the aftermath of a natural disaster. Work with a partner. Answer the following questions using examples from each reading. When you have finished, work individually and use this information to write a summary of the themes you discussed.

1. What is the <u>relationship between man (humans) and nature</u> in the two readings?

2. How does the <u>atmosphere or the environment change</u> in the aftermath of each disaster?

3. How do the <u>people's reactions and emotions change</u> over the period of time covered in the two readings?

4. How do the authors express the <u>feeling of helplessness</u>?

5 REVIEWING LANGUAGE

A. EXPLORING LANGUAGE

Work with a partner. Look at the adjectives in italics in the chart on page 87. Which ones can be used to describe the nouns that surround them? Write the adjectives beside the noun. Add more adjectives of your own. Some adjectives can be paired with more than one noun. An example has been done for you.

immense **LONELINESS**

immense **SKY**

immense **SEA**

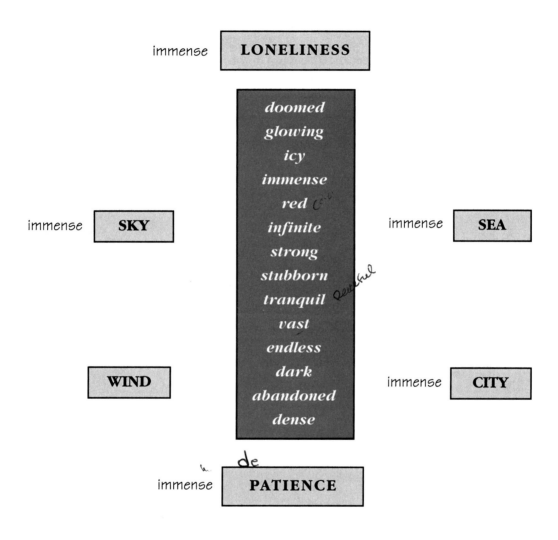

doomed
glowing
icy
immense
red *cold*
infinite
strong
stubborn *peaceful*
tranquil
vast
endless
dark
abandoned
dense

WIND

immense **CITY**

immense **PATIENCE** *de*

B. WORKING WITH WORDS: Synonyms

Work in a small group. Read the sentences below. In these sentences you can see how words from one reading can be used to express ideas from the other reading. Look for a synonym in the readings for each of the underlined words or phrases, and write the synonyms above them. Use the numbers in the parentheses to help you find the synonyms. The first number refers to the reading; the second number to the paragraph; and the third number to the line in the reading (1:1:13 means Reading One, paragraph 1, line 13). The first one has been done for you.

1. The <u>day was ending</u> [sun was setting] as great fires broke out all over San Francisco. (1:1:3)

2. In the aftermath of the earthquake, many people <u>put away</u> [stowed / to stow away] in secret places, belongings they could not take with them. (1:4:7)

3. San Franciscans tried to <u>wait</u> [holdout] as long as they could before leaving their homes. (1:4:9) [1:4:9]

4. As they left their homes, they had to <u>force</u> [to stuff] as much as they could in their suitcases. (1:4:12)

5. People were forced to <u>toss</u> [Fling / throw] what they couldn't carry anymore into the streets. (1:4:13)

6. The <u>ingenious</u> [clever] engineers who designed the life raft had never actually been at sea. (2:1:7)

7. The life raft had some interesting <u>devices</u> [*tool] such as a water filter to filter out salt from the water. (2:1:16)

8. Although he tried to remain hopeful, the sailor couldn't help feeling that he was <u>inevitably ruined</u> by his tragic situation. (2:2:8)

9. The sailor tried not to be <u>scared</u> [Panic-stricken], but being alone at night at sea was terrifying. (2:3:11)

10. When the sailor was on the ship living with many other sailors, he often felt <u>restricted</u>, quite the opposite of how he felt in his life raft in the middle of the sea. (2:7:3)

6 SKILLS FOR EXPRESSION

A. GRAMMAR: Identifying Adjective Clauses

1 *Examine the following sentences. Then discuss the questions with a partner.*

◆ I saw not one woman **who wept**, not one man **who was excited**, not one person **who was in the slightest degree panic stricken.**

◆ You've got a watch with a glowing dial **that you can't stop checking.**

◆ I began to look at my watch again as I had in the afternoon **when I searched the horizon for airplanes.**

a. In the first sentence, what kind of woman is being described? What kind of man? What kind of person?

b. In the second sentence, what does the writer say about the glowing dial?

c. In the last sentence, which afternoon is the writer describing?

d. What words begin the phrases printed in boldface letters? What words come just before these phrases?

Identifying Adjective Clauses

FOCUS ON GRAMMAR

See Adjective Clauses in *Focus on Grammar, High Intermediate.*

Identifying adjective clauses, sometimes called restrictive relative clauses, are groups of words (phrases) that act like adjectives to describe or identify a noun. These phrases come directly after the nouns they describe. They are introduced by relative pronouns that refer to the noun being described. Sentences with adjective clauses can be seen as a combination of two shorter sentences talking about the same noun.

I lived in **a house**. + **The house** was destroyed by a flood.
= I lived in **a house** *which* was destroyed by a flood.

The house was very old. + The flood destroyed **the house**.
= **The house** *which* **the flood destroyed** was very old.

Relative Pronouns

Identifying adjective clauses begin with a relative pronoun. The choice of pronoun is determined by the noun it describes. For example, use:

- ◆ **who** for a person or people

- ◆ **which** for a thing or things

- ◆ **that** for a person or people, and a thing or things (less formal than **which**)

- ◆ **when** for a time or times

- ◆ **where** or **in which** for a place or places

GRAMMAR TIP: Remember that the relative pronoun takes the place of the noun it describes; the noun is not repeated.

> I lived in **the town**. + The hurricane destroyed **the town**.
> = I lived in **the town** **which** a hurricane destroyed.

❷ *Complete the sentences with the appropriate relative pronoun. The first one has been done for you.*

1. The firefighter ___who___ helped save my family was given a medal
   (which/who)
   for heroism.

2. The town ___where___ I had lived the year before was destroyed by a
   (that/where)
   hurricane.

3. As he sat in the raft ___which___ protected him from the creatures of the
   (which/who)
   sea, the shipwrecked sailor reflected on his life.

4. The hospital ___in which___ I was born was destroyed by the volcano.
   (that/in which)

5. I was asleep at the time ___when___ the earthquake struck.
   (where/when)

to go of ...

6. The people had to evacuate the village when the dam __that__ held
   (who/that)
   back the lake broke.

7. Snowstorms __which__ happen early in the season often are the most
   (in which/which)
   devastating because people are not prepared.

8. The shipwrecked sailor built his raft out of wood __that__ he had
   (that/where)
   found on the island.

9. Despite repeated warnings of the possibility of an avalanche, many
   many
   people __who__ lived on the side of the mountain refused to leave
   (which/who)
   their homes.

10. The house __where__ we had slept the night before was completely
    (where/when)
    destroyed by the hurricane.

3 *Combine each pair of sentences into one sentence by using an identifying adjective clause. The first one has been done for you.*

1. __Many homes were damaged by the earthquake which registered__
   __6.3 on the Richter Scale.__

   a. Many homes were damaged by the earthquake.
   b. The earthquake registered 6.3 on the Richter Scale.

2. I lived in the town ~~where~~ *which was* destroyed by a tornado

   a. I lived in the town.
   b. The town was destroyed by a tornado.

3. Forest Fires kill many animals ~~which~~ *that* live
   in national parks.

   a. Forest fires kill many animals.
   b. Animals live in national parks.

4. *A hurricane is a tropical storm which has winds of at least 73 miles per hour.*

   a. A hurricane is a tropical storm.
   b. A tropical storm has winds of at least 73 miles per hour.

5. *We found the mountain climber, who had gotten lost during the storm.*

   a. We found the mountain climber.
   b. She had gotten lost during the storm.

6. *My flight was canceled because of the storm that dropped 32 inches of snow on the city.*

   a. My flight was canceled because of the storm.
   b. The storm dropped 32 inches of snow on the city.

7. *The avalanche occurred at night which trapped the climbers.*

   a. The avalanche occurred at night.
   b. The avalanche trapped the climbers.

8. *I spoke with a man who survived 38 days alone on a life raft*

   a. I spoke with a man.
   b. The man survived 38 days alone on a life raft.

9. *The house which had been in Mary's family for over 200 years destroyed the house.*

   a. The house had been in Mary's family for over 200 years.
   b. The flood destroyed the house.

10. *The reporter who was hit by lightning wrote a story about Hurricane Andrew*

   a. The reporter was hit by lightning.
   b. The reporter wrote a story about Hurricane Andrew.

11. *The afternoon when the forest fire broke out was sunny and hot.*

   a. The afternoon was sunny and hot.
   b. That afternoon the forest fire broke out.

B. STYLE: Descriptive Writing

1 *Examine each pair of sentences and circle the sentence (**a** or **b**) that is the most effective in describing the situation or event. With a partner, discuss why you think those sentences are more descriptive.*

1. **a.** There were ashes falling from the sky.

   b. A rain of ashes was falling.

2. **a.** The first bright star appeared in the night sky, and it didn't move.

   b. Like a yellow diamond in a wine colored sky, the first star appeared, immobile and perfect.

3. **a.** The water in the bay was dead calm.

   b. The water in the bay was not moving.

4. **a.** It seemed as if my body were glowing, with all the sun of the afternoon embedded under my skin.

   b. I felt sunburned and hot after being in the sun all day.

Descriptive Writing

Descriptive writing makes the reader's senses come alive. It makes the reader see, smell, hear, taste, or feel what is being described.

- -

Adjectives

Writers often use **adjectives** to add to a description. Notice how the following sentences come alive with the addition of a descriptive adjective. Adjectives can describe nouns, or further describe other adjectives.

Description without Adjective	Description with Adjective
◆ I watched with patience.	◆ I watched with **stubborn** patience.
◆ The wind whipped my shirt.	◆ The **icy** wind whipped my shirt.
◆ The bay was calm.	◆ The bay was **dead** calm.

> **Similes**
>
> A **simile** creates images by using the phrase **_like a_** . . . to compare two otherwise unrelated ideas. For example, García Marquez describes the first star appearing in the sky:
>
> ◆ **like a** yellow diamond
>
> ◆ **like a** signal
>
> **_As if, as though,_** and **_it seems (seemed)_** are other phrases used to describe a situation or feeling. They are used to give the reader the same impression or experience that the author had.
>
> ◆ **It seemed as if** my body were glowing, with all the sun of the afternoon embedded under my skin.
>
> ◆ From midnight on, my right knee began to hurt and I felt **as though** the water had penetrated my bones.
>
> ◆ **It seemed** to me, in the midst of that infinite solitude, in the midst of the sea's dark murmur, that if I spotted the light of only a single ship, I would let out a yell that could be heard at any distance.

2 *Add adjectives to make the following sentences more interesting.*

1. The fire destroyed the old house.

_____

2. The young sailor couldn't sleep during his first night at sea.

_____

3. The strong earthquake shook the city.

_____

4. The cows were carried away by the tornado.

_____

5. The flood swept away the garage.

_____

6. The people had to spend the night sleeping on the cold floor.

_____

3 *Complete the following sentences by using similes. Use as many descriptive details as possible. Share your sentences in small groups.*

1. The tornado knocked down the telephone poles like

_____

2. Wind and waves overcame our tiny boat. We felt as if we were

_____

3. During the earthquake the earth shook under our feet. It seemed as though

_____

4. The forest fire burned out of control. The smell was what I remember most. It was as if

_____

5. The typhoon destroyed the town completely. Houses were strewn across the fields like

_____

6. The rain was approaching quickly. It seemed the sky

_____

ON YOUR OWN

A. WRITING TOPICS

Choose one of the following topics. Write two or three paragraphs using some of the vocabulary, grammar, and style you learned in this unit.

1. In Exercise 1B (Sharing Information) you talked about a particular time in your life. Now write an essay describing that time, the event, and how you felt.

2. Have you ever seen a natural disaster on television or in the movies? Have you ever read a book that included a natural disaster as part of the story? Write a description of the disaster you saw or read about. Explain how it affected the people or the place involved. Be as descriptive as possible.

3. Have you ever been in a situation where you felt the power of nature (for example, in a heavy rainstorm, at the beach in a storm, in a strong windstorm)? Describe the event and how you felt.

B. FIELDWORK

PREPARATION

1. Work in a small group. Brainstorm a list of famous natural disasters you can think of from ancient times through the present day. Include earthquakes, floods, fires, hurricanes, tornadoes, typhoons, volcano eruptions.

2. Share your list with the class and make a master list of disasters on the chalkboard. As a class, discuss the disasters and what you know about them.

3. In a small group, select one disaster for your group to research. Discuss where you will find information (for example, library books, newspapers, the Internet).

RESEARCH ACTIVITY

Research the natural disaster your group selected and prepare a report that includes the following information:

- ◆ Date of disaster
- ◆ Type of disaster
- ◆ Description of disaster
- ◆ Any visuals of the disaster (photos, drawings, paintings)
- ◆ Aftermath (what happened as a result of the disaster: for example, an amazing survival story, type of help offered, a description of the damages and losses)

Present your report to the class. Use as much descriptive language as you can.

FROM TRASH TO TREASURE

1 APPROACHING THE TOPIC

A. PREDICTING

Look at the photograph and the title of this unit. Take some notes about the picture. What does it show? Why was this picture taken? What do you think "From Trash to Treasure" refers to? What do you think this unit will be about?

B. SHARING INFORMATION

Work with a partner. Take the Earth Quiz and discuss your answers. Check them against the answers at the bottom of the page.

Earth Quiz

1. Every year the United States produces enough solid waste to fill a line of garbage trucks which would reach _____.

   a. from New York to Los Angeles   **b.** around the world **c.** halfway to the moon

2. The world population has _____ since 1950.

   a. more than doubled   **b.** tripled   **c.** quadrupled

3. Close to _____ square kilometers of rain forest are destroyed each year.

   a. 160,000   **b.** 100,000   **c.** 300,000

4. _____ percent of the energy used by businesses worldwide comes from fossil fuels (oil, natural gas).

   a. 90   **b.** 75   **c.** 60

5. At the current rate of use, the world's known oil reserves will last _____ years.

   a. 100   **b.** 50   **c.** 35

6. Americans throw away enough food every day to feed the entire population of _____ for one day.

   a. New York City   **b.** Canada   **c.** Hawaii

Most people are surprised by the answers to the quiz. Discuss these questions in a small group.

1. What information from the quiz surprised you most?

2. What information did you already know? How did you know about it?

Answers: **1.** c **2.** a **3.** a **4.** a **5.** c **6.** b

PREPARING TO READ

A. BACKGROUND

Read this information.

More and more people and communities are changing their habits in order to protect the environment. One reason for this change is that space in landfills is running out and the disposal of waste has become difficult. As a result, the practices of recycling, reusing, and reducing waste are becoming more commonplace. In some countries the technology for disposing of, or getting rid of, waste has actually become big business. Individuals have also taken actions to reduce landfill waste; for example, people are recycling newspapers and donating clothes to charities. In addition, some people take leftover food and turn it into rich garden compost, an excellent fertilizer for vegetable and flower gardens.

Think about your home. How are the following items commonly disposed of? Check (✔) the category that best describes the disposal method you use. Work in small groups to share your answers.

ITEM	IN THE TRASH	RECYCLE/DONATE	OTHER (reuse, compost, burn)
Newspapers			
Bottles			
Cans			
Used computer paper			
Glass			
Aluminum foil			

Chart continues on next page.

ITEM	IN THE TRASH	RECYCLE/DONATE	OTHER (reuse, compost, burn)
Leftovers (non-meat)			
Batteries			
Cereal boxes			
Old toys, furniture			
Tires			
Clothes			

B. VOCABULARY FOR COMPREHENSION

Write the number of each underlined word next to its definition listed at the end of the text.

One job many <u>environmentalists</u> have today is to find different ways
(1)

to dispose of waste, or trash, rather than throwing it all in <u>landfills</u>.
(2)

Many landfills are filled to capacity; others are limited in their use. Of all

the waste in the United States, 25 percent is <u>organic</u> plant matter which
(3)

can actually be recycled. So rather than throwing <u>table scraps</u> and other
(4)

natural waste into landfills, people are looking for ways to use them

more productively.

One of the ways environmentalists have supported is <u>composting</u>,
(5)

the process of taking plant matter, breaking it down, and turning it into

a <u>nutrient</u>-rich organic material. <u>Microorganisms</u> break down, or
(6)   (7)

decompose, the plant matter with the help of sunlight and water. The
 (8)

sunlight and water keep the material warm and moist, which helps
 (9)

the decomposing process. Because the material, called compost, is high in

nutrients, individuals as well as large-scale agricultural operations use it

to fertilize gardens and crops.
 (10)

_____ **a.** add something to soil to improve its quality

_____ **b.** leftover food

_____ **c.** decay, or break down into its smallest parts

_____ **d.** a place to dispose of trash, a dump

_____ **e.** living organisms seen only through a microscope

_____ **f.** natural

_____ **g.** people who study our surroundings

_____ **h.** the changing of plant matter into organic matter used to
improve soil quality

_____ **i.** vitamins, proteins, and minerals

_____ **j.** wet

3 READING ONE: St. Paul Couple Give Composting a Worm Welcome

A. INTRODUCING THE TOPIC

The title of the article is "St. Paul Couple Give Composting a Worm Welcome." The title uses a ***pun***. A pun is a playful way to use words. It is formed by using words that sound alike or words that have more than one meaning. In the title of the article, the author uses a word that sounds like another word to make an expression.

Can you guess which word is the pun? What clue does the pun give about the topic of the article?

St. Paul Couple Give Composting a Worm Welcome

By Chuck Haga (from *The Star Tribune*)

1 They are not pets, of course, but footless soldiers in the garbage wars. A container not much larger than a cat's litter box holds 1,000 redworms, enough to turn a small household's table scraps into rich gardening compost.

2 "There's not much to watching them," Mergenthal said. "They're in there, and I put on a layer of scraps and the stuff disappears."

3 There's a fancy name for what Mergenthal and a growing number of Twin Cities[1] gardeners and environmentalists are doing: vermicomposting, from *vermis*, Latin for worm.

4 "Vermicomposting is like regular composting, except that you're using microorganisms and a community of worms to break down organic matter," according to "The Urban/Suburban Composter," a 1994 book by two Canadian gardening experts. The advantage with worms "is that they're fast and they excrete a nutrient-rich manure (called castings), which is great for plants."

5 To answer the second-most-asked question (after smells): No, you can't hear the worms eating, even in the still of the night.

6 Mergenthal feeds his worms potato peelings, apple cores, carrot stubs, bread scraps and other table leavings. (Banana peels should be OK, according to the composting guide, if covered.)

7 "Here's some cabbage leaves," Mergenthal said. He is not squeamish about working the moist, decomposing matter to haul out a representative worm or two. "It's only organic matter," he said patiently. "It's just a little more organic than most people are used to holding."

8 He returned a worm to its bedding and watched it tunnel in. "It's fun to dig around a little and see that they're doing their work," he said.

9 Mergenthal, 64, is manager of the bookstore at Luther Seminary, a few blocks from his home on Bourne Ave.[2] He grew up on a farm near Hillsboro, N.D.,[3] and he keeps models of John Deere[4] tractors in his study. He used to keep a

---

[1] *Twin Cities:* St. Paul and Minneapolis, Minnesota, USA
[2] *Ave.:* avenue
[3] *N.D.:* North Dakota, USA
[4] *John Deere:* name of a tractor company

large garden, but back problems complicated by arthritis have forced him to cut back.

10   "I'm interested in doing anything I can that's sustainable," he said. "I don't use commercial fertilizers, and I don't want to contribute any more than necessary to the landfills."

11   Last fall, he saw a magazine advertisement: "Worms will eat your garbage," it said, and that sounded like a good deal to Mergenthal. He ordered 1,000 redworms for about $20.00, he said, and a worm bin for about $50.00. (Redworms also are available from bait shops[5] and composters whose "worm communities" have grown too large.)

12   The worms, flat and shiny and a little more reddish than garden-variety angleworms, can reach a length of four inches. They reproduce well in captivity if handled properly, doubling or tripling in number in a few months.

13   They shouldn't be ordered late in the year because they don't travel well in winter. Mergenthal sent for his last fall, and his colony declined by the time he sorted the worms from their soil and started them in new bedding.

14   "This first time around, I wasn't a very good worm man," he said. "I shouldn't have lost worms. I should have gained."

15   His worm bin is about 2 feet by $2\frac{1}{2}$ feet and stands about 15 inches high. It is screened on the bottom for drainage.

16   No, he said, the worms will not try to escape. "They don't like the light," he said. "My wife was a little leery that we'd have them all over the kitchen floor, but they're happy where they are.

17   "Most people don't even notice it unless you point it out," he said. "Then they're interested. Kids are very interested. Usually they want to see the worms, and I don't mind showing them. It's a good way to get them thinking about natural life."

18   Mary Tkach, recycling program director at the St. Paul Neighborhood Energy Consortium, said vermicomposting "is not terribly popular yet, but it's definitely growing," especially as an environmental teaching tool for children. Call it the ant farm for the '90s. "We're also seeing apartment dwellers who don't have a place to compost outside," she said.

19   The Energy Consortium conducts "worm workshops" a couple of times a year, said Tkach, who has a worm bin in her house—in her kitchen, in fact. "It is a conversation piece," she said.

20   Mergenthal said the worms should be sorted and restarted in fresh bedding every four months or so. "You dump the contents out onto a tarp and slowly take off soil from the outside of the pile," he said. "The worms don't like the light, so they go to the middle. Eventually, you have all the worms in a ball."

21   The worm castings go onto the Mergenthals' garden. He makes new bedding of chopped box elder[6] leaves and shredded newspaper, wetted down. "Then I put the worms in and some table scraps so they have something to eat," he said, "and I let 'em go back to work."

22   Redworms, also known as manure worms, aren't as fussy as so-called higher forms, such as cats, but they do have their standards. They prefer moist bins, a temperature between 65 and 77 degrees and a neutral pH. When you feed them chopped orange peels or other acidic food, you should provide pulverized eggshells for balance. Meat scraps would create odors and shouldn't be added to the feed.

23   Some months ago, worried that Jennings' [Mr. Mergenthal's] worms weren't thriving, Mary Mergenthal placed a classified ad in a newspaper to ask for advice. That caused quite a few worm people to surface, Jennings said.

24   "I found one lady who really knows a lot," he said. "I'm told she really knows worms."

---

[5] *bait shop:* shop that sells worms used for fishing
[6] *box elder:* tree

B. READING FOR MAIN IDEAS

*Reading One can be divided into five main parts. Below are headings for each part. Number the headings in the order they would appear in the reading. Note that **d** can be found in two places.*

____ a. What Mergenthal does with his compost

____ b. The public's reaction to vermicomposting

____ c. Who Mergenthal is, why he practices vermicomposting, and how he heard about vermicomposting

____ d. Care, maintenance, and feeding of the worms

____ e. Definition of vermicomposting

C. READING FOR DETAILS

Emily Estey tried vermicomposting but failed miserably. According to the instructions for vermicomposting in Reading One, what did she do wrong? Read her letter to Mr. Mergenthal, circle her six mistakes, and make a list of what she should have done instead.

Dear Mr. Mergenthal,

I really need your help and advice. My worms seem to have all died and I can't understand why. Let me tell you what happened.

First I ordered my worms during the winter, in December. When they arrived, I put them in a cardboard shoe box under my dining room table. I filled the box with dry newspaper and began to feed them. Every night after dinner I would give them my table scraps: salad, apples, chicken, bread, orange peels. I worried that they were too cold and set my apartment temperature for 80 degrees. After six months of no luck, I decided to change their bedding and found out sadly that they had all died. What did I do wrong?

Sincerely,
Emily Estey

D. READING BETWEEN THE LINES

Work with a partner. Circle the best way to complete the following sentences. There can be more than one correct answer. Support your choices with examples from Reading One.

1. People are hesitant to practice vermicomposting because . . .

    a. of the cost.

    b. of the smell.

    c. it requires a lot of work.

2. Vermicomposting is appealing to apartment dwellers because . . .

    a. the worms are quiet.

    b. you can do your composting indoors.

    c. it does not take up much space.

3. Mrs. Mergenthal's reaction to the worms was . . .

    a. very enthusiastic.

    b. somewhat hesitant.

    c. totally unsupportive.

4. Mr. Mergenthal's first experience with worms was . . .

    a. very successful.

    b. moderately successful.

    c. a total failure.

5. The benefit(s) of vermicomposting is (are) . . .

    a. the resulting compost.

    b. the educational experience for children.

    c. the reduction of waste in landfills.

4 READING TWO: Earthship Homes Catch Old Tires on Rebound

A. EXPANDING THE TOPIC

An earthship home.

Work with a partner. Look at the picture, answer the questions, then read "Earthship Homes Catch Old Tires on Rebound."

1. Do you think this home looks comfortable?

2. Would you like to live here? Why or why not?

3. This home is very special. Can you guess why?

4. Why do you think it is called an "earthship"?

Earthship Homes Catch Old Tires on Rebound

By Eva Ferguson (from *The Calgary Herald*)

1 They're called earthships—an environmentalist's dream home made from up to 2,000 scrap tires, packed dirt, straw and concrete.

2 From the outside each looks like a berm[1] with a solarium in front. On the inside, it can be a luxurious mansion for everyday living or just a cozy one-room cabin with a great view.

3 Hundreds have been built in the U.S. Midwest for a wide range of homeowners, including environmentally conscious celebrities such as Dennis Weaver[2] and low income earners who want homes made of cheap materials and no heating bills—thanks to solar heating.

4 A handful of earthships are under construction in British Columbia [Canada] and now a Calgary entrepreneur is anxious to build them in Canmore, Crossfield, Exshaw [Alberta, Canada] or any remote area where Albertans are willing to try something unique that helps the environment too.

5 "Because the homes are totally self-sufficient, they're very affordable, and it's a way to get rid of used tires which have been such a headache for years" [said Michael Port]. In support of reusing old tires, Alberta's tire recycling management board launched the Recycling Industry Incentive Program, which provides up to $2 per tire for projects that use scrap tires in innovative ways.

6 To build a modest earthship, about 2,000 tires are stacked up atop each other and packed with dirt, straw, and cement to make up the main frame. An average sized home takes up to 90 to 135 square meters. The front, which faces south for maximum sunlight, is a solarium made of large glass windows. Because the earth and rubber from the tires trap heat, heating is never required, even in cold climates such as Alberta's. Ultimately the tires are completely covered, by drywall on the inside and earth on the outside. Solariums provide a great opportunity for gardens as well, allowing owners to grow their own vegetables at home.

7 Utilities like water, sewage, and electricity do not have to come from municipal sources. Running water and sewage storage is handled through underground tanks. "Photovoltaic" lights, which store solar energy in their own batteries, provide lighting at night. But for those who can't be without their TVs or microwaves, electricity can be installed.

8 Michael Reynolds, owner of Solar Survival Architecture, which initiated the idea and started successful construction in New Mexico, Colorado, and Idaho just a few years ago, said the homes are becoming popular in Japan, Australia, Europe, and South America.

9 "Housing itself is difficult to come by. Many people practically have to sell their souls to buy one. But these are affordable because they're made with old automobile tires, they don't create heating or cooling bills, and owners can even participate in their construction if they like."

10 The total price can range from $30,000 to $1 million, depending on size and amenities, he said.

---

[1] *berm:* a mound or bank of earth placed against the wall of a building to provide protection and warmth
[2] *Dennis Weaver:* an American actor

In your own words, write a brief description of an earthship home on a separate piece of paper.

B. LINKING READINGS ONE AND TWO

You have now read two articles dealing with alternative solutions to waste reduction. Work in groups to complete the following chart. Write about the two solutions (vermicomposting and earthship homes) and their impact on society. Discuss any other environmental program with which you are familiar, and write about it in the last column. Share other programs with the class and discuss the questions below the chart.

IMPACT ON SOCIETY	VERMICOMPOSTING	EARTHSHIP HOMES	OTHER
Benefits to the individual	Provides compost for the garden. Reduces waste in home.		
Benefits for the environment			
Ease of care or upkeep			
Cost			

1. Which, if any, of these programs would be possible to do in your community?

2. If a program is not possible, how could it be adapted to make it work in your community?

3. What are some inexpensive and easy everyday actions which individuals can do to help reduce waste?

5 REVIEWING LANGUAGE

A. EXPLORING LANGUAGE

Complete the sentences with the correct form of the words given. Use a dictionary if necessary. Check your answers with a partner. The first one has been done for you.

1. innovative, innovations

   a. There have been many great environmental _innovations_ in the last few years.

   b. In fact, some of the most _innovative_ ideas do not come from scientists, but from ordinary people who are concerned with the earth's future.

2. recycling, recyclable, recycle, recycled

   a. Every week Lisa Deering separates her glass and plastic and puts them in bins in order to _____ them.

   b. Lisa has recently realized that many items she once thought of as only trash are actually _____ .

   c. She is such a strong believer in the value of _____ that she has volunteered to help with her town's program.

   d. In Canada, _____ tires are used to build houses.

3. initiation, initiated

   a. Many recycling efforts are _____ by concerned citizens.

   b. The _____ of recycling programs has helped businesses around the world deal with the large amounts of used computer paper.

4. composting, compost

   a. _____ can be used to fertilize soil.

   b. In the United States, many towns provide residents with _____ bins.

5. reproductive, reproduce

    a. If handled correctly, worms _____ rapidly, doubling or tripling in number in a few months.

    b. A cold environment can slow down or stop the worm's _____ cycle.

6. storage, store

    a. Many people _____ their recyclable materials in their basements until they bring them to local recycling centers.

    b. Due to lack of _____ space, many landfills are already filled to capacity.

7. participation, participate

    a. The public's full _____ is necessary for any recycling effort to be successful.

    b. One reason the earthships are so economical is that the owners can _____ in their construction.

8. fertile, fertilization, fertility

    a. _____ is necessary for successful gardening.

    b. The deforestation of the rain forest is causing the once _____ soil to lose its valuable nutrients.

    c. In some areas the natives pray to the gods of _____ , hoping to increase the size of their harvest.

B. WORKING WITH WORDS

Circle the word in parentheses which best completes the sentence.

Public awareness of the value of (**1. innovative, recycling**) materials such as plastic, paper, and glass is increasing daily in all corners of the globe. In some countries these efforts are being (**2. initiated, fertilized**) by the local governments and in others, by individuals. Participation in these programs is at an all-time high.

In the small town of Truro in eastern Massachusetts, for example, space in the local (**3. landfill, store**) has run out; therefore, residents have had to think of new ways to dispose of their trash. With no room for items such as newspapers, bottles, and old lumber at the landfill, local residents have come up with many (**4. participation, innovative**) programs to recycle and/or reuse what was once thought of as only trash. For instance, yard waste such as leaves and grass which used to be thrown in the landfill is now broken down and made into (**5. worms, compost**) used by local people as fertilizer in their gardens. In addition, (**6. reproductive, recyclable**) plastics, newspapers, bottles, and cans are sold to a recycling company, thereby bringing in revenue for the town. The most popular local innovation, though, has been the founding of a "swap shop." This is a building to which people bring their unwanted clothing, books, and toys so that others who need them can take them.

Since there is so much (**7. fertilization, participation**) in all the recycling programs, the dump is seen as a place to meet with friends and neighbors and catch up on local news. There is even an annual September evening "dump dance," where locals dance to live music and have picnics by candlelight at the dump. This has become a highlight of the summer vacation season.

As humankind continues to (**8. reproduce, fertilize**) and the population grows, recycling efforts become even more important. These efforts must continue so that we will soon see new (**9. innovations, fertility**) and ideas concerning the use of recycled materials.

6 SKILLS FOR EXPRESSION

A. GRAMMAR: Advisability and Obligation in the Past

1 *Examine this sentence and answer the question that follows.*

◆ Emily Estey **should have written** to Mr. Mergenthal sooner.

What does the sentence mean?

a. Emily wanted to write to Mr. Mergenthal sooner than she did.

b. Emily needed to write sooner, but she didn't.

FOCUS ON GRAMMAR

See Advisability and Obligation in the Past in *Focus on Grammar, High Intermediate.*

Past Modals

To talk about actions that were advisable in the past, use the modals *should have, could have, ought to have*, and *might have*.

- -

Form of the Past Modals

Modal	+	Have	+	Past Participle
could		have		written
should		have		seen
ought to		have		studied
might		have		changed
should		not have		eaten

- -

Expressing Regret with Past Modals

Past modals can express regret about past possibilities and actions not taken. Look at the examples:

> Situation: I did not feed my worms the right food and they all died.

> Expressing regret: I **ought to have been** more careful with my worms.

> Situation: I threw away all my bottles and cans in the trash.
>
> Expressing regret: I **could have recycled** them instead.
>
> Situation: I threw meat scraps in my compost bin.
>
> Expressing regret: I **shouldn't have been** so careless.
>
> -
>
> **Expressing Blame with Past Modals**
>
> Past modals can also express blame. The blame is based on your opinion of a situation. Look at the example:
>
> Situation: Our governments have let big businesses pollute our air for a long time.
>
> Expressing blame: Our governments **should not have allowed** big businesses to continue to pollute for so many years.
>
> **GRAMMAR TIP:** We usually do not use **ought to have** in the negative. We use **should not have** instead.

2 *Read the following situations and write sentences using the modals given.*

1. Jack Bellingham ordered worms for his vermicomposter. They were sent to his house in Toronto, Canada, in January. Many of the worms died before they reached his house.

   <u>He should not have ordered his worms in winter.</u> (should not have)

   <u>He ought to have read the instructions for vermicomposting</u>

   <u>more carefully.</u> (ought to have)

2. Emily Estey often fed her worms orange and grapefruit peels, and her worms didn't seem to do well.

   _____ (should not have)

   _____ (should have)

3. Juan Carlos used all new tires when he built his earthship.

   _____ (could have)

   _____ (should not have)

4. Last year, Mr. Mergenthal threw out 300 pounds of compostable materials.

_____ (should not have)

_____ (ought to have)

5. The first time around, many of Mr. Mergenthal's worms died.

_____ (should not have)

_____ (might have)

6. Last year, a man built an earthship and faced all his windows to the north. His house was always cold and his indoor garden was not very successful.

_____ (should not have)

_____ (ought to have)

3 _Read the following situations. Write sentences expressing your opinion (blame or regret) using past modals._

1. America has begun to run out of landfills.

_____

_____

2. Fourteen billion pounds of garbage were dumped in the world's oceans last year.

_____

_____

3. Gas and oil costs have continued to rise because the planet is running out of fossil fuels.

_____

_____

4. Rain forests have been destroyed at an alarming rate.

_____

_____

B. STYLE: Cause and Effect

1 *Examine the sentences that follow and discuss the questions with the class.*

- Because the earth and rubber from the tires trap heat, heating is never required.

- The worms don't like the light, so they go to the middle of the pile.

- Since Mr. Mergenthal's worms weren't thriving, Mary Mergenthal placed a classified ad in the newspaper to ask for advice.

- The homes are totally self-sufficient; consequently, they are very affordable.

- As a result of these homes being made with old automobile tires, they are very affordable.

Each sentence has two clauses: one expresses a cause; the other expresses an effect.

a. In each sentence, can you identify the clause that expresses the cause?

b. Can you identify the result, or effect, clause?

c. What words connect the cause and effect clauses in each sentence?

Cause and Effect

Cause and effect sentences explain why something happened. There are two clauses in a cause and effect sentence. One clause (the cause) explains why something happened. The other clause (the effect) explains the result of what happened.

> **Cause:** Because the earth and rubber from the tires trap heat,

> **Effect:** heating is never required.

Conjunctions and Transitions

Conjunctions or transition words show the relationship between the two clauses. These include:

Words Introducing the Cause	Words Introducing the Effect
because	*as a result*
since	*consequently*
	for this reason
	so
	therefore
	thus

The Cause Clause

The **cause** is introduced by *because* or *since*. It can come at the beginning of the sentence. In this case the clauses are separated by a comma (,).

> ◆ *Because* **the earth and rubber from the tires trap heat,** heating is never required.

The cause can also come at the end, in which case there is no comma.

> ◆ Heating is never required *because* **the earth and rubber from the tires trap heat.**

The Effect Clause

The **effect** can be introduced by words like ***consequently, for this reason, therefore***. Cause and effect clauses can be combined into one sentence by using a semicolon (*;*) and a comma (*,*).

- ◆ Newspapers are the largest component of solid waste in land-fills; ***for this reason*, we need to promote newspaper recycling.**

They can also be two separate sentences.

- ◆ Newspapers are the largest component of solid waste in land-fills. ***For this reason*, we need to promote newspaper recycling.**

Notice the punctuation with ***so***:

- ◆ Newspapers are the largest component of solid waste in landfills, ***so* we need to promote newspaper recycling.**

② *Read the following paragraph. Underline the words that introduce the cause and effect clauses. Then, with a partner, complete the chart that follows.*

Houses in the United States are very expensive; as a result, many people have to invest all their savings to buy one. Thankfully, earthship homes are affordable because they are made with old automobile tires. In addition, because they are well insulated, they don't create high heating or cooling bills. Furthermore, since owners can participate in the construction, the cost is controlled.

CAUSE	EFFECT
1. Houses are very expensive.	
2.	Earthships are affordable.
3.	
4.	

❸ *For each sentence, first identify the cause (C) and the effect (E). Then combine the sentences with the transition words provided. The first one has been done for you.*

1. __C__ Emily ordered her worms in winter.

   __E__ The worms all died.

   (so)

   She ordered the worms in winter, **so** they all died.

2. _____ The ozone layer is becoming depleted.

   _____ There are more cases of skin cancer every year.

   (therefore)

   _____

3. _____ The world's rain forests are rapidly shrinking.

   _____ There will be fewer valuable medicines available.

   (consequently)

   _____

4. _____ There are more heat waves and cold snaps.

   _____ Climate changes from global warming are making weather patterns more extreme.

   (as a result)

   _____

5. _____ Drinking water near many landfills has become contaminated.

   _____ People have been throwing hazardous waste in landfills for years.

   (because)

   _____

6. _____ People have been cutting down large areas of forests.

   _____ Many animal species have become endangered.

   (for this reason)

   _____

7. _____ Julian didn't use fertilizer in his garden.

_____ His plants didn't grow very well.

(since)

_____

4 *Combine each set of sentences to show cause and effect. Use an appropriate transition word. Then put the sentences together to write a paragraph on acid rain.*

1. **a.** There are over 500 million gasoline-powered cars in the world.
   b. There are large amounts of dangerous gases in the air such as sulfur dioxide and nitrogen oxide from car emissions.

   _____

   _____

2. **a.** Sulfur dioxide and nitrogen oxide accumulate in the atmosphere.
   b. These gases return to earth in the form of acid rain.

   _____

   _____

3. **a.** Acid rain falls frequently in Europe.
   b. In Sweden, 40,000 out of 90,000 lakes are known to be acidified.

   _____

   _____

4. **a.** Acid rain is expensive to clean up.
   b. Billions of dollars are spent every year repairing damages from acid rain.

   _____

   _____

PARAGRAPH ON ACID RAIN

_____

_____

_____

_____

_____

_____

7 ON YOUR OWN

A. WRITING TOPICS

Choose one of the following topics. Write two or three paragraphs using some of the vocabulary, grammar, and style you learned in this unit.

1. Write a response to Emily Estey's letter (see page 104). Tell Emily what went wrong and explain how she could have prevented her worm disaster.

2. Imagine you are the Secretary of Housing in the United States. Write in support of the building of earthships to address low-income housing needs.

3. Describe an approach the United States or another country has taken to solve an environmental problem. Be sure to explain what has caused the government to take this approach and whether you think this approach has been successful or not.

4. Overpopulation is becoming a global problem. Some people believe that governments should help control the population by offering incentives for not having more than one child, such as by providing free birth control methods and abortions. Do you think that family size should be under government control, or should this be an issue of personal choice? Why or why not? Explain your answer.

B. FIELDWORK

PREPARATION

Answer the following questions with a partner or in small groups.

1. What are some important global environmental issues? What are some important environmental issues in your local community?

2. Of these issues, which one interests you the most?

3. What do you know about this issue?

4. What more would you like to know?

5. Where can you get information about this issue?

RESEARCH ACTIVITY: World Environmental Issues

Choose an environmental issue from your previous discussion or select one from the list below.

rain forest destruction
fossil fuels
global warming
species extinction
air and water pollution
overpopulation
waste disposal in the oceans
waste disposal in space
nuclear power
urbanization

Research your topic in one or more of the following ways:

◆ Go to a local library and find at least three different sources of information. These sources could be magazine articles, books, newspapers, reference books (encyclopedias, almanacs), or the Internet.

◆ Write a letter to an environmental organization and ask for information.

◆ Talk to a local environmental agency or group.

SHARING YOUR FINDINGS

Write a report on your research topic. The report should include a brief history of the issue, a description of the current status of the issue, and a discussion of what actions are being taken today to help resolve the issue. Share the report with your classmates.

REFERENCES

The following are addresses for international environmental groups.

Alp Action (Acid Rain)
Bellevue Foundation
P.O. Box 6
1211 Geneva, 3, Switzerland

Greenpeace International
Keizersgracht 176
1016 DW Amsterdam
The Netherlands

Rainforest Action Network
301 Broadway, Suite A
San Francisco, CA 94133
USA

World Wide Fund for Nature (WWF) International
World Conservation Centre
Avenue de Mont Blanc
CH-11996 Gland, Switzerland

Worldwatch Institute
1776 Massachusetts Avenue
Washington, DC 20036
USA

GIVE AND LEARN

1 APPROACHING THE TOPIC

A. PREDICTING

1. Philanthropy is a way of showing concern for other people. It is the act of giving money or property to individuals or organizations. It is also the act of volunteering—working without pay—to help needy people or worthy organizations. Look at the title of this unit. Briefly write what you think it means.

2. Look at the photograph. Discuss these questions with a partner. Who are these people? What are they doing? Why are they doing it?

B. SHARING INFORMATION

The quotations which follow represent a philosophy about philanthropy. Read these statements and write a few sentences explaining what you think that philosophy is. Give examples to illustrate your explanation. Share your ideas with the class.

"It is better to give than to receive."
—New Testament, Acts 20:35

"Practice random acts of love and kindness."
—Bumper sticker which is popular in the United States

"He who bestows his goods upon the poor,
Shall have as much again, and ten times more."
—Bunyan, *Pilgrim's Progress*, Vol. 2

The philosophy expressed in these quotations is:

_____

_____

For example:

_____

_____

2 PREPARING TO READ

A. BACKGROUND

Read the information and do the exercise that follows.

Across the United States more and more organizations—including corporate, educational, religious, and governmental groups—are sponsoring volunteer programs. And more and more people are volunteering. People volunteer for many different reasons: some for political or religious reasons; some for personal or social reasons; and others simply because it's mandatory, that is, required.

Read what the following people say about volunteering. Why do you think they donate, or give, their time? Match the people with their reason(s) for volunteering. Some people may have more than one reason. Share your answers in small groups. The first one has been done for you.

Reasons for Volunteering:

a. personal   **c.** medical research   **e.** mandatory

b. political   **d.** religious   **f.** environmental

1. Ralph Birdsong

Age 42

Raised $2,000 for AIDS research in the annual Boston to New York AIDS bicycle ride

"First of all, I'm trying to raise money for AIDS research in memory of my brother. Maybe this way what happened to him won't happen to others. Second, I enjoy biking and this way I can combine my hobby with a good cause."

Reasons: _____c and a_____

2. Greg Dean

Age 36

Donates his time as a Boy Scout leader

"I've always loved the outdoors and camping. By being a scout leader, I can do something I like and transmit my love of nature to another generation. Maybe they'll take care of it better than our generation has."

Reasons: _____

3. Ellen Bullard

Age 27

Volunteers in a soup kitchen for the homeless

"I've always been taught that we should help those who are less fortunate than we are. When Reverend Kingsford spoke at church last Sunday about all the good work being done here, I just knew I wanted to participate."

Reasons: _____

4. Jake Hutchings

Age 17

Spends three hours a week playing guitar for senior citizens in a nursing home

"I started working here last year because it was a school requirement. This year it's an extracurricular activity. I asked the director of the program if I could come back again this year because I really have a good time with these people. I think they like to listen to my music, too."

Reasons: _____

5. Marcia Pantani

Age 58

Spends five hours a week volunteering at a politician's headquarters

"I feel that this person is the best candidate. By volunteering for her, I can do more than just vote. I feel like I'm more involved in the whole political process."

Reasons: _____

B. VOCABULARY FOR COMPREHENSION

1 *Using the words on the left, identify the different parts of this bicycle. The first one has been done for you.*

a. seat

b. frame

c. pedal

d. spoke

e. brakes

f. wheel

g. grips

h. tire

2 *Work with a partner. In each set of words, two of the three words are similar in meaning to the boldface word. Cross out the word that does not belong. Use a dictionary if necessary. The first one has been done for you.*

1. judgment	decision	~~offer~~	opinion
2. proud	modest	pleased	content
3. challenge	allow	test	demand
4. satisfaction	happiness	pleasure	misery
5. determined	insistent	stubborn	uncertain
6. proposal	suggestion	order	recommendation
7. donate	contribute	give	sell
8. admire	respect	regard	hate
9. devote	dedicate	take	give
10. inspire	lessen	encourage	motivate
11. battered	broken	hurt	complete
12. thrilled	happy	saddened	excited

3 READING ONE: Justin Lebo

A. INTRODUCING THE TOPIC

Justin Lebo is a young boy who volunteers his own time and energy to help others.

Read the first two paragraphs of the story and answer the following questions. Work with a partner and compare your answers. Then read the rest of the story.

1. What condition is the bicycle in?

2. Why do you think Justin says the bicycle is "perfect"?

3. What do you think Justin will do with the bicycle?

Justin Lebo

BY PHILLIP HOOSE
(from *It's Our World, Too*)

1 Something about the battered old bicycle at the garage sale[1] caught ten-year-old Justin Lebo's eye. What a wreck! It was like looking at a few big bones in the dust and trying to figure out what kind of dinosaur they had once belonged to.

2 It was a BMX bike with a twenty-inch frame. Its original color was buried beneath five or six coats of gunky paint. Everything—the grips, the pedals, the brakes, the seat, the spokes—was bent or broken, twisted and rusted. Justin stood back as if he were inspecting a painting for sale at an auction. Then he made his final judgment: perfect.

3 Justin talked the owner down to $6.50 and asked his mother, Diane, to help load the bike into the back of their car.

4 When he got it home, he wheeled the junker into the garage and showed it proudly to his father. "Will you help me fix it up?" he asked. Justin's hobby was bike racing, a passion the two of them shared. Their garage barely had room for the car anymore. It was more like a bike shop. Tires and frames hung from hooks on the ceiling, and bike wrenches dangled from the walls.

5 Now Justin and his father cleared out a work space in the garage and put the old junker up on a rack. They poured alcohol on the frame and rubbed until the old paint began to yield, layer by layer. They replaced the broken pedal, tightened down a new seat, and restored the grips. In about a week, it looked brand new.

---

[1] *garage sale:* sale of used furniture, clothes, toys, etc. held at someone's home

6   Soon he forgot about the bike. But the very next week, he bought another junker at a yard sale[2] and fixed it up, too. After a while it bothered him that he wasn't really using either bike. Then he realized that what he loved about the old bikes wasn't riding them: it was the challenge of making something new and useful out of something old and broken.

7   Justin wondered what he should do with them. They were just taking up space in the garage. He remembered that when he was younger, he used to live near a large brick building called the Kilbarchan Home for Boys. It was a place for boys whose parents couldn't care for them for one reason or another.

8   He found "Kilbarchan" in the phone book and called the director, who said the boys would be thrilled to get two bicycles. The next day when Justin and his mother unloaded the bikes at the home, two boys raced out to greet them. They leapt aboard the bikes and started tooling around the semicircular driveway, doing wheelies and pirouettes, laughing and shouting.

9   The Lebos watched them for a while, then started to climb into their car to go home. The boys cried after them, "Wait a minute! You forgot your bikes!" Justin explained that the bikes were for them to keep. "They were so happy." Justin remembers. "It was like they couldn't believe it. It made me feel good just to see them happy."

10   On the way home, Justin was silent. His mother assumed he was lost in a feeling of satisfaction. But he was thinking about what would happen once those bikes got wheeled inside and everybody saw them. How could all those kids decide who got the bikes? Two bikes could cause more trouble than they would solve. Actually they hadn't been that hard to build. It was fun. Maybe he could do more . . .

11   "Mom," Justin said as they turned onto their street, "I've got an idea. I'm going to make a bike for every boy at Kilbarchan for Christmas." Diane Lebo looked at Justin out of the corner of her eye. She had rarely seen him so determined.

12   When they got home, Justin called Kilbarchan to find out how many boys lived there. There were twenty-one. It was already June. He had six months to make nineteen bikes. That was almost a bike a week. Justin called the home back to tell them of his plan. "I could tell they didn't think I could do it," Justin remembers. "I knew I could."

13   Justin knew his best chance to build bikes was almost the way General Motors or Ford builds cars: in an assembly line. He figured it would take three or four junkers to produce enough parts to make one good bike. That meant sixty to eighty bikes. Where would he get them?

---

[2] *yard sale:* garage sale

14   Garage sales seemed to be the only hope. It was June, and there would be garage sales all summer long. But even if he could find that many bikes, how could he ever pay for them? That was hundreds of dollars.

15   He went to his parents with a proposal. "When Justin was younger, say five or six," says his mother, "he used to give away some of his allowance[3] to help others in need. His father and I would donate a dollar for every dollar Justin donated. So he asked us if it could be like the old days, if we'd match every dollar he put into buying old bikes. We said yes."

16   Justin and his mother spent most of June and July hunting for cheap bikes at garage sales and thrift shops.[4] They would haul the bikes home, and Justin would start stripping them down in the yard.

17   But by the beginning of August, he had managed to make only ten bikes. Summer vacation was almost over, and school and homework would soon cut into his time. Garage sales would dry up when it got colder, and Justin was out of money. Still he was determined to find a way.

18   At the end of August, Justin got a break. A neighbor wrote a letter to the local newspaper describing Justin's project, and an editor thought it would make a good story. In her admiring article about a boy who was devoting his summer to help kids he didn't even know, she said Justin needed bikes and money, and she printed his home phone number.

19   Overnight, everything changed. "There must have been a hundred calls," Justin says. "People would call me up and ask me to come over and pick up their old bike. Or I'd be working in the garage, and a station wagon would pull up. The driver would leave a couple of bikes by the curb. It just snowballed."

20   The week before Christmas Justin delivered the last of the twenty-one bikes to Kilbarchan. Once again, the boys poured out of the home and leapt aboard the bikes, tearing around in the snow.

21   And once again, their joy inspired Justin. They reminded him how important bikes were to him. Wheels meant freedom. He thought about how much more the freedom to ride must mean to boys like these who had so little freedom in their lives. He decided to keep on building.

22   "First I made eleven bikes for the children in a foster home[5] my mother told me about. Then I made bikes for all the women in a battered women's shelter. Then I made ten little bikes and tricycles for children with AIDS. Then I made twenty-three bikes for the Paterson Housing Coalition."

---

[3] *allowance:* money that you are given regularly
[4] *thrift shops:* stores that sell used furniture, clothes, toys, etc., at a low price
[5] *foster home:* a temporary home where a child is taken care of by someone who is not the natural parent

23   In the four years since he started, Justin Lebo has made between 150 and 200 bikes and given them all away. He has been careful to leave time for his homework, his friends, his coin collection, his new interest in marine biology, and of course his own bikes.

24   Reporters and interviewers have asked Justin Lebo the same question over and over: "Why do you do it?" The question seems to make him uncomfortable. It's as if they want him to say what a great person he is. Their stories always make him seem like a saint, which he knows he isn't. "Sure it's nice of me to make the bikes," he says, "because I don't have to. But I want to. In part, I do it for myself. I don't think you can ever really do anything to help anybody else if it doesn't make you happy.

25   "Once I overheard a kid who got one of my bikes say, 'A bike is like a book; it opens up a whole new world.' That's how I feel, too. It made me happy to know that kid felt that way. That's why I do it."

B. READING FOR MAIN IDEAS

Complete the following statements. Share your answers with a partner.

1. Justin Lebo is _____

_____

_____

2. Justin is a special person because _____

_____

_____

3. His parents and the community have supported him by _____

_____

_____

4. Justin enjoys doing what he does because _____

_____

_____

C. READING FOR DETAILS

Look at the chart. It lists some benefits that can come from doing community service. Complete the chart with examples of how Justin Lebo benefited from his experience. The first one has been done for you.

THE BENEFITS OF COMMUNITY SERVICE	EXAMPLE OF JUSTIN LEBO
Encourages you to use your free time constructively	Justin spent his free time in the summer making bicycles for the children at the Kilbarchan Home for Boys.
Gives a sense of satisfaction and builds self-esteem	
Opens people's eyes to the great variety of people in need	
One successful community service experience leads to performing other services	
Helps you to find out who you are, what your interests are, and what you are good at	

D. READING BETWEEN THE LINES

Read each question and the three possible answers. Circle the answer which you feel is most correct. Refer to the reading to support your answer. Discuss your answers with a partner.

1. Which of the following statements best describes Justin's reaction to the first bike he saw at the garage sale?

   a. He knew immediately that the bike could be fixed up and used by someone who needed a bike.

   b. He wasn't exactly sure what he would do with the bike after he fixed it up.

   c. He knew he wanted to fix up the bike.

2. Which of the following statements best describes why Justin enjoyed fixing the first two bikes?

   a. He liked riding them.

   b. He liked taking them apart and putting them back together.

   c. He liked saving the bikes from being thrown away and giving them a second life.

3. Which of the following statements best describes what Justin was thinking about on his way home from the Kilbarchan Home for Boys?

   a. He knew he had to fix up enough bikes for all the children.

   b. He was satisfied with his work and felt very proud of himself.

   c. He was pleased that the boys enjoyed the bikes so much.

4. Which of the following statements best describes the director of the Kilbarchan Home's reaction to Justin's plan of making each boy a bicycle?

   a. He was pleased and knew Justin had the determination to complete his plan.

   b. He thought that Justin was an incredibly generous child.

   c. He was shocked and didn't really believe Justin could do it.

5. Which of the following events helped Justin most with his bike acquisitions?

   a. His parents' agreement to help him with money.

   b. The newspaper article written about his project.

   c. The fact that it was summer and there were many yard sales.

6. Which of the following statements best describes Justin's motivation for continuing to build and give away bikes?

    a. He loves bicycles and wants other people to have the opportunity to see how wonderful they are.

    b. He loves the challenge of repairing and restoring bicycles that would otherwise be thrown away.

    c. He loves the satisfaction of doing things for other people.

7. Which of the following statements best describes Justin Lebo?

    a. He is a young man with a wide range of interests and hobbies.

    b. He is a young man whose interests are centered on bike racing and repair.

    c. He is a young man who is continually changing his interests and hobbies.

8. Which of the following reasons describes why Justin Lebo does what he does?

    a. His parents have encouraged him to help others.

    b. It makes him happy to help others.

    c. Helping others is mandatory at his school.

READING TWO: Mandatory Volunteering

A. EXPANDING THE TOPIC

Many educational organizations (including the Department of Education) in the United States believe that students should be required to devote a certain number of hours outside classroom time to community service in order to graduate. Supporters of mandatory volunteering believe that the school's role should not only include preparing children to be academically successful, but also help them to be responsible citizens and active participants in their communities.

However, mandatory volunteering has not received unanimous support. Those opposed to the requirement believe that the term "mandatory volunteering" is an oxymoron, a contradiction of words; they believe that volunteering means something you do of your own free will. It is not something that is forced on you.

Before you read the two editorials about mandatory volunteering, write a short answer to the following question.

Do you believe mandatory volunteering is a good idea? Why or why not?

Some Take the Time Gladly

By Mensah Dean (from *The Washington Times*)

1　Mandatory volunteering made many members of Maryland's high school class of '97 grumble with indignation.

2　Future seniors, however, probably won't be as resistant now that the program has been broken in. Some, like John Maloney, already have completed their required hours of approved community service. The Bowie High School sophomore[1] earned his hours in eighth grade[2] by volunteering two nights a week at the Larkin-Chase Nursing and Restorative Center in Bowie.

3　He played shuffleboard, cards, and other games with the senior citizens. He also helped plan parties for them and visited their rooms to keep them company.

4　John, fifteen, is not finished volunteering. Once a week he videotapes animals at the Prince George County animal shelter in Forestville. His footage is shown on the Bowie public access television channel in hopes of finding homes for the animals.

5　"Volunteering is better than just sitting around," says John, "and I like animals; I don't want to see them put to sleep.[3]"

6　He's not the only volunteer in his family. His sister, Melissa, an eighth grader, has completed her hours also volunteering at Larkin-Chase.

7　"It is a good idea to have kids go out into the community, but it's frustrating to have to write essays about the work," she said. "It makes you feel like you're doing it for the requirement and not for yourself."

8　The high school's service learning office, run by Beth Ansley, provides information on organizations seeking volunteers so that students will have an easier time fulfilling their hours.

9　"It's ridiculous that people are opposing the requirements," said Amy Rouse, who this summer has worked at the Ronald McDonald House[4] and has helped to rebuild a church in Clinton.

10　"So many people won't do the service unless it's mandatory," Rouse said, "but once they start doing it, they'll really like it and hopefully it will become a part of their lives—like it has become a part of mine."

---

[1] *sophomore:* a student in the second year of high school (or college)
[2] *eighth grade:* The U.S. public school system begins with kindergarten and then continues
　with grades 1–12. A student in eighth grade would be approximately thirteen or fourteen years of age.
[3] *put to sleep:* killed in a humane way
[4] *Ronald McDonald House:* a residence, usually near a hospital, for the family of children
　who require a lot of time in the hospital because of serious illness

Mandatory Volunteering for High School Diploma Not a Good Idea

(From *The Sun Sentinel*)

1   Re proposals for mandatory service hours in order to graduate from high school: I am an active participant in the high school service program, and chairperson of a tutoring program run primarily by high school students such as myself. Volunteering is a personal choice and an extracurricular activity such as the debate team or school-sponsored sports.

2   Mandatory volunteering is not a good idea. First, many students do volunteer, and most do it with full force. By the time a volunteering student becomes a senior,[1] that student could earn as many as 1000+ service hours. If an entering freshman[2] is told that he or she must volunteer for a pre-set number of hours, the student might become resentful, complete the required hours, and never volunteer again. The volunteered hours would end up being less than the hours being volunteered now.

3   Many students do not have the time to volunteer. School goes from a set starting time to a set ending time. If the student's busy after-school schedule does not allow for extracurricular[3] activities, that is the student's own business. With the exception of homework, there is nothing that a student is required to do after school hours.

4   Finally, mandatory volunteering is an oxymoron. If students are required to volunteer it is no longer volunteering. The performed service becomes one more thing to do in order to graduate from high school. The quality of work can suffer greatly. If a student enjoys volunteering, he or she will volunteer without having to be told.

---

[1] *senior*: a student in the last year of high school
[2] *freshman*: a student in the first year of high school
[3] *extracurricular*: outside of the school requirement

Summarize the opinions in the editorials. Write them in the chart and share your summaries with the class.

FOR MANDATORY VOLUNTEERING	AGAINST MANDATORY VOLUNTEERING
1. _____	1. _____
2. _____	2. _____
3. _____	3. _____

Chart continues on next page.

4. _____   4. _____

5. _____   5. _____

6. _____   6. _____

B. LINKING READINGS ONE AND TWO

Imagine you are Justin Lebo and your school has just initiated a mandatory volunteering requirement. How would you react? Would you be for or against mandatory volunteering? How would your personal experience influence your reaction? Write a letter to the editor of your local paper expressing your opinion either for or against the requirement. Be sure to use your experience to support your position.

Justin Lebo

To the Editor:

I would like to express my opinion on the school's recent decision to adopt mandatory volunteering.

_____

_____

_____

_____

_____

_____

_____

_____

_____

_____

_____

_____

Sincerely,

Justin Lebo

5 REVIEWING LANGUAGE

A. EXPLORING LANGUAGE

*How do you think these people would answer the questions addressed to them? Read the questions and write their answers, using the words given. You may need to change the form of the words (for example, **devote** to **devoted**, or **determine** to **determination**). Share your responses with a partner. The first one has been done for you.*

1. To Diane Lebo.
   Your son Justin is quite remarkable, isn't he?

   devote   **determine**   **proud**

   "Yes, he is. I've never seen Justin so determined and
   devoted to a project before. I am very proud of him."

2. To Justin Lebo.
   After fixing the first bike, did you ever think you would end up repairing and donating over 150 more?

   passion   **challenge**   **snowball**

3. To the director of the Kilbarchan School for Boys.
   What did you think when Justin first told you he was planning on building a bicycle for every boy at Kilbarchan?

   thrilled   **proposal**   **manage**

4. To a Kilbarchan boy.
How did you feel when you rode one of Justin's bikes?

hope   inspire   admire

_____

_____

_____

5. To a student who supports mandatory volunteering.
Why do you support mandatory volunteering?

fulfilling   donate   volunteer

_____

_____

_____

6. To a student who is opposed to mandatory volunteering.
Why are you opposed to mandatory volunteering?

ridiculous   indignant   oppose

_____

_____

_____

B. WORKING WITH WORDS: Phrasal Verbs

A **phrasal verb** consists of two or three words. This combination of words often has a meaning that is very different from the meaning of its parts.

Work in a small group. Read the sentences and circle the best explanation for each underlined phrasal verb.

1. Proponents of mandatory volunteering say volunteering for a community service is time better spent than <u>sitting around</u> all day watching television or playing computer games.

   sit around

   a. do nothing special

   b. sit with friends in a circle

   c. not take part in something

2. Little boys and girls love to <u>tear around</u> on bicycles that Justin Lebo made.

   tear around

   a. play so hard you rip your clothes

   b. move quickly in all directions

   c. destroy things

3. Students who have lots of free time like to <u>tool around</u> town on bikes or in cars.

   tool around

   a. play with hammers, screwdrivers, and other tools

   b. terrorize a place in a vehicle

   c. take a ride in or on a vehicle

4. At first, Justin could not <u>figure out</u> what to do with his two bikes.

   figure out

   a. resolve a problem

   b. make a plan

   c. take part in

5. Justin had so many bikes that he had to <u>clear out</u> his basement and start building them there.

   clear out

   a. make room on a table

   b. clean a small area

   c. empty an area or space

6. When the students <u>found out</u> the new graduation requirements, they were furious.

   find out

   a. create something

   b. discover something lost

   c. learn about a new fact

7. Justin Lebo <u>talked</u> the bicycle owner <u>down</u> $3.00.

   talk down

   a. discuss a situation

   b. speak disrespectfully to someone

   c. persuade someone to reduce a price

8. People fear that if students do not do community service, they will <u>end up</u> being uncaring and unsympathetic individuals.

   end up

   a. complete a project

   b. finish in a certain way

   c. stop something

9. When people donate old clothes to a community center, the center staff will often come to the house and <u>pick up</u> the donations.

   pick up

   a. start to increase

   b. clean something

   c. collect something

10. Justin was afraid that the garage sales would <u>dry up</u> by the end of the summer.

    dry up

    a. be dull and uninteresting

    b. slowly come to an end

    c. become useless

6 SKILLS FOR EXPRESSION

A. GRAMMAR: Tag Questions

1 *Examine these sentences and discuss the questions that follow with a partner.*

- ◆ Justin Lebo is a philanthropist, <u>isn't he</u>?

- ◆ Justin Lebo doesn't sell his bikes, <u>does he</u>?

- ◆ He and his father fixed bikes, <u>didn't they</u>?

a. There are two parts to a tag question. What are they?

b. What are the tags in these questions?

c. When the verb in the statement is affirmative, what is the verb in the tag part? What happens to the tag when the verb in the statement is negative?

FOCUS ON GRAMMAR

See Tag Questions in *Focus on Grammar, High Intermediate.*

Tag Questions

Tag questions are like *yes/no* questions. They are often used to check information or ask for agreement. They usually mean, "Isn't the statement I've just made true? Aren't I right?" Tag questions are answered in the same way as *yes/no* questions.

- ◆ He is a philanthropist, **isn't he?**   **Yes**, he is./**No**, he isn't.

Affirmative and Negative Forms

Tag questions are made up of two parts: a statement and the tag. If the verb in the statement is affirmative, the verb in the tag is negative. If the verb in the statement is negative, the verb in the tag is affirmative. The negative verb in the tag is always a contraction.

- ◆ Justin **is** young, **isn't** he?

- ◆ Justin **isn't** old, **is** he?

Subject Agreement

The subject of the tag agrees with the subject of the statement. The subject in the tag is always a subject pronoun.

- **Mandatory volunteering** is ridiculous, isn't **it**?
- **Many students** are volunteers, aren't **they**?
- **Justin** doesn't have to volunteer, does **he**?

Verb Agreement

The verb in the tag is the same tense as the verb in the statement and agrees with the statement verb in number and person. The verb in the tag is always a form of *be* or an auxiliary verb.

Statement	Tag
1. be (main verb)	**be**
• Volunteering **wasn't** a requirement,	**was** it?
2. be (auxiliary)	**be**
• You **were** going to volunteer last week,	**weren't** you?
3. have (auxiliary verb)	**have**
• Justin **has fixed** more than 200 bikes,	**hasn't** he?
4. Modal (auxiliary)	Modal
• You **will** help us with the project,	**won't** you?
• They **can't** graduate until they volunteer,	**can** they?
5. Other verbs (main verb)	**do**
• Justin's mother **helped** him collect bikes,	**didn't** she?
6. have (main verb)	**do**
• You **have** some free time to volunteer,	**don't** you?

2 *Match the tags with the following statements. The first one has been done for you.*

STATEMENTS

1. Nearly all civilizations have practiced some form of philanthropy, __l__

2. Private donations helped establish churches, hospitals, libraries, and universities, _____

3. Many corporations give money to support the arts, _____

4. Volunteering in soup kitchens can really make a difference, _____

5. Some people haven't reacted well to the idea of forcing community service, _____

6. Mandatory volunteerism is an oxymoron, _____

7. You won't forget to take food to the homeless shelter, _____

8. Mandatory volunteering isn't a good idea, _____

9. Students shouldn't have to do mandatory volunteering, _____

10. You have a good feeling about yourself and others when you volunteer, _____

11. You would like to do something like Justin is doing, _____

12. By Christmas, she had baked over 1,000 cookies for children in foster care, _____

TAG

a. isn't it?

b. will you?

c. should they?

d. don't they?

e. is it?

f. didn't they?

g. wouldn't you?

h. can't it?

i. hadn't she?

j. have they?

k. don't you?

l. haven't they?

3 *Some of the following tag questions have grammatical errors. Find the errors and make the necessary corrections. Not all the sentences have errors. The first one has been done for you.*

1. Justin Lebo fixed three bicycles yesterday, ~~doesn't~~ *didn't* he?

2. John is not finished volunteering, is John?

3. Corporations have been donating more and more to the needy, hasn't she?

4. It's ridiculous for people to oppose the requirements, is not it?

5. Students shouldn't be forced to do volunteer work, shouldn't they?

6. Students who volunteer will be more likely to attend four-year colleges, won't they?

7. Students who volunteer in high school will continue to volunteer throughout their lives, aren't they?

8. People's reaction to mandatory volunteering is mixed, isn't it?

9. The bikes weren't that hard to build, didn't they?

10. Justin used to give away some of his allowance to help others in need, didn't he?

B. STYLE: Punctuation

1 *Examine the punctuation in the sentences on page 146 and discuss the questions that follow with a partner.*

◆ I like animals; I don't want to see them put to sleep.
◆ Justin stood back as if he were inspecting a painting for sale at an auction and then made his final judgment: perfect.
◆ Everything—the grips, the pedals, the brakes, the seat, the spokes—was bent or broken, twisted and rusted.

a. In which sentence does the punctuation set off a list of extra information?

b. In which sentence does the punctuation separate two closely related statements?

c. In which sentence does the punctuation set off a word which identifies and clarifies other words that come before it?

d. Can you name the different types of punctuation in these sentences?

Punctuation

The Semicolon

A semicolon looks like this **;**

Use a semicolon to

◆ connect two independent clauses with very closely related ideas.

A bike is like a book; it opens up a whole new world.

The Colon

A colon looks like this **:**

Use a colon to

◆ illustrate or give further information about a noun or noun phrase.

Justin knew his best chance to build bikes was almost the way General Motors or Ford builds cars: in an assembly line.

◆ introduce a quotation. This is a more formal way to introduce quotations than the use of a comma (,).

Reporters and interviewers have asked Justin Lebo the same question over and over: "Why do you do it?"

The Dash

A dash looks like this ▬

Use a dash to

- set off extra information, especially if the information has a series of commas.

    Everything—the grips, the pedals, the brakes—was broken.

- indicate a sudden break in thought or parenthetical information.

    Volunteering for community service—whether it be mandatory or not—is a great way to get students involved in society.

- emphasize or summarize a thought.

    Hopefully it will become a part of their lives—like it has become a part of mine.

2 *Look at the following pairs of sentences. Circle the letter of the sentence in each pair that correctly uses colons, semicolons, and dashes. Review the explanations in the chart and explain the use of punctuation in each sentence. The first one has been done for you.*

1. **(a.)** Justin stood back as if he were inspecting a painting for sale at an auction. Then he made his final judgment: perfect.

    b. Justin stood back as if he were inspecting a painting for sale at an auction. Then he made his final judgment—perfect.

    The colon is used to give further information about a noun or

    noun phrase.

2. **a.** All of Lev's work—which is a lot—has been focused on the homeless.

    b. All of Lev's work: which is a lot, has been focused on the homeless.

    _____

    _____

3. **a.** In order to fix the bicycles, Justin Lebo needed to have lots of spare parts; chains, pedals, seats, and cables.

    b. In order to fix the bicycles, Justin Lebo needed to have lots of spare parts: chains, pedals, seats, and cables.

    _____

    _____

4. **a.** There are many types of community service—working in soup kitchens, working in nursing homes, working at homeless shelters—which high school students can choose to do.

   b. There are many types of community service; working in soup kitchens, working in nursing homes, working at homeless shelters; which high school students can choose to do.

   _____

   _____

5. **a.** Most volunteers at some time ask themselves the same question— "Why is it important for me to do this?"

   b. Most volunteers at some time ask themselves the same question: "Why is it important for me to do this?"

   _____

   _____

6. **a.** Volunteering is becoming more and more important in the college application process: many colleges look more favorably on students who have volunteered in high school.

   b. Volunteering is becoming more and more important in the college application process; many colleges look more favorably on students who have volunteered in high school.

   _____

   _____

3 *Add the correct punctuation to this paragraph. Use a colon (:), semi-colon (;), or dash (—). The first one has been done for you.*

I began volunteering at the age of fourteen. At the time, there was no mandatory volunteering requirement __;__ volunteering was a
(1)
personal choice based on my own interest. My interests centered on helping children _____ especially children with special needs. At our
(2)
school we had a special needs classroom with a number of special needs children. Twice a week I would work as the teacher's helper. Through the work I did, I realized two things _____ I was happiest when I volunteered,
(3)
and I was good at helping special needs students. I am now much older, have a college degree in special education, and still do volunteer work at a community center for troubled teenagers. I guess I would say that the volunteer work I did at age fourteen changed my life _____ forever.
(4)

ON YOUR OWN

A. WRITING TOPICS

Choose one of the following topics and write two or three paragraphs about it. Try to use the ideas, vocabulary, grammar, and style from this unit in your writing.

1. Imagine you are responsible for setting up a community service program in your city. What kind of program would you start? Who would it serve? Would there be volunteers? Who would the volunteers be? What would you hope to accomplish? Be as specific as possible.

2. In your opinion, what are the pros and cons of mandatory volunteering in high school? Describe both sides of the issue.

3. Many large corporations are involved in philanthropic work. They often say that they want to give something back to the people and community that have supported them and their products. Their money and efforts do much good; however, skeptics would say that they are really just looking for a "tax break" and/or a cheap way to buy good-will (good publicity for the company). What is your opinion on corporate philanthropy? Give examples to support your opinion.

4. There are many different ways to practice "random acts of love and kindness." Write about some of these ways and why you think people perform these acts.

B. FIELDWORK

PREPARATION

As a class, brainstorm a list of community centers or community work being done in your area, or list types of community centers you have heard about. Discuss the type of services these centers offer: serving food, offering shelter, meeting medical or educational needs, helping repair homes, cleaning up the neighborhood, or others.

RESEARCH ACTIVITY

In small groups, research one of the centers or community projects.

Individually, or in groups, go to a center or project headquarters and gather information to complete the chart below. If there is not a center or project near you, go to the library and find information about activities in another area.

Combine your information and prepare a report of your findings for the class. Use the chart to organize your report and take notes on the reports of your classmates.

Name of center or project				
History of center: When was it started? Who started it? Why?				
Type of people the center helps				
Type of people who work in the center: Are there volunteers? How many? Who are they?				
Funding for the center: How does the center pay for its activities? How is it funded?				

HOMING IN ON EDUCATION

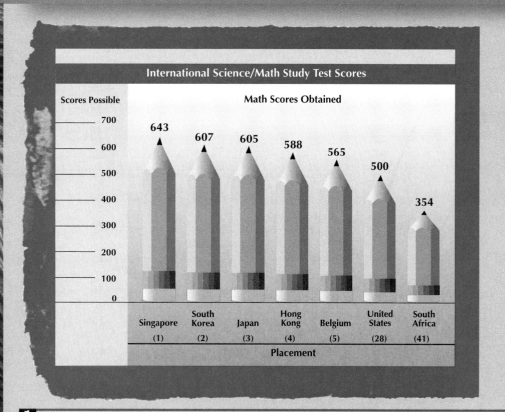

International Science/Math Study Test Scores

Math Scores Obtained

Scores Possible

Singapore (1)	643
South Korea (2)	607
Japan (3)	605
Hong Kong (4)	588
Belgium (5)	565
United States (28)	500
South Africa (41)	354

Placement

1 APPROACHING THE TOPIC

A. PREDICTING

Look at the graph. It shows test scores from a recent International Science/Math Study. The math test was given to 500,000 students in forty-one countries. The test compared academic performance among the participating countries. The average score was 513. The graph shows the results of seven countries. Working in small groups, study the results and answer the questions.

1. What countries are among the top five? Where did the United States place?
2. What are your reactions to the test results?
3. Why do you think the students from the top countries scored so well?

B. SHARING INFORMATION

According to research, some of the factors listed below contribute to a student's success, and some do not. Check (✓) each factor you believe contributed to the success of the top scoring countries in the International Science/Math Study. Discuss your opinions with the class. Then, compare your opinions with the answers at the bottom of the page.

Students in the top scoring countries:

_____ **1.** spend more time on homework.

_____ **2.** spend less time watching television.

_____ **3.** have easy access to computers and books in the home.

_____ **4.** have better trained and qualified teachers.

_____ **5.** spend more time in class.

_____ **6.** have more challenging coursework (curricula).

_____ **7.** spend less time playing with friends after school.

_____ **8.** have smaller class sizes.

Answers: 3, 4, and 6.

PREPARING TO READ

A. BACKGROUND

Read this information and do the exercise that follows on page 154.

The term *home schooling* or *home tuition,* as it is called in England, means educating children at home or in places other than a (**1**) <u>mainstream</u> setting such as a public or private school. There are many reasons why parents choose home schooling for their children. Some parents are dissatisfied with the quality of education in the public schools. Others do not want their children to have to worry about (**2**) "<u>peer pressure</u>," or social pressure from friends. They say it may interfere with the child's studies. These parents fear this type of pressure will lead to negative behavior such as smoking, drinking alcohol, and taking drugs. (**3**) <u>Bullying</u> and harassing from other students is another concern. Still other parents choose this type of education for religious reasons. Whatever the reasons may be, it is evident that more and more children are being taken out of mainstream schools every year. As a result, many questions have (**4**) <u>emerged</u>, encouraging the debate over home schooling versus public schooling.

What then is the future of education? Will this (**5**) <u>marginal</u> model of schooling replace traditional schools and conventional methods? Will computers and the Internet replace our classrooms and teachers? Will public schools be a (**6**) <u>thing of the past</u>? As the debate over home schooling versus public schooling continues, so do the questions about what home schoolers are studying at home. How can parents (**7**) <u>ensure</u> that their children are prepared academically for college? How are home schoolers (**8**) <u>assessed</u> to make sure they are getting the basics, the same educational standards that mainstream students must have? Finally, there are questions regarding the children's emotional development. Are they too (**9**) <u>isolated</u> from their peers? Are they (**10**) <u>missing out on</u> the social benefits of being in a large classroom of their peers? As with any (**11**) <u>debatable</u> issue, the answers to these questions are neither simple nor one-sided.

Complete these sentences.

1. The main reasons for home schooling are _____

_____

_____

2. People are worried about home schooling because _____

_____

_____

3. I might (or I might not) teach a child at home because _____

_____

_____

B. VOCABULARY FOR COMPREHENSION

Look at the underlined words in the background reading on page 153. Write the number of each word beside its synonym below. The first one has been done for you.

_11_ **a.** controversial, questionable

_____ **b.** developed, arisen

_____ **c.** guarantee

_____ **d.** losing an opportunity for

_____ **e.** uncommon or unconventional

_____ **f.** separated or secluded from

_____ **g.** social demands from your "group"

_____ **h.** something that is not used anymore or is obsolete

_____ **i.** tested, evaluated

_____ **j.** threatening, teasing

_____ **k.** traditional, conventional

READING ONE: Teaching at Home Hits New High with Internet

A. INTRODUCING THE TOPIC

Read the title of the article and the first paragraph. Then write three questions which you would like the article to answer. Use the question words given.

1. Where? _____

2. How? _____

3. Why? _____

Teaching at Home Hits New High with Internet; As Schools Fight for a Future 15,000 Families Join the Trend Towards Teaching Children at Home

By Dorothy Lepkowska (from *The Evening Standard*)

1   Record numbers of children are being taken out of school and educated by their parents at home. Up to 100 children a month nationally are leaving the classroom because of their parents' disillusionment with the education system. Around 15,000 families are now teaching their youngsters at home, a rise of 50 per cent from last year, according to latest figures.

2   The popularity of home tuition has traditionally been blamed on the rigidity of the examination system, parents being unable to get their children into the school of their choice, and dissatisfaction with teaching methods. Some parents also prefer to keep their children at home because of bullying and a lack of discipline in schools. Academics now claim, however, that a significant proportion of families educating at home do so because they feel that the concept of institutionalised education is a thing of the past. They believe that schools could be obsolete within 20 years as parents turn instead to media technology, such as the Internet, to educate their children.

3   Under the law, parents must ensure their children are educated, whether at school or at

home. It is the responsibility of local authorities to safeguard their schooling. Professor Roland Meighan, a senior lecturer in education at Nottingham University, said parents were fed up with the constrictions of the existing education system. He said: 'Schools have become an outdated concept from the days of the town crier,[1] when information was scarce and a central figure was needed to impart knowledge. Parents are now coming to the conclusion that education is moving on, and they do not want their children to be stifled by conventional methods.'

4   Professor Meighan said many academics now thought schools as we know them could become obsolete within 20 years. Instead, children will be taught at home using the Internet, computers, and video. He said: 'The schools of the future will be small pockets of children, sharing equipment in each others' homes, with teachers taking on a new role as advisers, sorting through the available information.'

5   The future of institutionalised schooling was recently called into question by Sir Christopher Ball, the director of learning at the Royal Society of Arts. He predicted the education system of the future would include a global curriculum and a worldwide qualifications[2] system. He said: 'Some existing marginal models of schooling will move into the mainstream—community schools and home schooling, for example. No doubt, other models as yet unseen will emerge.'

How Opting Out Brings *O-Level* Success at 13

6   Leslie Barson is already running a prototype of the type of school educationalists predict will educate children in the future. Based partly at a community centre in Brent and partly in family homes, the Otherwise Club is comprised of some 35 families around north London. Professional teachers are brought in where necessary to help with more specialised subjects, but for the most part parents and children work together on projects such as study of the Greeks and the American

Civil War, reading up on events, making costumes, and learning how people used to live.

7   Parents opting out of school claim the flexibility of home learning means some children sit one of two GCEs[3] by the age of 13. Ms Barson's own children, Luis, age 12, and 7-year-old Lilly, have never attended school. She pays around £2,000 a year for private tutors to help in specialised areas. She set up the Otherwise Club six years ago with just a handful of youngsters. She said: 'The whole idea of educating children should be to develop their self-confidence. Our children do not see adults as disciplinarians.' Her son agrees. Luis, who is currently teaching himself math, said: 'I like the freedom to learn things that interest me, particularly music. I don't feel I am missing out on anything by not being at school because I am a member of various clubs and have friends who attend normal school.'

The 'Danger' of Isolating Children

8   Home schooling could affect children's relationships with their peers and other adults because of prolonged periods spent with their parents, educationalists have claimed. Most academics concede that education will in the future be increasingly centred around the home, and fear children could become isolated and withdrawn. Professor Michael Barber, of London University's Institute of Education, said pupils could spend half their time at school and half at home as a compromise. He said home tuition would play an increasingly significant role in educating children in the coming years. 'I believe very strongly that children need to have the experience of school,' he added. 'There is the quality control issue of ensuring pupils are taught the basics and assessed. Children also need to spend time with their peers to learn the rules of work in a democratic society and learn to deal with relationships with adults other than their parents.' Margaret Rudland, head teacher of Godolphin and Latymer School, Hammersmith, said children needed to experience the 'rough and tumble'[4] of peer associations.

---

[1] *town crier:* in the past, a person employed by a town to make public announcements—usually by shouting in the streets
[2] *qualifications:* completion of necessary requirements for graduation
[3] *sit one of two GCEs:* take one of two standardized tests
[4] *"rough and tumble":* hard or demanding aspects

B. READING FOR MAIN IDEAS

*Which of the following sentences are the main ideas of the text and which are supporting details? Mark each sentence as either main idea (**MI**) or supporting detail (**SD**). The first one has been done for you.*

___MI___ **1.** Home schooling is increasing in popularity.

_____ **2.** Around 15,000 families now educate their children at home.

_____ **3.** Many parents are unhappy with the traditional schools.

_____ **4.** Some educators believe traditional schools will not exist in the future.

_____ **5.** Some people think the Internet and modern technology will replace the teacher and the classrooms of today.

_____ **6.** Sir Christopher Ball believes future educational systems will include a worldwide qualifications system.

_____ **7.** Some people believe isolating home schoolers from their peers can be dangerous.

_____ **8.** Home schooling may affect children's socialization skills because they spend too much time alone.

C. READING FOR DETAILS

In each set, circle the two choices that accurately complete the sentence. Then discuss your answers with a partner.

1. It was reported that in England

    a. about 15,000 students were taken out of school.

    b. no more than 100 children per month are being taken out of school.

    c. more than 100 children per month are being taken out of school.

2. Academics who support home schooling believe

  a. institutionalized education is still important.

  b. schools could be obsolete in 20 years.

  c. media and the Internet will become increasingly important in education.

3. Sir Christopher Ball, director of learning at the Royal Society of Arts, predicts education systems in the future will

  a. have a global curriculum.

  b. include more home schooling and community schools.

  c. have a qualifications system based only on community needs.

4. In the Otherwise Club

  a. students develop self-confidence.

  b. teachers are brought in to teach many of the main subjects.

  c. students attend various clubs and have friends in normal schools.

5. Some educationalists believe home schooling can affect students' relationships with their peers because

  a. the students spend long periods of time with their parents.

  b. the students' lives are centered around their homes.

  c. the students study for many long hours.

D. READING BETWEEN THE LINES

How do you think the following issues are dealt with in a traditional school and in a home school? Complete the chart. Refer to the reading for help. Discuss your answers with a partner. An example has been done for you.

ISSUES	TRADITIONAL SCHOOL	HOME SCHOOL
peer pressure and bullying		Students don't have to worry about this because they study at home.
socialization skills		
teaching methods/materials		
role of teachers/role of parents		
self-discipline and motivation		
student interest in learning		

4 READING TWO: The Fun They Had

A. EXPANDING THE TOPIC

The following story was written by Isaac Asimov in 1951. It addresses the question of computerized home schooling. At that time this type of home schooling was regarded as science fiction.

Read the first three paragraphs of the story. Then write a short answer to the following questions. What do you think was one of Isaac Asimov's fears about the future of books? Do you think we are headed in the direction he feared?

The Fun They Had

BY ISAAC ASIMOV
(from *Earth Is Room Enough*)

1   Margie even wrote about it that night in her diary. On the page headed May 17, 2157, she wrote, "Today Tommy found a real book!"

2   It was a very old book. Margie's grandfather once said that when he was a little boy his grandfather told him that there was a time when all stories were printed on paper.

3   They turned the pages, which were yellow and crinkly,[1] and it was awfully funny to read words that stood still instead of moving the way that they were supposed to—on a screen, you know. And then, when they had turned back to the page before, it had the screen words on it that it had had when they read it the first time.

4   "Gee," said Tommy, "what a waste. When you're through with the book, you just throw it away, I guess. Our television screen must have had a million books on it and it's good for plenty more. I wouldn't throw it away."

5   "Same with mine," said Margie. She was eleven and hadn't seen as many books as Tommy had. He was thirteen.

6   She said, "Where did you find it?"

7   "In my house." He pointed without looking, because he was busy reading. "In the attic."

8   "What's it about?"

9   "School."

10   Margie was scornful. "School? What's there to write about school? I hate school."

11   Margie had always hated school, but now she hated it more than ever. The mechanical teacher[2] had been giving her test after test in geography and she had been doing worse and worse until her mother had shaken her head sorrowfully and sent for the County Inspector.

12   He was a round little man with a red face and a whole box of tools with dials and wires. He smiled at Margie and gave her an apple, then took the teacher apart. Margie hoped he wouldn't know how to put it together again, but he knew how all right, and after an hour or so, there it was again, large and square and ugly, with a big screen on which all the lessons were shown and the questions were asked. That

---

[1] *crinkly:* dried out
[2] *mechanical teacher:* a computer

wasn't so bad. The part Margie hated most was the slot[3] where she had to put homework and test papers. She always had to write them out in a punch code they made her learn when she was six years old, and the mechanical teacher calculated the mark[4] in no time.

13   The Inspector had smiled after he was finished and patted Margie's head. He said to her mother, "It's not the little girl's fault, Mrs. Jones. I think the geography sector was geared a little too quick. Those things happen sometimes. I've slowed it up to a ten-year level. Actually, the over-all pattern of her progress is quite satisfactory." And he patted Margie's head again.

14   Margie was disappointed. She had been hoping they would take the teacher away altogether. They had once taken Tommy's teacher away for nearly a month because the history sector had blanked out[5] completely.

15   So she said to Tommy, "Why would anyone write about school?"

16   Tommy looked at her with very superior eyes. "Because it's not our kind of school, stupid. This is the old kind of school that they had hundreds and hundreds of years ago." He added loftily, pronouncing the word very carefully, "Centuries ago."

17   Margie was hurt. "Well, I don't know what kind of school they had all that time ago." She read the book over his shoulder for a while, then said, "Anyway, they had a teacher."

18   "Sure they had a teacher, but it wasn't a regular teacher. It was a man."

19   "A man? How could a man be a teacher?"

20   "Well, he just told the boys and girls things and gave them homework and asked them questions."

21   "A man isn't smart enough."

22   "Sure he is. My father knows as much as my teacher."

23   "He can't. A man can't know as much as a teacher."

24   "He knows almost as much, I betcha.[6]"

25   Margie wasn't prepared to dispute that. She said, "I wouldn't want a strange man in my house to teach me."

26   Tommy screamed with laughter. "You don't know much, Margie. The teachers didn't live in the house. They had a special building and all the kids went there."

27   "And all the kids learned the same thing?"

28   "Sure, if they were the same age."

29   "But my mother says a teacher has to be adjusted to fit the mind of each boy and girl it teaches and that each kid has to be taught differently."

---

[3] *slot:* an opening
[4] *mark:* a grade
[5] *blanked out:* erased
[6] *I betcha:* I'll bet you. I'm sure.

30   "Just the same they didn't do it that way then. If you don't like it, you don't have to read the book."

31   "I didn't say I didn't like it," Margie said quickly. She wanted to read about those funny schools.

32   They weren't even half-finished when Margie's mother called, "Margie! School!"

33   Margie looked up. "Not yet, Mama."

34   "Now!" said Mrs. Jones. "And it's probably time for Tommy, too."

35   Margie said to Tommy, "Can I read the book some more with you after school?"

36   "Maybe," he said nonchalantly. He walked away whistling, the dusty old book tucked beneath his arm.

37   Margie went into the schoolroom. It was right next to her bedroom and the mechanical teacher was on and waiting for her. It was always on at the same time every day except Saturday and Sunday, because her mother said little girls learned better if they learned at regular hours.

38   The screen was lit up, and it said: "Today's arithmetic lesson is on the addition of proper fractions. Please insert yesterday's homework in the proper slot."

39   Margie did so with a sigh. She was thinking about the old schools they had when her grandfather's grandfather was a little boy. All the kids from the whole neighborhood came, laughing and shouting in the schoolyard, sitting together in the schoolroom, going home together at the end of the day. They learned the same things, so they could help one another on the homework and talk about it.

40   And the teachers were people . . .

41   The mechanical teacher was flashing on the screen: "When we add the fractions 1/2 and 1/4 —"

42   Margie was thinking about how the kids must have loved it in the old days. She was thinking of the fun they had.

The School Museum: "They had a special building."

In what way is the home schooling described by Asimov different from and similar to the home schooling described in Reading One? Complete the chart with a partner.

	TEACHING AT HOME HITS NEW HIGH WITH INTERNET	THE FUN THEY HAD
1. Is there a teacher? If yes, what kind of teacher is he/she?		
2. Where does the "school" take place?		
3. Who determines what the students learn and at what pace they learn?		
4. Who monitors the progress of the students?		
5. When and where do students socialize with friends?		
6. How do the students feel about home school compared to traditional school?		

B. LINKING READINGS ONE AND TWO

Discuss these questions in small groups. After your discussion, choose one question and write your own answer in a paragraph on a separate piece of paper.

1. Margie says that kids had fun in the old days. Do you agree? Why or why not?

2. Do you believe that schools today are headed in the direction of the home schooling described in "The Fun They Had"? If yes, how? If no, why not?

3. What do you think are the biggest advantages of home schooling? What do you think are the biggest problems facing home-schooled students? What solutions can you think of for the problems?

4. How would home schooling or traditional schooling meet the three requirements for educational success (the answers to the quiz) mentioned on page 152 in Sharing Information?

5 REVIEWING LANGUAGE

A. EXPLORING LANGUAGE

*How do you think these people would answer the questions asked to them? Read the question and write their answer, using the words given. You may need to change the form of the words (for example, **outdate** to **outdated**). Share your responses with a partner. The first one has been done for you.*

1. To Professor Meighan.
   What do you think will happen to schools in the next twenty years?

obsolete   outdate   constrict   stifle

"I believe that present-day schools will become obsolete and
outdated. Schools these days constrict the students' freedom
and stifle their creativity."

2. To Luis Barson, home schooler.
   What do you like about home schooling?

freedom   peer pressure   bullying   self-confidence

3. To Leslie Barson, home schoolers' mother.
   Why are you so unhappy with traditional schools?

disillusioned   disappointed   teaching methods   rigidity

4. To Professor Michael Barber.
   What concerns do you have about home schooling?

isolation   withdrawal   peers   relationships

5. To Margie, from "The Fun They Had."
   What do you think about twentieth-century schools?

doubtful   surprised   curious   lonely

B. WORKING WITH WORDS:
American and British Spelling

Reading One comes from a British newspaper. Many words are spelled differently than in American English. In the late 1700s, Noah Webster published a book called *The American Spelling Book*. In this book he attempted to simplify British spelling by dropping the "u" in words like *colour* and *harbour*. In other changes, *centre* became *center*, *traveller* became *traveler*. Unfortunately, Webster was not consistent. Words like *glamour* and *acre* never changed from their British spelling. In addition, many words have both an accepted British and American spelling, such as *gray/grey* and *ax/axe*.

Look at the following words. Some of the words are spelled in British English. Others are spelled in American English. Write the American or British equivalents. Use your dictionary if necessary. Discuss the spelling with your classmates. Do you see any patterns?

BRITISH SPELLING	AMERICAN SPELLING
specialise	specialize
institutionalised	
	behavior
	honor
	canceled
connexion	
learnt	
neighbour	
mediaeval	
	spelled
memorise	
	equaling
smelt	

6 SKILLS FOR EXPRESSION

A. GRAMMAR: Direct and Indirect Speech

1 *Examine the following sets of sentences and discuss the questions that follow with a partner.*

Direct Speech	Indirect Speech
◆ Professor Roland Meighan said, "Schools have become an outdated concept."	◆ Professor Roland Meighan said that schools had become an outdated concept.
◆ Professor Meighan said, "Schools will become obsolete."	◆ Professor Meighan said that schools would become obsolete.
◆ He said, "I believe children need experience."	◆ He said that he believed children needed experience.

a. What are the differences in punctuation between direct and indirect speech?

b. What other differences are there between direct and indirect speech? Which words are different? Can you explain how they change?

FOCUS ON GRAMMAR

See Direct and Indirect Speech: Tense Changes in *Focus on Grammar, High Intermediate.*

Direct and Indirect Speech

Speech (and writing) can be reported in two ways:

Direct speech (also called quoted speech) reports the speaker's exact words. **Indirect speech** (also called reported speech) reports what the speaker said without using the exact words.

Punctuation

For direct speech, put quotation marks before and after the words you are quoting. Use a comma to separate the words in quotation marks from the reporting verbs such as *say, tell, report.*

For indirect speech, you do not need any special punctuation.

Verb Changes

For indirect speech, when the reporting verb is in the past tense (*said, told, reported*), the verbs inside the quotation marks change. Here are some examples:

Direct Speech		Indirect Speech
do/does (simple present)	→	**did** (simple past)
am/is/are doing (present progressive)	→	**was/were doing** (past progressive)
did (simple past)	→	**had done** (past perfect)
was/were doing (past progressive)	→	**had been doing** (past perfect progressive)
has/have done (present perfect)	→	**had done** (past perfect)
will (modal)	→	**would** (past modal)
can (modal)	→	**could** (past modal)
may (modal)	→	**might** (past modal)

Time and Location Changes

For indirect speech, time and location phrases may change to keep the speaker's original meaning. Here are some examples:

Direct Speech		Indirect Speech
now	→	**then/at that time**
tomorrow	→	**the next (following) day**
ago	→	**before/earlier**
here	→	**there**
this	→	**that**

Pronouns and Possessives

For indirect speech, pronouns and possessives change to keep the speaker's original meaning. Here are some examples:

Direct Speech	Indirect Speech
Mrs. Barson said, "**I** . . ."	Mrs. Barson said **she** . . .
Mrs. Barson said, "**Our** children . . ."	Mrs. Barson said **their** children . . .

---

2 *Read the first sentence in each set and circle the letter of the direct speech that is being reported. The first one has been done for you.*

1. She said that she learned more outside of school than she did in school.

   a. "I have learned more outside of school than I have in school."

   b. "I had learned more outside of school than I did in school."

   c. "I learn more outside of school than I do in school."

2. She reported that Luis had never attended school.

   a. "Luis has never attended school."

   b. "Luis never attends school."

   c. "Luis may never attend school."

3. He said that in order to succeed in life, he had to do well in school and follow all the rules.

   a. "In order to succeed in life, I will have to do well in school and follow all the rules."

   b. "In order to succeed in life, I have to do well in school and follow all the rules."

   c. "In order to succeed in life, I have had to do well in school and follow all the rules."

4. Professor Michael Barber told us that pupils would spend half their time at school and half at home.

   a. "Pupils spend half their time at school and half at home."

   b. "Pupils spent half their time at school and half at home."

   c. "Pupils will spend half their time at school and half at home."

5. Margaret Rudland said that students at her school felt that they might benefit from some home schooling.

   a. "Students at my school feel that they benefited from some home schooling."

   b. "Students at my school feel that they may benefit from some home schooling."

   c. "Students at my school feel that they will benefit from some home schooling."

6. Professor Meighan reported that many students were studying at home.

   a. "Many students are studying at home."

   b. "Many students studied at home."

   c. "Many students had been studying at home."

7. Margie said that they hadn't had time to think about the book.

   a. "We don't have time to think about the book."

   b. "We didn't have time to think about the book."

   c. "We may not have time to think about the book."

3 *Change the following direct speech to indirect speech. Remember to keep the speaker's original meaning. The first one has been done for you.*

1. Tommy said, "My father knows as much as my teacher."

   Tommy said his father knew as much as his teacher.

2. The inspector told Margie's mother, "I think the geography sector was a little too difficult."

3. He added, "I've slowed it up to a ten-year level."

4. Tommy said, "This is the old kind of school that they had hundreds and hundreds of years ago."

5. Margie told Tommy, "My mother says a teacher has to be adjusted to fit the mind of each boy and girl it teaches."

6. Tommy told Margie, "You can read the book with me again tomorrow."

B. STYLE: Concessions

1 *Read the letter on page 172 and discuss the questions that follow with a partner.*

"Inadequately prepared parents" and "weak curricula" are two of the main concerns critics have of home schooling. As a home schooled student, I would like to address these concerns.

During my third and fourth grade years I was taken out of school to be taught by my mother. When I was put back in school at the beginning of fifth grade, I was at the head of my class. Although my mother was not a trained teacher, she was not only able to keep up with the material, but also enjoyed learning and exploring the material with me. Moreover, despite the fact that traditional school teachers are highly qualified, it seems they waste a lot of time disciplining students rather than actually teaching them.

Critics say that home schoolers have a weak curriculum. This issue is true of public schools as well. I was actually taken out of public school because the curricula did not challenge me. In addition, I would like to point out that even though home schoolers are not under the rigid curricula of traditional schools, they often spend more time on the subjects or topics that really interest them. Because of this, children can actually learn more than what the curriculum requires. Further-more, for many home schoolers, learning is not confined just to the home. In fact, learning takes place everywhere and all the time: at museums, during family vacations—twelve months a year! This may explain why home-taught students are doing 25 percent better than the state's public school average.

In conclusion, I believe our educational system must rise to the highest level that it can so that we students remain in school and remain interested in learning. When that finally happens, maybe we won't need to be home schooled. By the way, I'm at home again.

—*Max Andrew Jacobs, Grade 11*
Amarillo, Texas

1. Which of the two types of schooling described in the letter does the writer prefer?

2. What two concerns about home schooling does the writer address?

3. How does the writer defend these concerns—by presenting only his opinion, or by acknowledging the side of the traditional schools and then presenting his own opinion?

4. Which opinion do the words *although*, *even though*, and *despite the fact* introduce—do they introduce the opinion of the traditional school or the home school?

Concessions

In expressing your opinion (or position), it is important to support your opinion but, at the same time, recognize and describe the opposing opinion (or position). Admitting similarities and differences in contrasting points of view can make your argument stronger.

Concession Clauses

The following words are used to concede (acknowledge) similarities or differences between two contrasting ideas. Note that these words do not introduce a complete thought. They introduce dependent clauses. They need the main clause to complete the sentence. The main clause usually describes the point that is more important.

although	**in spite of the fact that**
though	**despite the fact that**
even though	

◆ *Although* **my mother was not a trained teacher**, she was able to keep up with the material.

> Opposing position: Only trained teachers should teach children.

> Writer's opinion: She wasn't trained, but she had no problems keeping up with the material.

◆ *Even though* **home schoolers are not under the rigid curricula of traditional schools**, they often spend more time on the subjects or topics that really interest them.

> Opposing position: Children learn more under the controlled curricula of traditional schools.

> Writer's opinion: Home schoolers learn more because they can spend more time on the topics that interest them.

Punctuation

When the sentence begins with the dependent clause, a comma separates it from the main clause.

◆ **Although my mother was not a trained teacher,** she was able to keep up with the material.

When the dependent clause comes after the main clause, there is no comma.

◆ My mother was able to keep up with the material **although she was not a trained teacher.**

2 *Combine the sentences. Use the words in parentheses. The first one has been done for you.*

1. Supporters of home schooling say that the children have enough social contact.
Critics say children should be in a school setting surrounded by peers.

(even though)

Supporters of home schooling say that the children have enough

social contact **even though** they are not in a school setting

surrounded by peers.

2. Critics maintain that there is no way to assess home schoolers.
Supporters of home schooling say that they are following a standard curriculum.

(though)

_____

_____

_____

3. Critics question whether home schoolers are being taught the basics.
Home schoolers are gaining in numbers every year.

(although)

_____

_____

_____

4. Critics worry that traditional school students do not take school seriously.
Many successful students graduate from traditional schools every year.

(in spite of the fact that)

_____

_____

_____

5. Home schooling is apparently very successful.
Many people still believe in the benefits of traditional schooling.

(despite the fact that)

_____

_____

_____

3 *The educational issues highlighted in this exercise have been addressed throughout this unit. For each issue, think about the position of home schooling and traditional schooling. Write a sentence that expresses your opinion while showing concession to the other position. Use the concession words below. The first one has been done for you.*

| although | even though | in spite of the fact that |
| though | despite the fact that | |

1. peer pressure, bullying, socialize

Although students in traditional schools experience more peer pressure and bullying, they also learn how to socialize with their peers.

2. teaching methods

_____

_____

3. curriculum

_____

_____

4. teacher qualifications

_____

_____

5. students' self-discipline and self-motivation

_____

_____

6. students' interest in learning

_____

_____

ON YOUR OWN

A. WRITING TOPICS

Choose one of the following topics. Write two or three paragraphs that express your opinion on the topic. Use the grammar, vocabulary, and style that you have learned in this unit.

1. Do you think home schooling is a good idea? Why or why not?

2. Do you believe that teachers are the critical factor in a student's success? Why or why not?

3. Do you believe that peer pressure weakens a student's ability to learn? Why or why not?

4. Of the three requirements identified by the quiz in Sharing Information on page 152, which do you believe is the most important to a student's success? Why? Are there other requirements you feel are more important?

B. FIELDWORK: Researching Home Schooling

PREPARATION

In small groups, prepare a list of questions you would like to answer in doing research about home schooling.

RESEARCH ACTIVITY

Research a home school organization through your local library or the Internet (*keywords: home schools, home schooling*).

SHARING YOUR FINDINGS

Share your research with your group. Combine your information and prepare a group report to present to the class. Your report should follow this basic outline:

Part I: Introduction

- A brief introduction to your topic (home schooling)

- An explanation of what information you were looking for (your original questions)

- An explanation of where and how you found your information

Part II: Results

- The information you collected and the answers to your questions

Part III: Conclusions

- Final conclusions and opinions you have about home schooling

REFERENCES

The following are addresses you can use for information about home schools.

Organizations in the United States

American Homeschool Association
P.O. Box 3142
Palmer, AK 99645
tel. (509) 486-2477
AHAonline@aol.com

Home Education Magazine
P.O. Box 1083
Tonasket, WA 98855
http://www.home-ed-press.com

National Homeschool Association
P.O. Box 290
Hartland, MI 48353
http://www.alumni.caltech.edu/~casner/nha.html

International Organizations

Australia

Alternative Education Resource Group
c/7 Bartlett St.
Moorabbin, VIC 3189
Australia
tel. (03) 553-4720

Canada

Ontario Federation of Teaching Parents
83 Fife Rd.
Guelph, Ontario, N1H 6X9
Canada

England

Education Otherwise
36 Kinross Rd.
Leamington Spa, Warwickshire, CV32 7EF
England
tel. (0926) 886828

Germany

Rhein Main Homeschoolers
c/o AAFES
PSC 05, Box 2134
APO AE 09057
Germany
tel. 011-49-6150-14788
(international number)
06150-14788 (in Germany)

Japan

Otherwise Japan
P.O. Kugayama Suginami-ku
Tokyo, Japan
tel. 81 3-3331-6554
jab02521@nifyserve.or.jp

WE'VE COME A LONG WAY

1 APPROACHING THE TOPIC

A. PREDICTING

Take five minutes to write your answers to these questions. Then share your answers with a partner.

Neil Armstrong and "Buzz" Aldrin were the first people to walk on the moon. During that first walk, Neil Armstrong said, "This is one small step for man and one giant leap for mankind." What did he mean? Look at the title. What do you think it refers to? How have we come a long way?

B. SHARING INFORMATION

1 *Read this letter written in 1961 by an elementary school child to President John F. Kennedy. Then work with a partner and answer the questions.*

> Las Cruces, New Mexico
> April 13, 1961
>
> Dear Mr. Kennedy,
> My class and I would like you to raise the taxes on boxing and racing and cigarets + liquor, because we want to get some rockets on the moon before the Russians get to the moon and paint a hammer + sickle.[1] We want to greet the Russians with coffee, cookies + sandwiches.
>
> Your friend,
> Micheil Scott Third

What do you think the feeling of the American people was toward the Russians and the Soviet Union at the time the letter was written? How does the letter show this feeling? What does the child's letter tell you about life in the United States in the 1960s?

2 *What do you know about the history of space exploration? Answer these questions in a small group.*

1. When did the first man go up in space? What country was he from?

2. When did the first woman go up in space? What country was she from?

3. When was the first moon walk? What country were the astronauts from?

4. When did the Russians and Americans shake hands in space for the first time?

5. What is the name of the Russian space station in which both Russians and Americans have lived and worked recently?

6. What other facts do you know about the history of space exploration?

---

[1] *hammer and sickle:* symbols on the flag of the former Soviet Union

PREPARING
TO READ

A. BACKGROUND

Study the time line. Then answer the questions that follow.

Time Line of Significant Space Pioneers in Space History

April 12, 1961 — First manned spaceflight. *Cosmonaut:* Yuri Gagarin. *Country:* Soviet Union	*Astronauts:* Frank Borman, James Lovell, and William Anders. *Country:* United States
February 20, 1962 — First American in orbit. *Astronaut:* John Glenn	**July 20, 1969** — First walk on the moon. *Astronauts:* Neil Armstrong and "Buzz" Aldrin. *Country:* United States
June 16, 1963 — First woman in space. *Cosmonaut:* Valentina Tereshkova. *Country:* Soviet Union	**May 25, 1973** — First visit to Skylab. *Astronauts:* Charles Conrad, Joseph Kerwin, and Paul Weitz. *Country:* United States
March 18, 1965 — First spacewalk. *Cosmonaut:* Alexi Leonove. *Country:* Soviet Union	
June 3, 1965 — First American spacewalk. *Astronaut:* Edward White	**July 17, 1975** — First time Americans and Russians shake hands in space. Apollo-Soyuz Test Project
March 16, 1966 — First docking in space. *Astronauts:* Neil Armstrong and David Scott. *Country:* United States	**1986** — Mir space station launched. *Country:* Soviet Union
	1995 — First American astronaut joins Mir
December 21, 1968 — First mission to escape from the Earth's gravity by traveling to the moon and back.	**April 1997** — First joint U.S.–Russian spacewalk

1. The relations between Russia and the United States have changed dramatically over the years. How does the time line reflect these changes?

2. Do you think the race to conquer space (the "space race") of the 1960s and 1970s between the former Soviet Union and the United States was beneficial to scientific advancement? If so, how?

3. Do you think the present-day cooperation on space station Mir encourages both scientific discovery and peacetime relations between Russia and the United States? If so, how?

4. Do you think the space station Mir influences our life on earth? If so, how?

B. VOCABULARY FOR COMPREHENSION

Read each sentence. Look at the underlined words. Then answer these questions. Circle the letter of the word or phrase that best completes each sentence. The first one has been done for you.

1. When Yuri Gagarin was in space, up and down no longer existed. He watched as pens, notebook, and other objects magically <u>drifted</u> in front of him.

   What did the pens, notebook, and other objects do? They _____ in front of him.

   a. floated

   b. gathered

   c. disappeared

2. Yuri Gagarin was a <u>wide-eyed</u> boy, curiously watching his parents' world change quickly.

   What kind of boy was he? He was _____ .

   a. naive and inquisitive

   b. not sleepy

   c. a child whose eyes were placed widely apart

3. His family <u>foraged</u> food from the fields, looking for anything they could eat.

   What did his family do? They _____ food.

   a. planted

   b. cooked

   c. searched for

4. Young Yuri Gagarin <u>crammed</u> day and night, in school and at home, so that one day he would pass his exams to become a pilot.

   What did Yuri do day and night? He _____ .

   a. ate a lot

   b. studied hard

   c. worked hard

5. Gagarin <u>swept through</u> the difficult cosmonaut training program, completing it without any problems.

   How did he do in the training program? He _____ through it.

   a. went quickly

   b. suffered

   c. was a janitor

6. The <u>crew</u> of the spaceship checked everything twice.

   Who checked the spaceship? The _____ did.

   a. officers

   b. workers

   c. rowers

7. Technicians helped Gagarin through the <u>hatch</u> of the spacecraft.

   Where did he go? He went through the _____ of the spacecraft.

   a. helmet

   b. window

   c. small door

8. On the ground, the people watched as the spaceship was <u>launched</u> into the sky.

   What did the people see? They saw the spaceship _____ into space.

   a. sent up

   b. introduced to

   c. held back

9. The acceleration <u>generated</u> a force of six times normal gravity.

   What did the acceleration do? It _____ a force of six times normal gravity.

   a. killed

   b. produced

   c. maintained

10. When Yuri Gagarin jumped out of the spacecraft, he <u>deployed</u> his personal parachute and fell to earth.

What did he do? He _____ his parachute.

a. put away

b. lined up

c. put into use

11. The ringing of the telephone awakened Alan Shepard from a deep <u>slumber</u>.

Where was he? He was in a deep _____ .

a. pile of wood

b. sleep

c. hole

READING ONE: First in Space

A. INTRODUCING THE TOPIC

Read the first paragraph of the story and answer the questions below. Then read the rest of the story.

1. The person discussed in this paragraph is Yuri Gagarin. Where is he?

2. What is he thinking about? Why do you think he is thinking about this?

First in Space

BY ALAN SHEPARD AND DEKE SLAYTON
(Adapted from *Moon Shot*)

1   For a long time he drifted between sleep and wakefulness. It had been that way throughout the night. Floating between memories as if the sounds drifted through the walls of his room. Strange, he couldn't tell if the sounds were from the past memories or the present, but he accepted the ones that reminded him of his father. A carpenter, a skilled craftsman who had worked hard to make so special their wooden home in the village of Klushino, near Smolensk of the western Soviet Union.

2   Harsher memories intruded. Great guns firing, shells exploding. Earth-shaking rumble of German tanks moving through his home-town. He was a wide-eyed boy then, watching his parents' world coming apart as they fell under enemy occupation. They obeyed the Nazis, and whenever possible they foraged food from the fields and the scattered wreckage of their village. Another sound grew louder, and he seized it in his dream state. Airplane engines. At first only German. Then other planes came by with red stars on their wings, and there was terrible fighting and the tanks that pushed into Klushino were Russian. As quickly as that war[1] ended, young Yuri A. Gagarin crammed day and night, in school and at home, so that one day he would qualify to become a pilot in the Red Air Force.[2]

3   They moved to the larger town of Gzhatsk. Yuri completed school, completed special courses, and in 1955 entered the Air Force. Two years later he won the coveted wings of a jet fighter pilot. He had become an expert parachutist as well. For two years he served in operational units and then, in 1959, he volunteered for an exciting new program.

4   Cosmonaut! He swept through the rigorous training, excelling in everything he did. On April 8, 1961, only four days before this night of dreams, his commander gave him the news. "You will be the first to travel through space."

5   Unreal. It all seemed unreal. But it was true. And his close friend, German Stepanovich Titov, would be his backup. Today was the day. His door opened.

---

[1] *that war:* World War II
[2] *Red Air Force:* Soviet Union Air Force

6 Sleep and dreams vanished. He met with Titov, technicians, doctors, engineers, the political commissar.[3] Everything moved smoothly through breakfast, final medical checks. Sensors were attached to his body before he donned the pressure suit and heavy helmet. Fully protected from space, his teammates helped him into the bright orange flight suit that would aid the recovery crews in spotting him after launching.

7 Sunrise was still to come as he arrived at the launch pad. He stood quietly for several minutes, studying the enormous SS-6 ICBM[4] that would send him into orbit. No warhead atop the big rocket. It had been replaced with the *Swallow*, the Vostok spacecraft of more than five tons.

8 Gagarin stood on a ramp partway up the stairs to the elevator. He turned to the select group who would witness the moment that would separate the past from the future. He spoke clearly to those men:

9 "The whole of my life seems to be condensed into this one wonderful moment," he began. His audience stood silently transfixed. "Everything that I have been, everything that I have done, was for this," Gagarin added. Yielding to the emotion of the moment, he lowered his head, regained control.

10 He looked up again, smiling. "Of course I'm happy," he said, his voice stronger. "Who would not be? To take part in new discoveries, to be the first to enter the cosmos, to engage in a single-handed duel with nature . . ." His smile broadened. "Could anyone dream of more?"

11 His words spoken, he waved farewell and entered the elevator to the top of the support tower. There he climbed a short ladder to the platform alongside his Vostok spacecraft. Technicians and his close backup team assisted him through the hatch. They secured his harness to the specially designed seat. Gagarin nodded, signaling he was ready. The hatch closed and was sealed.

12 Moscow time: 9:07 A.M. America slept, unaware of Gagarin's jubilant cry from his ascending fire machine. "Off we go!" he cried aloud, bringing smiles and grins to the crews in the launch control.

13 Through the increasing g-loads,[5] Gagarin maintained steady reports. He was young and muscular, and he absorbed the acceleration punishment easily. With the strap-on boosters jettisoned[6] and the main core engines burning, the acceleration generated a force of six times normal gravity.

14 The miracle was at hand. A human being was falling around the earth at 17,500 miles an hour. Gagarin in *Swallow* had entered orbit

---

[3] *commissar:* official title of a government leader in the USSR
[4] *ICBM:* intercontinental ballistic missile
[5] *g-loads:* force caused by acceleration of gravity
[6] *jettison:* throw things overboard to lighten the aircraft

with a low point above earth of 112.4 miles, soaring as high as 203 miles before starting down again.

15   He felt as if he were a stranger in his own body. He was not sitting or lying down. Up and down no longer existed. He was suspended in physical limbo, kept from floating about loosely only by the harness strapping him to his contoured couch. About him the magic of weight-lessness appeared in the form of papers, a pencil, his notebook, and other objects drifting, responding to the gentle tugs of air from his life support system.

16   He had circled the globe in eighty-nine minutes.

17   He had plunged across East Africa and now began his return to earth, flying backward.

18   Thirteen thousand feet above the ground he separated from the ejection seat and deployed his personal parachute. He breathed in deeply the fresh spring air. What a marvelous ride down!

19   On the ground, two startled peasants and their cow working in a field watched as a man wearing a bright orange suit, topped with a white helmet, drifted out of the sky. The man hit the ground running. He tumbled, rolled over, and immediately regained his feet to gather his parachute. Gagarin unhooked the parachute harness and looked up to see a woman and a girl staring at him.

20   "Have you come from outer space?" asked the astonished woman.

21   "Yes, yes, would you believe it?" Gagarin answered with a wide grin. "I certainly have."

22   The shrill ringing penetrated the fog of his sleep—annoying, persistent. For a moment Alan Shepard remained confused, extricating himself from deep slumber. Only for the moment. Then he reached for the clamoring telephone in his motel room.

23   "What?" he barked into the phone.

24   The voice at the other end of the call was soft, polite. Considerate. "Commander Shepard?"

25   "Uh-huh. Yeah, this is Shepard."

26   "Have you heard?"

27   He was sharply attentive now. He didn't like those words. "Heard what?" he asked cautiously.

28   "The Russians have put a man in orbit."

29   The phone almost slipped from Shepard's hand. He sat quietly another few moments to brush away the last fog of sleep from his mind. Then his disbelief found voice. "You've got to be kidding."

30   Shepard managed a courteous response, thanked the man, and replaced the phone in its cradle. A single phrase kept repeating itself over and over again in his mind:

31   I could have been up there three weeks ago . . .

B. READING FOR MAIN IDEAS

Put the following main ideas in the correct sequence according to the story, numbering from 1 to 6. When you have finished, check your sequencing by looking back at the story.

_____ Gagarin goes up in space and makes space history.

_____ American astronaut Alan Shepard is notified about Gagarin's flight.

_____ As a young man, Gagarin worked and studied very hard.

_____ Before going up in space, there were extensive preparations and ceremonies.

_____ Gagarin was chosen to go on the space mission and be the first man in space.

_____ As a child, Gagarin lived through times of war and hunger.

C. READING FOR DETAILS

Circle the word which best completes the sentence. Compare your answers with your classmates'.

1. Gagarin's father was a skilled _____ .

   a. mechanic   **b.** engineer   **c.** craftsman

2. Gagarin was a child during _____ .

   a. the Vietnam War   **b.** World War II   **c.** World War I

3. Gagarin became a cosmonaut _____ years after entering the Air Force.

   a. six   **b.** four   **c.** two

4. Gagarin learned he was to go into space _____ before his flight.

    a. four days   **b.** four weeks   **c.** four months

5. As Gagarin spoke to the audience, they were _____ .

    a. crying   **b.** clapping   **c.** quietly listening

6. Gagarin sped around the earth at _____ miles an hour.

    a. 12,500   **b.** 15,500   **c.** 17,500

7. He circled the globe in _____ minutes.

    a. eight   **b.** ninety-eight   **c.** eighty-nine

8. He parachuted back down to earth and landed in a(n) _____ .

    a. field   **b.** ocean   **c.** forest

9. Alan Shepard was _____ when he heard the news.

    a. happy   **b.** in disbelief   **c.** relieved

D. READING BETWEEN THE LINES

The story in Reading One begins and ends with two different men awakening to two very different days. How do you think the two astronauts, Yuri Gagarin and Alan Shepard, felt when they first woke up on the morning of April 12, 1961?

Write a paragraph for their personal journals expressing their feelings. The first line of each paragraph has been written for you.

Yuri Gagarin

April 12, 1961

I couldn't believe it when I woke up this morning.

ALAN SHEPARD

April 12, 1961

I couldn't believe it when I woke up this morning.

4 READING TWO: Pink Socks and Jello

A. EXPANDING THE TOPIC

Shannon Lucid was the first American woman astronaut to stay on the Russian space station Mir (*mir* means "peace"). She remained in space with two Russian cosmonauts for six months (188 days), setting a new women's record for most consecutive days in space.

Not only was Shannon Lucid away from her home and family for six months, her crew mates, Yuri and Yuri, were not from the United States.

Imagine you were in Shannon's situation and answer the questions below with a partner. Then read the letter on page 191 that Shannon wrote while in space.

◆ What would you do to overcome feelings of isolation and loneliness?

◆ What would you bring with you to help with the isolation? (Remember, room on space station Mir is very limited.)

By Shannon Lucid

Pink Socks and Jello

Sunday, May 19, 1996

Dear Everybody!!

1   Here it is, another Sunday on Mir!!! And how, you might ask, do I know that it's Sunday? Easy!!! I have on my pink socks and Yuri, Yuri, and I have just finished sharing a bag of Jello!!!

2   When light follows darkness every forty-five minutes, it is important that I have simple ways of marking the passage of time. The pink socks were found on STS-76[1] and Kevin, the commander, said that they were obviously put on as a surprise for me, so I took them with me over to Mir and decided to wear them on Sundays.

3   And the Jello? It is the greatest improvement in space flight since my first flight over ten years ago. When I found out that there was a refrigerator on board Mir, I asked the food folks at JSC[2] if they could put Jello in a drink bag. Once aboard Mir, we could just add hot water, put the bag in the refrigerator and, later, have a great treat. Well, the food folks did just that and sent a variety of flavors with me to try out. We tried the Jello first as a special treat for Easter. It was so great that we decided the Mir 21-NASA[3] 2 crew tradition would be to share a bag of Jello every Sunday night. (Every once in a while, Yuri will come up to me and say, "Isn't today Sunday?" and I will say, "No, it's not. No Jello tonight!!!")

4   There have been a lot of changes here on Mir since I arrived. And no, the changes were not because I am here!!!

5   The first big change was the arrival of Priroda, the final segment[4] that is to be added to Mir. This segment is called Priroda

[1] *STS:* Space Transportation System, a shuttle vehicle to take crew to Mir
[2] *JSC:* Star City cosmonaut training center in Russia
[3] *NASA:* National Aeronautics and Space Administration (U.S.)
[4] *segment:* a section

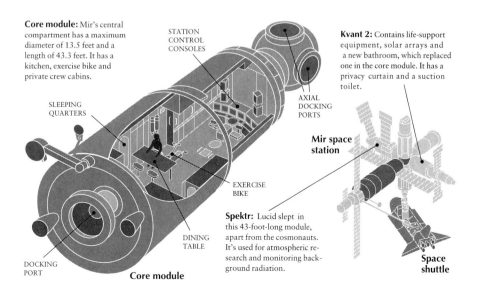

Core module: Mir's central compartment has a maximum diameter of 13.5 feet and a length of 43.3 feet. It has a kitchen, exercise bike and private crew cabins.

STATION CONTROL CONSOLES

SLEEPING QUARTERS

AXIAL DOCKING PORTS

EXERCISE BIKE

DINING TABLE

DOCKING PORT

Core module

Kvant 2: Contains life-support equipment, solar arrays and a new bathroom, which replaced one in the core module. It has a privacy curtain and a suction toilet.

Mir space station

Spektr: Lucid slept in this 43-foot-long module, apart from the cosmonauts. It's used for atmospheric research and monitoring background radiation.

Space shuttle

because that's the Russian word for nature and there are sensors on the outside of the segment to study the Earth. The U.S. science equipment is located inside this segment.

6 The other big change, although it is not permanent, was the arrival of *Progress*, the resupply vehicle. Usually about every six weeks one is sent to Mir with food, equipment, clothes—everything that, on Earth, you would have to go to the store and buy in order to live. Because it had deployed solar batteries, it was easier to spot while approaching the station than Priroda had been.

7 I saw it first. There were big thunderstorms out in the Atlantic, with a brilliant display of lightning like visual pom poms.[5] The cities were strung out like Christmas lights along the coast—and there was *Progress* like a bright morning star skimming along the top!!! Suddenly, its brightness increased dramatically and Yuri said, "The engine just fired." Soon, it was close enough so that we could see the deployed solar arrays. To me, it looked like some alien insect headed straight toward us. All of a sudden I really did feel like I was in a "cosmic outpost"[6] anxiously awaiting supplies—and really hoping that my family did remember to send me some books and candy!!!

8 Soon after it docked, the three of us began opening the hatch. When Yuri opened a small valve to equalize the pressure, we could smell the air that was in *Progress*. Yuri said, "Smell the fresh food." I will admit it was a fruit smell, but I thought it smelled more like the first time you open your refrigerator after a two-week vacation only to discover you had forgotten to clean out the vegetable compartment.

9 The first things we took out were our personal packages and, yes, I quickly peeked in to see if my family had remembered the books and candy I'd requested. Of course they had. Then we started to unpack. We found the fresh food and stopped right there for lunch. We had fresh tomatoes and onions; I never have had such a good lunch. For the next week we had fresh tomatoes three times a day. It was a sad meal when we ate the last ones!!!

10 After our impromptu lunch, we took the rest of the afternoon off, looking at our mail that was in the packages and enjoying the apples and oranges that were also on board. Yuri commented that for the first time all six of the docking ports were now occupied—a Guinness Book[7] record!

11 Like I said, I had a wonderful bag of new books on *Progress*. My daughters had hand-selected each one, so I knew I'd enjoy them. I picked out one and rapidly read it. I came to the last page and the hero, who was being chased by an angry mob, escaped by stepping through a mirror. The end. Continued in Volume Two. And was there Volume Two in my book bag? No. Could I dash out to the bookstore? No. Talk about a feeling of total isolation and frustration!!!! You would never believe that grown children could totally frustrate you with their good intentions while you were in low earth orbit, but let me tell you, they certainly can. Suddenly, August and home seem a long way away!!!!

Shannon

---

[5] *pom-poms:* big bright balls
[6] *outpost:* a basic fort or encampment for soldiers used during the time when the western United States was first being explored; these forts were located very far away from civilization
[7] *Guinness Book:* a book which lists world records

Write short answers to the following questions.

1. Why was the arrival of *Progress* so important to the crew of Mir?

2. What did *Progress* have on it that helped the crew with isolation, boredom, and loneliness?

B. LINKING READINGS ONE AND TWO

How has space exploration and travel changed since Yuri Gagarin's first space flight? Complete the chart. Compare Yuri Gagarin's and Shannon Lucid's space missions. Use examples from the readings to support your ideas. When you have finished, write a paragraph which summarizes the chart and expresses these changes. Be sure to include your examples. Discuss your paragraph with a partner.

	YURI GAGARIN'S MISSION	SHANNON LUCID'S MISSION
Objective or goal of the mission		
Length of the mission		
Number of people on the mission		
Nationality of the people involved		
Physical conditions of the spaceship		

5 REVIEWING LANGUAGE

A. EXPLORING LANGUAGE: Paraphrasing

Paraphrasing means to restate an idea using different words, while keeping the meaning the same.

*Read the pairs of sentences. Decide if the second sentence paraphrases the first sentence. In other words, decide if the two sentences have similar meaning. Circle **similar** or **different**. If different, explain why. The first one has been done for you.*

1. **a.** For two years Gagarin served in operational units and then, in 1959, he volunteered for an exciting new program.

   b. It was a thrilling day for Gagarin in 1959 when, after two years, he was chosen for an exciting new program.

   similar   (different)

   If different, why?

   Sentence **a** says he volunteered. Sentence **b** says he was chosen.

2. **a.** After our impromptu lunch, we took the rest of the afternoon off.

   b. We rested for the remaining part of the afternoon after our scheduled lunch.

   similar   different

   If different, why?

   _____

3. **a.** Gagarin swept through the rigorous training, excelling in everything he did.

   b. Although the training was demanding, Gagarin did extremely well.

   similar   different

   If different, why?

   _____

4. **a.** He turned to the select group who would witness the moment that separated the past from the future.

   b. He faced the elite group that would see history being made.

   similar   different

   If different, why?

   _____

5. **a.** America slept, unaware of Gagarin's jubilant cry from his ascending fire machine.

   b. Americans were not aware of Gagarin's space flight or his intense feelings of joy.

   similar   different

   If different, why?

   _____

6. **a.** "Have you come from outer space?" asked the astonished woman.

   b. The woman was shocked when she asked if he had come from outside.

   similar   different

   If different, why?

   _____

7. **a.** It (the Jello) was so great that we decided the crew tradition would be to share a bag of Jello every Sunday night.

   b. The crew's idea of sharing a bag of Jello every Sunday night was excellent.

   similar   different

   If different, why?

   _____

8. **a.** Sensors were attached to his body before he donned the pressure suit and heavy helmet.

   b. After sensors had been attached to his body, he took off the pressure suit and heavy helmet.

   similar   different

   If different, why?

   _____

B. WORKING WITH WORDS: Phrasal Verbs

A **phrasal verb** consists of two or three words which, when used together, have a different meaning from the meanings of the individual parts.

Work with a partner. Try to guess the meaning of each phrasal verb in the following sentences. Circle the letter of the phrase or word with the same meaning as the underlined word. Use your dictionary if necessary. The first one has been done for you.

1. He was a wide-eyed boy then, watching his parents' world coming apart as they <u>fell under</u> enemy occupation.
   a. fought against
   b. were dominated by
   c. lived under the ground

2. "To <u>take part in</u> new discoveries, to be the first to enter the cosmos, to engage in a single-handed duel with nature . . ." His smile broadened.
   a. separate from
   b. do something alone
   c. participate in

3. "<u>Off</u> we <u>go</u>!" he cried aloud, bringing smiles and grins to the crews in the launch control.
   a. depart
   b. explode
   c. continue

4. When I <u>found out</u> that there was a refrigerator on board Mir, I asked the food folks at JSC if they could put Jello in a drink bag.
   a. discovered
   b. detected
   c. believed

5. Well, the food folks did just that and sent a variety of flavors with me to <u>try out</u>.
   a. attempt
   b. put on
   c. test

6. Every once in a while, Yuri will <u>come up to</u> me and say, "Isn't today Sunday?"

   a. awaken

   b. approach

   c. imagine

7. I thought it smelled more like the first time you open your refrigerator after a two-week vacation only to discover you had forgotten to <u>clean out</u> the vegetable compartment.

   a. polish

   b. take all the money from

   c. empty

8. After our impromptu lunch, we <u>took</u> the rest of the afternoon <u>off</u>.

   a. stopped working

   b. undressed

   c. flew for a period of time

SKILLS FOR EXPRESSION

A. GRAMMAR: Phrasal Verbs

1 *Examine these sentences and discuss the questions that follow with a partner.*

- NASA called off the space flight launch because of bad weather.

- Many astronauts dropped out of the training program.

- Yuri Gagarin often thought back on his first flight in space.

a. What is the verb in each sentence?

b. What is the difference between <u>call</u> and <u>call off</u>?

c. What is the difference between <u>drop</u> and <u>drop out</u>?

d. What is the difference between <u>think</u> and <u>think back on</u>?

FOCUS ON GRAMMAR

See Phrasal Verbs in *Focus on Grammar, High Intermediate.*

Phrasal Verbs

A **phrasal verb** consists of two or three words put together to make one verb. Phrasal verbs are often used in informal English.

Form of Phrasal Verbs

Phrasal verbs (also called two-part or two-word verbs) combine a verb with a particle to form a new meaning.

VERB	+	PARTICLE	=	MEANING
talk	+	over	=	discuss
look	+	over	=	examine
give	+	up	=	quit

Some phrasal verbs (also called three-part or three-word verbs) combine with a preposition to form a new meaning.

PHRASAL VERB	+	PREPOSITION	=	MEANING
come up	+	with	=	imagine
think back	+	on	=	remember

Meaning of Phrasal Verbs

The words in a phrasal verb are usually common ones, but their meaning changes when the words are used together to make a phrasal verb. Therefore it is not always possible to guess the meaning of the verb from its individual parts.

call off = cancel

drop out of = quit

Some phrasal verbs can have more than one meaning.

- ◆ She **took off** her space suit. = She **removed** her space suit.
- ◆ She **took off** at 7:00 A.M. = She **departed** at 7:00 A.M.
- ◆ She **took** the day **off**. = She **didn't work** that day.

Some verbs can be combined with several different particles or prepositions. Each combination creates a phrasal verb with a different meaning.

- She **came up with** a plan.   = She **developed** a plan.
- She **came up to** me.   = She **approached** me.
- She **came out with** a new book.   = She **published** a new book.

2 *Work in small groups. Read each sentence and write the word or phrase that has the same meaning as the underlined phrasal verb. The first one has been done for you.*

1. invented   regained consciousness   approached

   a. The director of the program <u>came up to</u> Shannon Lucid to ask her some questions. <u> approached </u>

   b. After months of testing, the Russian space scientists <u>came up with</u> a space suit that works better than any in history. _____

   c. Alan Shepard fainted because of lack of oxygen, but with the doctor's help he <u>came to</u> in a few minutes. _____

2. disassemble   participate   dominate

   a. A successful space flight is a group effort. Everyone must <u>take part in</u> all aspects of the project. _____

   b. If there is a mechanical problem, the technicians will have to <u>take the engine apart</u>. _____

   c. The race to the moon would <u>take over</u> the space program of the 1960s after Gagarin's successful space flight. _____

3. review   continue   leave

   a. Without adequate funding from the government, the space program wouldn't have been able to <u>go on</u>. _____

   b. Alan Shepard decided to <u>go off</u> to visit his mother before his first space flight. _____

   c. Being an astronaut is not easy. You have to <u>go over</u> all the information necessary for your flight many times. _____

4. break   be dominated by   lose speed

   a. The Americans didn't want to <u>fall behind</u> in the space race with the Russians during the cold war. _____

   b. If the new space shuttle pilot is a good leader, the entire crew will <u>fall under</u> his influence. _____

   c. If the spacecraft is not adequately constructed, it will <u>fall apart</u> during reentry into the atmosphere. _____

5. departed   not work   removed

   a. After completing a space journey, it is customary for the astronauts to <u>take</u> a few days <u>off</u>. _____

   b. On April 12, 1961, Yuri Gagarin <u>took off</u> in the first manned space capsule. _____

   c. When Yuri Gagarin landed, he <u>took off</u> his parachute harness and looked up to see a woman and a girl staring at him. _____

❸ *Rewrite the paragraphs. Use a phrasal verb from Exercise 2 above in place of the underlined verbs. Be sure to use the correct tense in the phrasal verb.*

1. Moments before Shannon Lucid <u>departed</u> on her first space mission, a reporter <u>approached</u> her and asked what her thoughts were. She replied that she was extremely proud to <u>participate</u> in such an important project. A few seconds passed, and she added with a quick smile that what she was really hoping was that the spaceship would not <u>break</u> during liftoff!

2. Did you know that many of the products we use every day are the result of technology designed specifically for space flight? For example, scientists <u>invented</u> Velcro as a way to attach things easily and securely in antigravity situations. The orange-flavored Tang and other powdered drinks that <u>dominated</u> the juice market in the 1960s were also designed specifically for space travel. Therefore, we can say that by using these products, we are all <u>participating</u> in the space experience. Hopefully, scientists will <u>continue</u> creating new products that benefit us all.

B. STYLE: Chronological Order—Expressing Time

1 *Examine these sentences and discuss the questions with a partner.*

◆ The crew of Mir had quite a smelly surprise <u>when they opened *Progress*</u>.

◆ <u>As soon as Shepard heard about Gagarin's successful space flight</u>, he became depressed.

◆ <u>A year and a half after Gagarin's flight</u>, John Glenn was launched into orbit.

◆ Gagarin felt wonderful <u>while he was in space</u>.

◆ We will have to spend more money on space research <u>before we can even think about living on other planets</u>.

◆ <u>During the time they are in space</u>, crew members do valuable scientific research.

a. Each of these sentences talks about two events and the time relationship between the events. In the first sentence, the two events (<u>had a smelly surprise</u> and <u>opened *Progress*</u>) happened at the same time. Which other sentences describe two events happening at the same time?

b. In which sentence does one action take place immediately after another action?

c. What are the time relationships in the remaining sentences?

Expressing Time: Adverbial Time Clauses

When describing two events in a single sentence, you may have to use words that indicate to the reader how the events relate to each other chronologically. A single sentence made up of an **adverbial time clause** (dependent clause) and a main clause (independent clause) is an effective way to do this.

Time Words with Dependent Clauses

A dependent clause is not a complete sentence. It needs an independent clause or main clause to complete it. The following time words are commonly used to introduce dependent clauses.

before/after	**during (the time)**
while	**as soon as**
when	**since/until**

◆ **Before Shannon Lucid became an astronaut**, she trained extensively.
         (dependent clause)   (independent clause)

Time Clauses and Verb Tense

The relationship of the verb tenses in the two clauses is very important. The tenses listed below show this relationship. The tenses can also be in the progressive or perfect form.

IF THE VERB IN THE MAIN CLAUSE IS:		THE VERB IN THE TIME CLAUSE IS:
present	→	present
future	→	present
past	→	past
imperative	→	present

◆ Astronauts **train** for many months before they **go** into space.

◆ Shannon Lucid **will not be** able to write about her mission until she **has** more time.

◆ Alan Shepard **(had) trained** for many months before he **went** into space.

◆ **Use** the radio to call NASA as soon as you **have** a problem.

Punctuation

The adverbial time clause (the dependent clause) can come at the beginning or at the end of the independent (the main) clause. When the sentence begins with a dependent clause, a comma separates it from the main clause.

◆ **Before Shannon Lucid became an astronaut**, she had extensive training.

When a dependent clause comes after the main clause, no comma is needed.

◆ Shannon Lucid had extensive training **before she became an astronaut**.

---

2 *Think about the information in Readings One and Two. Then combine each pair of sentences below to make one sentence. Use **one** of the boldface time words. The first one has been done for you.*

1. **after/during the time**
   a. The war ended.
   b. Gagarin went to school.

   <u>After the war ended, Gagarin went to school.</u>

2. **while/after**
   a. Yuri completed special courses and entered the Air Force.
   b. He became a fighter pilot.

   _____

3. **as soon as/while**
   a. Lucid asked for Jello.
   b. She discovered there was a refrigerator on board Mir.

   _____

4. **after/while**
   a. The three astronauts opened the hatch.
   b. *Progress* docked on Mir.

   _____

5. **before/after**
   a. Lucid arrived with different food.
   b. The cosmonauts had never eaten Jello.

   _____

6. as soon as/before
   a. The astronauts started to open the hatch to *Progress*.
   b. They smelled the food.

_____

7. after/during the time
   a. The Russians and Americans were enemies.
   b. The space programs began.

_____

8. until/when
   a. The cold war ended.
   b. There was not a lot of cooperation in space exploration.

_____

❸ *Choose the correct time clause to complete the sentences. Pay attention to verb tenses. The first one has been done for you.*

1. After *Progress* arrives, <u>the crew will have fresh food.</u>
   a. the crew will have fresh food.
   b. the crew had fresh food.

2. Shannon Lucid told the Russians,

   _____ , be careful.”
   a. “When you will open the hatch
   b. “When you open the hatch

3. Satellites circle the earth _____
   a. while we are sleeping.
   b. while we were sleeping.

4. _____ , pharmaceutical

   companies use the information to develop new products.
   a. As soon as space research provided new medical information
   b. As soon as space research provides new medical information

5. _____ , space exploration was

   extremely important.
   a. During the time the Russians and Americans are enemies
   b. During the time the Russians and Americans were enemies

6. People hadn’t thought living on other planets was possible

   _____
   a. before astronauts landed on the moon.
   b. before astronauts land on the moon.

ON YOUR OWN

A. WRITING TOPICS

Choose one of the following topics and write two or three paragraphs about it. Try to use the ideas, vocabulary, grammar, and style from this unit in your writing.

1. Some people believe that competition between two companies is good because it pushes them to create better and better products. Others believe cooperation is the best way. This can be said for the space programs as well. During the 1960s, space exploration was well funded and moving ahead at great speed. What were the benefits of competition during the space race in the 1960s? What are the benefits of cooperation at the present time?

2. Look at the time line on page 181. How do these important space events reflect the movement from competition to cooperation between the United States and Russia? Describe the movement toward cooperation over time. Use examples from the time line.

3. In the beginning of space exploration, the relationship between man and nature was "man against nature": We were trying to conquer space. Nowadays, this feeling can be expressed more as "man studying nature": We are trying not only to protect nature (for example, by studying the earth from space), but to use nature to help us (for example, through medical research on Mir). Why do you think this relationship has changed? What do you think the future will bring?

4. There have always been people who are critical of the space programs. Some say that the tremendous amount of money used for space exploration could be better used right here on earth. Some argue that we are polluting space with satellites and space garbage. And others have made even more critical assessments of space projects. How do you feel about space exploration? If possible, use examples from the unit to support your opinions.

B. FIELDWORK

PREPARATION

In small groups, make a list of past and present space programs and space-related activities (satellite communication, scientific exploration, etc.). Discuss what you know about these programs. Include, for example, names of sponsoring countries, dates, objectives of the programs, and people involved.

Share your information with the class. You may want to write the information on the board.

Then, in small groups, choose a program that interests your group. Brainstorm a list of places you can get information about this program.

RESEARCH ACTIVITY

Research the space program your group selected. Include information about the history of the program, its objectives, and its results.

Discuss your research with your group. Combine the group's research and write a group report. Present the report to the class.

THE GRASS IS ALWAYS GREENER

Martina Navratilova
Born: Prague, Czechoslovakia
  October 18, 1956
Occupation: Tennis pro
  (retired)
Immigrated to the U.S.
  in 1975

Jamaica Kincaid
Born: Antigua,[1] 1949
Occupation: Writer
Immigrated to the U.S.
  in 1966

Henry A. Kissinger
Born: Furth, Germany
  May 27, 1923
Occupation: Former U.S.
  Secretary of State to
  Presidents Richard
  Nixon and Gerald Ford
Immigrated to the U.S.
  in 1938

[1] *Antigua:* an island in the Caribbean

1 APPROACHING THE TOPIC

A. PREDICTING

Look at the photographs and read the information about each person.
Answer these questions with a partner.
1. What do these people have in common?
2. What personal history do you think they share?
3. Look at the title of the unit. What does "the grass is always greener"
   mean to you?

B. SHARING INFORMATION

Work in groups. Brainstorm a list of reasons why people immigrate. Think about economic, political, and personal reasons. Write as many reasons as you can in the chart, and share your reasons with the class. If you wish, share any personal experiences you have had.

ECONOMIC REASONS	POLITICAL REASONS	PERSONAL REASONS

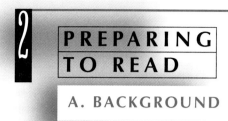

PREPARING TO READ

A. BACKGROUND

Read the information and complete the exercise that follows.

The story you are about to read is from the novel *Lucy* by Jamaica Kincaid. As a young woman Jamaica Kincaid left her home in Antigua to come to New York. She was only sixteen years old when she came to the United States to work in the home of an American family as a nanny, taking care of the children. After working at several domestic jobs,[1] in and around New York, Kincaid entered college and eventually began writing for the *New Yorker* magazine. She became a highly successful and respected author. She has written many short stories about her native island and her family.

Imagine you are sixteen years old and have left your home on a tropical island. This is your first time away from the island and your family. You arrive in New York in the wintertime. What kinds of problems do you think you will face? Write down some ideas. For example, think about the differences you will find in the food, climate, and living conditions. Share your ideas with a partner.

B. VOCABULARY FOR COMPREHENSION

Work with a partner. Read the sentences. Each underlined word has two meanings. Circle the meaning of the word as it is used in the sentence. This is the meaning of the word as it is used in Reading One.

1. <u>Bouts</u> with one's enemies usually never end peacefully.

    a. fights or contests between two opponents

    b. periods of time spent in a particular way

---

[1] *domestic job:* a job in which you work in a home cleaning, cooking, or taking care of children

2. New York City is filled with many wonderful <u>spectacles</u> such as the World Trade Center, the Statue of Liberty, and the Empire State Building.

    a. things that are remarkable or impressive

    b. eyeglasses

3. I was no longer in a tropical zone and I felt cold inside and out, the first time such a <u>sensation</u> had come over me.

    a. big event causing great public excitement

    b. feeling or emotion

4. We sat on the <u>bank</u> and watched the sunset while eating our picnic.

    a. money-lending and savings institution

    b. side of a river

5. Agatha Christie's books have sold millions of copies around the world because her stories always have great <u>plots</u>.

    a. pieces of land

    b. actions or events

6. After living abroad for many months, she began to <u>long for</u> her mother's cooking.

    a. relatively great distance

    b. desire or yearn for

7. The child became bored and started to <u>twist</u> in his chair during the long movie.

    a. dance by moving his hips

    b. wriggle or squirm

8. The Statue of Liberty is probably the most famous <u>sight</u> in New York City.

    a. ability to see

    b. spectacle or view

9. He was in a state of <u>rage</u> after his airline tickets and travelers checks were stolen.

    a. anger

    b. popular trend or fad

READING ONE: Poor Visitor

A. INTRODUCING THE TOPIC

Read the first paragraph of the story on page 212 and write short answers to the questions below.

1. Which words from the paragraph tell you about Lucy's emotions on her first day in New York? How does she feel?

2. What do you think will happen? What do you think the author will describe in the rest of the story?

Share what you have written with a partner. Then read the rest of the story.

Poor Visitor

BY JAMAICA KINCAID
(from *Lucy*)

1   It was my first day. I had come the night before, a gray-black and cold night before—as it was to be in the middle of January, though I didn't know that at the time—and I could not see anything clearly on the way in from the airport, even though there were lights everywhere. As we drove along, someone would single out[1] to me a famous building, an important street, a park, a bridge, that when built was thought to be a spectacle. In a daydream I used to have, all these places were points of happiness to me; all these places were lifeboats to my small drowning soul, for I would imagine myself entering and leaving them, and just that—entering and leaving over and over again—would see me through a bad feeling I did not have a name for. I only knew it felt a little like sadness but heavier than that. Now that I saw these places, they looked ordinary, dirty, worn down by so many people entering and leaving them in real life, and it occurred to me that I could not be the only person in the world for whom they were a fixture of fantasy. It was not my first bout with the disappointment of reality and it would not be my last. The undergarments that I wore were all new, bought for my journey, and as I sat in the car, twisting this way and that to get a good view of the sights before me, I was reminded of how uncomfortable the new can make you feel.

2   I got in an elevator, something I had never done before, and then I was in an apartment and seated at a table eating food just taken from a refrigerator. In the place I had just come from, I always lived in a house, and my house did not have a refrigerator in it. Everything I was experiencing—the ride in the elevator, being in an apartment, eating day-old food that had been stored in a refrigerator—was such a good idea that I could imagine I would grow used to it and like it very much, but at first it was all so new that I had to smile with my mouth turned down at the corners. I slept soundly that night, but it wasn't because I was happy and comfortable—quite the opposite; it was because I didn't want to take in anything else.

3   That morning, the morning of my first day, the morning that followed my first night, was a sunny morning. It was not the sort of bright-yellow sun making everything curl at the edges, almost in fright, that I was used to, but a pale-yellow sun, as if the sun had grown

---

[1] *single out:* point out, show

weak from trying too hard to shine; but still it was sunny, and that was nice and made me miss my home less. And so, seeing the sun, I got up and put on a dress, a gay dress that I would wear if I were at home and setting out for a day in the country. It was all wrong. The sun was shining but the air was cold. It was the middle of January, after all. But I did not know that the sun could shine and the air remain cold; no one had ever told me. What a feeling that was! How can I explain? Something I had always known—the way I knew my skin was the color brown of a nut rubbed repeatedly with a soft cloth, or the way I knew my own name—something I took completely for granted, "the sun is shining, the air is warm," was not so. I was no longer in a tropical zone, and this realization now entered my life like a flow of water dividing formerly dry and solid ground, creating two banks, one of which was my past—so familiar and predictable that even my unhappiness then made me happy now just to think of it— the other my future, a gray blank, an overcast seascape on which rain was falling and no boats were in sight. I was no longer in a tropical zone and I felt cold inside and out, the first time such a sensation had come over me.

4   In books I had read—from time to time, when the plot called for it—someone would suffer from homesickness. A person would leave a not so very nice situation and go somewhere else, somewhere a lot better, and then long to go back where it was not very nice. How impatient I would become with such a person, for I would feel that I was in a not so nice situation myself, and how I wanted to go some-where else. But now I, too, felt that I wanted to be back where I came from. I understood it, I knew where I stood there. If I had to draw a picture of my future then, it would have been a large gray patch surrounded by black, blacker, blackest.

5   What a surprise this was to me, that I longed to be back in the place that I came from, that I longed to sleep in a bed I had outgrown, that I longed to be with the people whose smallest, most natural gesture would call up in me such a rage that I longed to see them all dead at my feet. Oh, I had imagined that with my one swift act—leaving home and coming to this new place—that I could leave behind me, as if it were an old garment never to be worn again, my sad thoughts, my sad feelings, and my discontent with life in general as it presented itself to me. In the past, the thought of being in my present situation had been a comfort, but now I did not even have this to look forward to, and so I lay down on my bed and dreamt I was eating a bowl of pink mullet and green figs cooked in coconut milk, and it had been cooked by my grandmother, which was why the taste of it pleased me so, for she was the person I liked best in the world and those were the things I liked best to eat also.

B. READING FOR MAIN IDEAS

*Read each sentence and write **T** if it is true or **F** if it is false. If it is false, correct the sentence.*

_____ **1.** Lucy feels very comfortable in the new country.

_____

_____ **2.** Lucy finds everything very much the same as she expected and very similar to her own country.

_____

_____ **3.** Lucy is unsure of her future.

_____

_____ **4.** Lucy was a happy young girl in her native country.

_____

_____ **5.** Lucy is surprised that she is homesick.

_____

_____ **6.** Lucy's dreams became reality in the new country.

_____

C. READING FOR DETAILS

Imagine that Lucy wrote the following letter to her grandmother. In it she describes her new life in the United States. There are, however, eight factual errors in what she writes. Read the letter, think back to the reading, and underline any incorrect information that Lucy has given her grandmother. Be prepared to explain the incorrect information by referring to the story. Discuss your findings with a partner.

Dear Grandmother,

I had a wonderful trip. The weather was warm and sunny, and I loved traveling by boat. Driving through the city, I saw many of the famous sights that I had dreamt about before my trip. They were beautiful! The apartment building where I am staying has an elevator. As you know, I had never seen one before, much less been in one! It's great not to have to walk up the stairs. The apartment is furnished and it has a brand new refrigerator, just like the one we have at home. After a good night's sleep, I awoke to another bright, sunny day. I put on a pretty summer dress. It was just the right thing. Despite the warm weather, I felt a feeling of homesickness coming over me. It's hard to explain why this would happen, but it did. Perhaps it has to do with the insecurity I feel about my future. If you had told me before I left that I would miss my life back home, I wouldn't have believed you. Nevertheless, that is what has happened. Don't worry about me, I'll be fine. I'll write again as soon as I have more to tell you.

Love,
Lucy

P.S. I enjoyed eating the pink mullet and green figs that you cooked for me to eat on my trip. It made me feel less homesick.

D. READING BETWEEN THE LINES

Work with a partner. Read the following sentences from "Poor Visitor" and answer the questions. Share your answers with the class.

1. In a daydream I used to have, all these places were points of happiness to me; all these places were <u>lifeboats to my small drowning soul.</u>

   What does Lucy mean by "lifeboats to my small drowning soul"?

   _____

   _____

2. I was reminded of how <u>uncomfortable the new can make you feel.</u>

   What does Lucy mean by this?

   _____

   _____

3. But at first it was all so new that I had to <u>smile with my mouth turned down at the corners.</u>

   Why does Lucy smile with her mouth turned down?

   _____

   _____

4. But now I, too, felt that I wanted to be back where I came from. I understood it, I knew where I stood there.

   Why does Lucy want to be back in her native country?

   _____

   _____

5. Oh, I had imagined that with my one swift act—leaving home and coming to this new place—that I could leave behind me, as if it were an old garment never to be worn again, my sad thoughts, my sad feelings, and my discontent with life in general as it presented itself to me.

   What does Lucy realize about herself and her feelings?

   _____

   _____

READING TWO: Nostalgia¹

A. EXPANDING THE TOPIC

The following poem was written by a Puerto Rican poet who describes his nostalgia for his homeland. Before you read the poem, answer the following question. Share your answer with a classmate.

What things about your native country do you (or would you) miss if you are (or were) in another country?

Nostalgia

BY VIRGILIO DÁVILA (1869–1943)

1 "Mamma, Borinquen² calls me,
this country is not mine,
Borinquen is pure flame
and here I am dying of the cold."

2 In search of a better future
I left the native home,
and established my store
in the middle of New York.
What I see around me
is a sad panorama,³
and my spirit calls out,
wounded by much nostalgia,
for the return to the home nest,
Mamma, Borinquen calls me!

3 Where will I find here
like in my *criollo*⁴ land
a dish of chicken and rice,
a cup of good coffee?

---

¹ *nostalgia:* longing for the past
² *Borinquen:* the name the people of Puerto Rico use when referring to their homeland;
the Borinquen Indians, or Boriqueños, were the original inhabitants of Puerto Rico
³ *panorama:* view, scene, sight
⁴ *criollo:* Spanish American

Where, oh where will I see
radiant in their attire
the girls, rich in vigor,
whose glances bedazzle?[5]
Here eyes do not bedazzle,
this country is not mine!

4 If I listen to a song here
of those I learned at home,
or a *danza*[6] by Tavarez,
Campos, or Dueño Colón,
my sensitive heart
is more enflamed with patriotic love,
and a herald[7] that faithful proclaims
this holy feeling
the wail "Borinquen is pure flame!"
comes to my ears.

5 In my land, what beauty!
In the hardest winter
not a tree is seen bare,
not a vale[8] without green.
The flower rules the garden,
the river meanders talkative,
the bird in the shadowy wood
sings his arbitrary song,
and here . . . The snow is a shroud,[9]
here I am dying of the cold.

---

[5] *bedazzle:* impress, enchant
[6] *danza:* dance music from the nineteenth century
[7] *herald:* messenger
[8] *vale:* valley
[9] *shroud:* covering or burial garment

Answer the following questions.

What does Virgilio Dávila miss about his native country? Are these things similar to or different from the things you said you miss (or would miss)?

B. LINKING READINGS ONE AND TWO

Think of at least four similar themes or topics described in both "Poor Visitor" and "Nostalgia." Write them in the chart. Give examples of each theme. Discuss your answers with a partner. The first theme is done for you.

THEME	EXAMPLE FROM "POOR VISITOR"	EXAMPLE FROM "NOSTALGIA"
1. weather		
2.		
3.		
4.		

5 REVIEWING LANGUAGE

A. EXPLORING LANGUAGE: Compound Words

Compound words are formed by combining two separate words. Recognizing two separate words within one word can help you guess the new meaning of the compound noun, verb, or adjective. For example, the compound noun *homework* is formed from the words *home* and *work*. Homework is work that you do at home. *Footpath* is formed from the words *foot* and *path*. A footpath is a path that is only used by people on foot, not by motor vehicles or bicycles.

Work with a partner. For each word, find the two words that make the compound word. Discuss the meaning. Add your own example using one of the words that make up the compound word. Use your dictionary if necessary. The first one has been done for you.

COMPOUND WORD	FIRST WORD	SECOND WORD	YOUR EXAMPLE
1. lifeboat	life	boat	lifetime
2. undergarment			
3. homesickness			
4. daydream			
5. overcast			
6. outgrown			
7. grandmother			

B. WORKING WITH WORDS: Sentence Completion

Use compound words from Part A on page 220 to complete the sentences.

1. Some people think that by moving to a new country they can discard their problems like clothes they have _____ .

2. Our second day in the new country was a dark and stormy day. The sky was _____ .

3. I miss my _____ very much; she would always cook my favorite food.

4. Many immigrants often _____ about their native country and their lives there.

5. The ship was sinking rapidly, and the passengers were hurrying to get into the _____ (s).

6. Many people consider _____ to be a normal part of adaptation to a new country or culture.

7. People from warm climates are often unprepared for the cold winters in New York. To keep warm they should always wear several layers of _____ (s) under their clothes.

SKILLS FOR EXPRESSION

A. GRAMMAR: Past Perfect

❶ *Examine the following sentences, and discuss the questions with a partner.*

- ◆ By the time Lucy arrived in New York, she <u>had</u> already <u>imagined</u> what New York would look like.

- ◆ Lucy <u>had</u> just <u>put</u> on her summer dress when she realized it was cold outside.

- ◆ Before Lucy moved to New York, she <u>had longed</u> to go there.

a. In the first sentence, did Lucy arrive in New York first, or did she imagine what New York looked like first?

b. In the second sentence, did Lucy realize it was cold outside before she put on her summer dress?

c. In the third sentence, which happened first—Lucy's move to New York, or her longing to go there?

d. What helped you decide the order of events in these sentences?

FOCUS ON GRAMMAR

See Past Perfect in *Focus on Grammar, High Intermediate.*

Past Perfect

The **past perfect** form of a verb is used to show that something happened before a specific time or event in the past.

Form of the Past Perfect

The past perfect is formed with **had** + past participle.

- ◆ Lucy **had** never **been** in an elevator before.

Past Perfect and a Specific Time or Event in the Past

To show that something happened before a specific time in the past, use the past perfect with *by* + a certain time in the past.

 ◆ **By the next morning,** Lucy **had become** very homesick.

Past Perfect with Two Past Events

When talking about two events that happened in the past, use the past perfect to show the event that happened first (the earlier event). The simple past is often used to show the second event. In other words, the event in the past perfect happened before the event in the simple past.

Time words such as ***after*** and ***as soon as*** are used to introduce the first event (past perfect).

 ◆ **As soon as** she **had put on** her summer dress, she had a strange sensation.

Before and ***by the time*** are used to introduce the second event (simple past).

 ◆ Lucy **had lived** with her grandmother **before** she moved to New York. (First she lived with her grandmother. Then she moved to New York.)

When can be used to introduce either the first or the second event. Notice the difference.

 ◆ Lucy **had put on** her dress **when** she realized the weather was cold. (First she put on her dress. Then she realized the weather was cold.)

 ◆ Lucy **put on** her dress **when** she realized the weather was cold. (First she realized the weather was cold. Then she put on her dress.)

Already, Never, and *Ever*

These words are often used with the past perfect to emphasize the event that happened first.

- ◆ Lucy **had never eaten** food from a refrigerator before then.
- ◆ No one **had ever told** Lucy that the sun could shine and the air remain cold.

GRAMMAR TIP: As in all sentences with two clauses, when the sentence begins with a dependent clause (the clause beginning with a time word), a comma separates it from the main clause. When the sentence begins with the main clause, no comma is necessary.

---

2 *Each of the following sentences talks about two events which happened in the past. Which event happened first? Write 1 for the first event and 2 for the second event. The first one has been done for you.*

1. By the time Lucy arrived in New York, she had already imagined what New York would look like.

   __2__ Lucy arrived in New York.

   __1__ Lucy imagined what New York looked like.

2. Before Virgilio Dávila established his store in New York, he had lived in Puerto Rico.

   _____ Dávila established his store in New York.

   _____ Dávila lived in Puerto Rico.

3. The immigrants had already seen the Statue of Liberty when the spectacle of Ellis Island came into view.

   _____ The immigrants saw the Statue of Liberty.

   _____ Ellis Island came into view.

4. Dávila had never felt so alone before he moved to New York.

   _____ Dávila moved to New York.

   _____ Dávila never felt so alone.

5. After Lucy had woken up, she put on a gay summer dress.

_____ Lucy woke up.

_____ Lucy put on a gay summer dress.

6. The immigrants had never studied a second language before they moved to the new country.

_____ The immigrants never studied a second language.

_____ The immigrants moved to a new country.

7. By the time Dávila established his store in New York, he had grown very nostalgic for his homeland.

_____ Dávila was nostalgic for his homeland.

_____ Dávila established his store in New York.

8. As soon as Jamaica Kincaid had moved from Antigua to New York, she needed to find a job and a place to stay.

_____ Jamaica Kincaid moved from Antigua to New York.

_____ She needed to find a job and a place to stay.

3 *Study the time line of Jamaica Kincaid's life. Use the time line to complete the sentences that follow. Use the past perfect or the simple past as necessary. The first one has been done for you.*

JAMAICA KINCAID'S LIFE

1949	born as Elaine Potter Richardson in St. Johns, Antigua	**1979**	married Allen Shawn, son of *New Yorker* publisher
1965	left West Indies	**1983**	published first short story collection
1966	worked at domestic jobs in New York City		
1969	was a college student	**1985**	moved to Bennington, Vermont, with husband
1973	published first magazine article (*Ingenue* magazine) and changed name to Jamaica Kincaid	**1988**	published a long essay, *A Small Place*
1974	published story in the *Village Voice* newspaper	**1990**	published *Lucy*
		1996	published *Autobiography of My Mother*
1976	worked as a staff writer at the *New Yorker* magazine	**1997**	published *My Brother*

1. <u>After</u> Elaine Potter Richardson had changed her name to Jamaica Kincaid, <u>she published a story in the Village Voice</u>.

2. Jamaica Kincaid had moved to Bennington, Vermont, <u>before</u>

_____ .

3. <u>As soon as</u> _____ ,
she found a domestic job in New York.

4. <u>By the time</u> she published _Lucy,_ _____

_____ .

5. <u>By 1983,</u> _____

_____ .

6. <u>When</u> _____

_____ .

7. She had <u>already</u> _____

_____ .

8. She had <u>never</u> _____

_____ .

B. STYLE: Comparisons and Contrasts

① _Examine the paragraph, and answer the questions with a partner._

Lucy faces many changes upon her arrival in New York City. First she is struck with the change in climate. Her native climate is warm and the sun is brilliant <u>while</u> New York in January is very cold and the sun is lifeless. Her living conditions are different, too. In New York she lives in an apartment building. <u>In contrast</u>, she lived in a house in her native country. In addition, she finds herself eating food that has just been taken from the refrigerator <u>whereas</u> she always ate her grandmother's freshly cooked meals in her homeland. The most important aspect of her life remains the same, though; Lucy faces many different problems and issues in New York <u>in the same way</u> she did in Antigua. She has learned that she cannot leave her troubles behind like clothes she has outgrown.

1. Look at the underlined words. Which words introduce things that are similar? Which words introduce things that are different?

2. Four topics are compared and contrasted in this paragraph. What are they?

Comparisons and Contrasts

Comparisons point out things that are similar. Contrasts point out things that are different.

Subordinating Conjunctions

Subordinating conjunctions are used to contrast the ideas in two clauses. They join the independent (main) clause to the dependent clause being contrasted. The subordinating conjunctions include *while* and *whereas*. Note that these words do not introduce a complete thought. They introduce dependent clauses. They need the independent clause to complete the sentence or idea. The main clause usually describes the point that is being emphasized or is more important.

- Her native climate is warm and the sun is brilliant **while** New York in January is very cold and the sun is lifeless.

More emphasis: The weather in her native country is warm.

Less emphasis: The weather in New York is cold.

- **Whereas** the sun in New York is lifeless, the sun in her native country is brilliant.

Less emphasis: The sun in New York is lifeless.

More emphasis: The sun in her native country is brilliant.

Punctuation

See the Grammar Tip on page 224. The same punctuation rules apply for dependent and independent clauses.

Transition Words

Transition words show the relation between two independent clauses (two sentences).

Transition words for comparisons include:	Transition words for contrasts include:
similarly	*in contrast*
in the same way	*on the other hand*
likewise	*however*

Two independent clauses can be combined in one sentence by using a semicolon (;) and a comma (,):

- ◆ In New York she lives in an apartment building; **however,** she lived in a house in her native country.

The two independent clauses can also be written as separate sentences:

- ◆ In New York she lives in an apartment building. **However,** she lived in a house in her native country.

The two independent clauses can also be combined as a simple sentence with **_in the same way_** or **_in contrast to_**:

- ◆ Lucy came to New York in search of a better future **in the same way** Dávila did.

❷ *Combine the following pairs of sentences to make comparisons and contrasts. Use the boldface words given. The first one has been done for you.*

1. likewise
 a. Lucy feels homesick.
 b. Virgilio Dávila feels nostalgic.

 Lucy feels homesick; likewise, Dávila feels nostalgic. .

2. in the same way
 a. Dávila dislikes harsh winter with its bare trees.
 b. Lucy dislikes the pale winter sun.

 _____ .

3. similarly
 a. Lucy misses her grandmother's home cooking.
 b. Dávila misses his country's native food.

 _____ .

4. on the other hand
 a. Dávila opened his own store in New York.
 b. Lucy worked for a family as a nanny.

 _____ .

5. in contrast
   a. Lucy is a young woman.
   b. Dávila is an older man.

   _____.

6. while
   a. "Poor Visitor" was written in the last half of the twentieth century.
   b. "Nostalgia" was written in the first half of the twentieth century.

   _____.

7. whereas
   a. Dávila misses his culture.
   b. Lucy misses her family.

   _____.

8. however
   a. Jamaica Kincaid was born in Antigua.
   b. Dávila was born in Puerto Rico.

   _____.

3 *Write a short paragraph either comparing or contrasting Dávila's life in Puerto Rico and his new life in New York. Use appropriate conjunction and transition words. Write your paragraph on a separate piece of paper.*

ON YOUR OWN

A. WRITING TOPICS

Choose one of the following topics. Write two or three paragraphs using some of the vocabulary, grammar, and style you learned in this unit.

1. Compare similar themes in "Poor Visitor" and "Nostalgia." Use specific examples from the two readings. Refer to the chart in Exercise 4B on page 219 for possible themes to discuss.

2. Have you ever left your homeland to live in another country? What were your feelings about your homeland when you first arrived in the new country? What feelings did you have after being away for a while? Did you experience any bouts of nostalgia? If so, what did you do to overcome the sensation?

3. Living in another language means growing another self, and it takes time for that other self to become familiar.

—Allistair Reed

Discuss the meaning of this quote and how it applies to you and your experiences. Has studying English changed your life? If yes, how has English changed your life? What is different about you now, as opposed to before you knew English? Are these positive or negative changes?

B. FIELDWORK: Immigrants' Stories

PREPARATION

In small groups, brainstorm a list of famous immigrants. Write as much information as you know about them—for example, occupation, country of origin, country of immigration.

RESEARCH ACTIVITY

Choose an immigrant you would like to know more about. Choose someone from the Predicting exercise at the beginning of the unit or from the brainstorming list in your Fieldwork preparation. Research this person at the library or through the Internet, and write a short report. Present your report to the class.

TAKE IT OR LEAVE IT

who needs all this **technology** anyway?!

I wish it would all go away!!! microprocessors... microwaves... frozen corn on the cob... operating systems named BOB.

well o.k... maybe a **little** technology.

©1998 Bill Layne

1 APPROACHING THE TOPIC

A. PREDICTING

Work with a partner. Read the cartoon and answer the questions that follow.

1. How do you think the character in the cartoon feels about technology?
2. Are these feelings similar to or different from your own feelings about technology? Explain your answer.
3. Look at the title of the unit. What do you think "take it or leave it" means? What would be the consequences of your taking—or leaving— technology?

B. SHARING INFORMATION

How has technology made our lives easier? What technology is considered necessary, and what technology is considered a luxury?

Look at the following chart and check (✓) whether you feel the technology is a necessity or a luxury. Add any technology you feel is missing from the list. When you are finished, compare your opinions in small groups.

TECHNOLOGY	NECESSITY	LUXURY
electricity		
running water		
automatic dishwasher		
washing machine		
lights that go on automatically when you enter a room and go off when you leave		
air conditioning		
vacuum cleaner		
a TV in every room		
computers		
CD player		
automatic garage-door opener		
automatic sprinklers for a lawn		
microwave oven		
Internet access		

2 PREPARING TO READ

A. BACKGROUND

Read the information and complete the exercise that follows.

Bill Gates is the owner of Microsoft© Corporation and one of the wealthiest people in the United States. He has built a state-of-the-art home near Seattle, Washington. His home incorporates "Smart Home" technologies. A Smart Home is a home that has many mechanical or electronic conveniences, many controlled by computers that help make life easier and often save energy.

The picture below illustrates some Smart Home technologies. Try to guess what each mechanical or electronic device does in each room, and write a few sentences describing it. Check your answers with the answers at the bottom of the page.

Smart Home: The house of tomorrow won't just shelter you and your family. It will take care of you.

Answers: Ring the doorbell. Your picture appears on the TV screen, and the TV remote control opens the door. Open the garage door by remote control: the Motion sensors turn on the lights. Use the telephone to turn on the stove or oven.

B. VOCABULARY FOR COMPREHENSION

Work with a partner. Complete the sentences with words from the list. If necessary, use your dictionary.

console   image browsing
database   visual recognition
interface   unobtrusive
information highway   remote control
monitor   ostentatious
network

1. Some people are _____ with their technology; they like to have all the latest technology just to impress their friends.

2. Some technology is very obvious, like dishwashers and washing machines. Other technology is _____, like automatic lighting and house alarms; it is not noticeable.

3. It might be possible in the future to have a camera system with _____ capabilities that could identify house guests just from their photographs.

4. Today it isn't necessary to touch the television to change the channel. You can change channels from a distance by using a _____ .

5. The screen of a computer is called a _____ .

6. One of the most unusual electronic features in Bill Gates's house is a _____ , or computer storage place, of more than a million still images, including photographs and reproductions of paintings.

7. The _____ is not really a road or street at all. It is a term that refers to information available through the infrastructure of the Internet, phone lines, satellites, and/or e-mail.

8. A _____ is a place where people keep a computer screen, television, or stereo. It is often designed to hide the electronic device by making it look like a piece of furniture.

9. Another term for the Internet is _____ , which refers to the way in which the Internet is interconnected with computers around the world. Actually, "net" in Internet comes from this word.

10. The _____ refers to the way in which a person connects with a computer. Computer programs are designed to make this connection "user friendly."

11. Another term for looking at pictures on the Internet is _____ . With this technology you can see any painting or photograph you want, all in the comfort of your own home, without having to go to a library or bookstore.

3 READING ONE: Inside the House

A. INTRODUCING THE TOPIC

Write a short answer to the following questions. Share your answer with a partner.

What kind of a "dream" house would you want? Where would it be located? What kind of technology would you have in the house?

Bill Gates's dream house.

Inside the House

BY BILL GATES
(from *The Road Ahead*)

1   I began thinking about building a new house in the late 1980s. I wanted craftsmanship but nothing ostentatious. I wanted a house that would accommodate sophisticated, changing technology, but in an unobtrusive way that made it clear that technology was the servant, not the master.

2   I found some property on the shore of Lake Washington within an easy commuting distance of Microsoft. Living space will be about average for a large house. The family living room will be about fourteen by twenty-eight feet, including an area for watching television or listening to music. And there will be cozy spaces for one or two people, although there will also be a reception hall to entertain one hundred comfortably for dinner.

3   First thing, as you come in, you'll be presented with an electronic pin to clip on your clothes. This pin will tell the home who and where you are, and the house will use this information to try to meet and even anticipate your needs—all as unobtrusively as possible. Someday instead of needing the pin, it might be possible to have a camera system with visual-recognition capabilities, but that's beyond current technology. When it's dark outside, the pin will cause a moving zone of light to accompany you through the house. Unoccupied rooms will be unlit. As you walk down a hallway, you might not notice the lights ahead of you gradually coming up to full brightness and the lights behind you fading. Music will move with you, too. It will seem to be everywhere, although, in fact, other people in the house will be hearing entirely different music or nothing at all. A movie or the news or a phone call will be able to follow you around the house, too. If you get a phone call, only the handset nearest you will ring.

4   You won't be confronted by[1] the technology, but it will be readily and easily available. Hand-held remote controls and discreetly visible consoles in each room will put you in charge of your immediate environment and of the house's entertainment system. You'll use the controls to tell the monitors in a room to become visible and what to display. You'll be able to choose from among thousands of pictures, recordings, movies, and television programs, and you'll have all sorts of options available for selecting information.

5   If you're planning to visit Hong Kong soon, you might ask the screen in your room to show you pictures of the city. It will seem to

---

[1] *be confronted by:* have to deal with; be forced to meet

you as if the photographs are displayed everywhere, although actually the images will materialize on the walls of rooms just before you walk in and vanish after you leave. If you and I are enjoying different things and one of us walks into a room where the other is sitting, the house might continue the audio and visual imagery for the person who was in the room first, or it might change to programming both of us like.

6   I will be the first home user for one of the most unusual electronic features in my house. The product is a database of more than a million still images, including photographs and reproductions of paintings. If you are a guest, you'll be able to call up portraits of presidents, pictures of sunsets, airplanes, skiing in the Andes, a rare French stamp, the Beatles in 1965, or reproductions of High Renaissance paintings, on screens throughout the house.

7   I believe quality images will be in great demand on the information highway. This vision that the public will find image-browsing worthwhile is obviously unproven. I think the right interface will make it appealing to a lot of people.

8   A decade from now, access to the millions of images and all the other entertainment opportunities I've described will be available in many homes and will certainly be more impressive than those I'll have when I move into my house. My house will just be getting some of the services a little sooner.

9   One of the many fears expressed about the information highway is that it will reduce the time people spend socializing. Some worry that homes will become such cozy entertainment providers that we'll never leave them, and that, safe in our private sanctuaries, we'll become isolated. I don't think that's going to happen. As behaviorists keep reminding us, we're social animals. We will have the option of staying home more because the highway will create so many new options for home-based entertainment, for communication—both personal and professional—and for employment. Although the mix of activities will change, I think people will decide to spend almost as much time out of their homes.

10   The highway will not only make it easier to keep up with distant friends, it will also enable us to find new companions. Friendships formed across the network will lead naturally to getting together in person. This alone will make life more interesting. Suppose you want to reach someone to play bridge with. The information highway will let you find card players with the right skill level and availability in your neighborhood, or in other cities or nations.

11   I enjoy experimenting, and I know some of my concepts for the house will work out better than others. Maybe I'll decide to conceal the monitors behind conventional wall art or throw the electronic pins into the trash. Or maybe I'll grow accustomed to the systems in the house, or even fond of them, and wonder how I got along without them. That's my hope.

B. READING FOR MAIN IDEAS

"Inside the House" can be divided into three main ideas. What does the reading say about each idea? Circle the letter of the sentence that gives the best summary.

1. Description of the house

   a. Even though the house is larger than an average house, Bill Gates does not want it to feel cold or unfriendly.

   b. Bill Gates designed the house to accommodate one hundred people.

2. Description of the technology in the house

   a. The technology is designed to be impressive and complex.

   b. The technology is designed to be easy to use and energy efficient.

3. Analysis of the technology

   a. The information highway is a necessary part of everyone's life.

   b. Although the information highway has both positive and negative aspects, it is basically a positive technology.

C. READING FOR DETAILS

The following exercise is based on an outline of Reading One. An outline is the skeleton of a text, showing the main ideas, supporting details, and examples. Outlines are useful when taking notes from texts or when organizing an essay. Some people prefer very specific outlines showing all the details, while others prefer a more general outline without including the specific details. This is an example of a detailed outline.

Complete the outline with the missing information: main ideas, supporting ideas, and examples from the text. You may need to look back at the reading while you are working. When you have completed the outline, compare your work with a classmate's.

MAIN IDEA **I.** Began thinking about home in the late 1980s

    SUPPORT **A.** Style preferences

        EXAMPLE **1.** _____

        EXAMPLE **2.** not ostentatious

    SUPPORT **B.** Must accommodate sophisticated and changing technology

        EXAMPLE **1.** not obtrusive

        EXAMPLE **2.** functions as servant, not master

II. Selected the perfect property

    A. Location

        1. _____

        2. easy commuting distance

    B. Living space—average size

        1. living room

            a. size = _____

            b. area for _____ or _____

        2. other cozy spaces for one or two people

        3. _____

            a. accommodates one hundred

III. _____ controls the home environment

    A. Tells the home _____ and _____

    B. House uses pin information to meet your needs

        1. _____ follows you

        2. _____ follows you

        3. _____ follows you

IV. Other readily and easily available technology

    A. Hand-held remotes and consoles in each room

        1. controls tell monitors:

            a. _____

            b. _____

    B. Visual displays

        1. large choice

            a. thousands of pictures

            b. _____

            c. _____

        d. television programs

        e. many options for selecting information

    2. house can control visual displays

        a. materialize when you _____ and vanish when you _____

        b. house can change programming depending on _____

V. Home has a state-of-the-art database

    A. First homeowner to have it

    B. Database has more than _____

        1. includes photographs

        2. includes _____

    C. Guests can call up anything they like

        1. _____

        2. pictures of sunsets

        3. skiing in the Andes, etc.

VI. Future availability of quality images

    A. On the information highway

    B. In homes

VII. Fears about _____

    A. Reduce the time people spend socializing

        1. homes will become too cozy and self-contained

        2. people will become _____

    B. Not in agreement

        1. people are social animals

        2. highway only provides more entertainment and _____ options

            a. _____

            b. _____

            c. _____

        3. people will decide to spend as much time out of their homes

VIII. Benefits of the information highway

    A. Makes it easier to:

        1. maintain _____

        2. find _____

B. Makes life more interesting
  1. people will meet in person
  2. meet people with common interests
IX. Conclusion: Experimenting and the future
  A. Bill Gates enjoys experimenting and may decide to:
    1. _____
    2. _____
  B. Hopes
    1. may like everything
    2. wonder how _____

D. READING BETWEEN THE LINES

The following statements can be inferred from the reading. Find an example from the reading that would support each inference.

1. Technology should make life easier; it should not take over your life.
Example:

_____

2. A large home can be intimate.
Example:

_____

3. Homes should have energy-saving devices.
Example:

_____

4. A home should make guests feel comfortable by providing entertainment.
Example:

_____

5. The information highway allows people to be in the comfort of their home but, at the same time, stay connected to the world.
Example:

_____

6. The design of a home should be current but also allow for changes over time.
Example:

_____

READING TWO: Thoreau's Home

A. EXPANDING THE TOPIC

Thoreau's home

In 1845, the American philosopher Henry David Thoreau moved to the woods of Massachusetts. He chose to live a life that reflected his philosophy: Live life in the simplest of ways. He did not believe luxuries or comforts were necessary; in fact, he felt they actually stopped human progress.

Before you read "Thoreau's Home," write a few sentences to answer the following question. Share your ideas with a partner.

What ways can you think of by which technology may actually stop or interfere with human progress?

Thoreau's Home

BY HENRY DAVID THOREAU
(Edited, from *Walden*)

1   Near the end of March 1845, I borrowed an axe and went down to the woods by Walden Pond[1] nearest to where I intended to build my house, and began to cut down some tall arrowy white pines, still in their youth, for timber.[2] . . . It was a pleasant hillside where I worked, covered with pine woods, through which I looked out on the pond, and a small open field in the woods where pines and hickories were springing up.[3] The ice on the pond was not yet dissolved, though there were some open spaces, and it was all dark colored and saturated with water. . . .

2   So I went on for some days cutting and hewing timber, and also studs and rafters,[4] all with my narrow axe, not having many communicable or scholar-like thoughts, singing to myself,

---

[1] *Walden Pond:* pond located in Lincoln, Massachusetts
[2] *timber:* wood used for building or making things
[3] *springing up:* growing
[4] *studs and rafters:* beams and pieces of wood that form the structure of a building

Men say they know many things;
But lo! they have taken wings—
The arts and sciences,
And a thousand appliances;
The wind that blows
Is all anybody knows.

3   My days in the woods were not very long ones; yet I usually carried my dinner of bread and butter, and read the newspaper in which it was wrapped, at noon, sitting amid the green pine boughs which I had cut off, and to my bread was imparted some of their fragrance, for my hands were covered with a thick coat of pitch.[5] . . .

4   Before winter I built a chimney, and shingled the sides of my house, which were impervious to[6] rain. . . .

5   I have thus a tight shingled and plastered house, ten feet wide by fifteen feet long, and eight-feet posts, with a garret[7] and a closet, a large window on each side, two trap doors, one door at each end, and a brick fireplace opposite. The exact cost of my house, paying the usual price for such materials as I used, but not counting the work, all of which was done by myself, was as follows; and I give the details because very few are able to tell exactly what their houses cost, and fewer still, if any, the separate cost of the various materials which compose them:

Boards	8.03\frac{1}{2}$	Mostly shanty boards.
Refuse shingles for roof and sides	4.00	
Laths	1.25	
Two second-hand windows with glass	2.43	
One thousand old bricks	4.00	
Two casks of lime	2.40	That was high.
Hair	0.31	More than I needed.
Mantle-tree iron	0.15	
Nails	3.90	
Hinges and screws	0.14	
Latch	0.10	
Chalk	0.01	
Transportation	1.40	I carried a good part on my back.
In all	28.12\frac{1}{2}$	

---

[5] *pitch:* pine sap
[6] *impervious to:* protected against
[7] *garret:* a small room in the top of a house

Write short answers to these questions. Work in a small group and compare answers. Why do you think Thoreau wanted to build his own house? Was building his own home more satisfying than having it built? If so, in what ways?

B. LINKING READINGS ONE AND TWO

Work with a partner. One of you imagines you are Bill Gates, and the other Henry David Thoreau. Imagine you could write to each other and ask each other questions. What questions would you ask? For example: How big is your house? What luxuries do you have in your house? Write five questions you would ask.

Exchange your questions with your partner, and write an answer to each question based on your understanding of Readings One and Two.

REVIEWING LANGUAGE

A. EXPLORING LANGUAGE: Word Forms

Work with a partner and identify the words in the left-hand column as nouns, verbs, or adjectives. Write the words under the correct heading. Then try to complete the chart with the other forms of the words. Sometimes the words have more than one noun, verb, or adjective form. Sometimes the words do not have all of the forms. Use a dictionary if necessary. The first one has been done for you.

WORD	NOUN	VERB	ADJECTIVE
availability	availability	x	available
behaviorist			
brightness			
communicable			
conventional			
entertainment			
friendship			
information			
materialize			
ostentatious			
television			
visible/visual			

B. WORKING WITH WORDS

Complete the sentences with an appropriate form of the words given. If necessary, refer to the word forms in Part A above. The first one has been done for you.

1. vision   **entertainment**

     a. The monitors in Bill Gates's home will not be _____ visible _____ until you turn them on.

     b. Bill Gates believes that one of the goals of technology is to

        _____ .

c. _____ , however, is not the only goal of technology; improving the quality of life is also important.

d. Bill Gates has many _____ for the future of technology.

e. The use of _____-recognition cameras is one of Bill Gates's future plans.

f. He suggests some very _____ uses of the information highway.

2. communication   information

a. One of the advantages of the information highway is that it allows people to _____ with co-workers without actually traveling to the office.

b. Personal computers, modems, e-mail, and fax machines have increased the speed of _____ dramatically.

c. Unfortunately, not all the _____ available over the Internet is correct.

d. Some of the data and facts are _____ and useful, but other information is just not true.

e. Because Bill Gates's house was out of the ordinary, it was necessary for him to _____ the architects and builders exactly what he wanted.

3. friendship   material

a. Bill Gates feels that the information highway can be used to foster _____ .

b. Some of Thoreau's contemporaries felt that he was not _____ because he often kept to himself.

c. In a Smart Home your favorite pictures will _____ on the walls of the rooms just before you walk in.

d. Thoreau used many reused _____ when building his home; this was part of his belief in living economically and simply.

e. Thoreau rejected the _____ world.

SKILLS FOR EXPRESSION

A. GRAMMAR: Future Progressive

1 *Read the following paragraph, and discuss the questions that follow with a partner.*

As technology advances, our lives <u>will be changing</u> day by day. In the future more and more people <u>will be building</u> smart homes like Bill Gates's. People in general <u>are going to be using</u> technology more and more in their everyday lives. We <u>will be using</u> the information highway for a wide range of activities such as banking, shopping, studying, and telecommuting. Our children certainly <u>won't be living</u> as we live; they will have many more electronic conveniences, but also some inconveniences. For example, today if we have a complaint or suggestion about some product or service, we are usually able to make it to a "live" person. In the future our children may not have this option. They probably <u>won't be complaining</u> to a person, but to a machine. Although technological advances are designed to improve the quality of life, you <u>will be talking</u> about the "good old days" when life was simpler, just as your parents did before you. Technology may change our lifestyle, but not our human nature. As the French say, the more things change, the more they stay the same!

a. Is the paragraph describing past, present, or future events?

b. Is the focus of the paragraph on the events themselves or on the fact that the events are ongoing?

FOCUS ON GRAMMAR

See Future Progressive Tense in *Focus on Grammar: High Intermediate.*

Future Progressive

The **future progressive** tense is used to talk about actions that will be in progress at a specific time in the future. It is also used to emphasize the ongoing nature of the action.

Form of the Future Progressive

The future progressive is formed with

will (not) + _be_ + base form + **_ing_**

OR

be (not) going to + _be_ + base form + **_ing_**

- ◆ Tomorrow at 4:00, I **will be talking** to friends in Colombia by e-mail.

- ◆ I **won't be sending** faxes at that time.

- ◆ I**'m going to be using** the computer all day.

As with all progressive tenses, the future progressive is not usually used with non-action (stative) verbs.

- ◆ Bill Gates **will be** in New York at 6:00 P.M. tomorrow.

  (NOT _will be being_)

Future Progressive with Time Clauses

If there is a time clause in the sentence, the time clause is in the present tense, not the future.

- ◆ After he **finishes,** he**'ll be flying** to Spain.

---

2 _Complete the following paragraph. Use the future progressive when possible. The first one has been done for you._

Matt Olsen is a very busy man. Every day he has a full schedule.

Tomorrow, for example, before he even eats breakfast,

he_'ll be communicating__ with associates in France on the information
    1. (communicate)
highway. At 9:00 A.M. he _____ with Microsoft
                          2. (meet)
development engineers. At 9:45 he _____ out a
                          3. (try)
new version of "Windows 2001." From 10:30 to 11:00 he

_____ letters to his secretary. After he
    4. (dictate)

_____ to his wife on the phone, he _____
     5. (talk)   6. (eat)
lunch with his plant manager. After lunch, he and his staff

_____ the visual recognition capabilities of the new
     7. (test)
"smart camera." Don't try calling him after 3:00 P.M., however, because

he is going to be spending some time exercising in his personal gym. At

4:45 he _____ back in his office. Before he
             8. (be)

_____ dinner, he _____ to his Japanese
     9. (eat)   10. (talk)
business associates for about 30 minutes. For dinner, he

_____ a fresh salad, salmon steaks, and couscous.
     11. (have)
Remember not to call him after 10:00 P.M. because he

_____ . He certainly _____ for your call.
     12. (sleep)   13. (not wait)

3 _Imagine the following scenario:_

Ms. Allison Joan Smith, a high school history teacher, has been reading
all of Henry David Thoreau's writing recently. She has decided to take a
year off from her teaching job and try to follow in Thoreau's footsteps.
She will recreate some of his famous trips and projects. Look at the
tentative calendar she has planned for next year.

Plans for Next Year			
JANUARY	**FEBRUARY**	**MARCH**	**APRIL**
Go on winter camping excursion in western Massachusetts	Visit Walt Whitman's home in New York	Build full-size model of cabin at Walden Pond	Walk the beaches of Cape Cod and write about experiences
MAY	**JUNE**	**JULY**	**AUGUST**
(Continue to) build full-size model of cabin at Walden Pond	Live in model of Walden Pond cabin	Travel by boat on the Concord River	Study transcendentalist philosophy
SEPTEMBER	**OCTOBER**	**NOVEMBER**	**DECEMBER**
Take railroad from Concord, Massachusetts, to Bangor, Maine	Live in the back-woods of Maine	Travel by boat on the Merrimack River	Write about experiences following the footsteps of H. D. Thoreau

After contacting all the people and places involved in her plan, Allison was forced to make some changes in her schedule. The calendar below shows her final plans for next year.

Use the information in both calendars, and complete the sentences that follow. Be careful—the information given in each sentence is according to her tentative plans. In many cases, these plans have been changed. Check the revised calendar carefully, and complete the sentences appropriately. Use the future progressive. The first one has been done for you.

Revised Plans for Next Year			
JANUARY	**FEBRUARY**	**MARCH**	**APRIL**
Visit Walt Whitman's home in New York	Go on winter camping excursion in western Massachusetts	Build full-size model of cabin at Walden Pond	(Continue to) build full-size model of cabin at Walden Pond
MAY	**JUNE**	**JULY**	**AUGUST**
Live in model of Walden Pond cabin	Walk the beaches of Cape Cod and write about experiences	Travel by boat on the Concord River	Take railroad from Concord, Massachusetts, to Bangor, Maine
SEPTEMBER	**OCTOBER**	**NOVEMBER**	**DECEMBER**
Live in the backwoods of Maine	Travel by boat on the Merrimack River	Study transcendentalist philosophy	Write about experiences following the footsteps of H. D. Thoreau

1. In January, Allison <u>won't be going on a winter camping excursion in</u>
(go / winter camping excursion)
<u>western Massachusetts. She will be visiting Walt Whitman's home in</u>
<u>New York.</u>

2. In February, Allison _____
(visit / Walt Whitman's home in New York)

_____

3. In March, Allison _____
(build / model of cabin)

_____

4. In April, Allison _____
(walk / beaches of Cape Cod)

_____

_____

5. In May, Allison _____
(build / model of cabin)

_____

_____

6. In June, Allison _____
(live / model of Walden Pond cabin)

_____

7. In July, Allison _____
(travel / boat on Concord River)

_____

_____

8. In August, Allison _____
(study / transcendentalist philosophy)

_____

_____

9. In September, Allison _____
(take / railroad from Concord, Massachusetts)

_____

_____

10. In October, Allison _____
(live / backwoods of Maine)

_____

_____

11. In November, Allison _____
(travel / boat on Merrimack River)

_____

_____

12. In December, Allison _____
(write / experiences)

_____

_____

B. STYLE: Outlining

1 *Work with a partner. Examine the following outline from part of "Inside the House," and discuss the questions that follow.*

I. Fears about the information highway
  A. Reduce the time people spend socializing
    1. homes will become too cozy and self-contained
    2. people will become isolated
  B. Not in agreement
    1. people are social animals
    2. highway only provides more entertainment and communication options
      a. personal
      b. professional
      c. employment
    3. people will decide to spend as much time out of their homes

II. Benefits of the information highway
  A. Makes it easier to:
    1. maintain distant relationships
    2. find new companions
  B. Makes life more interesting
    1. people will meet in person
    2. meet people with common interests

a. What are the main ideas discussed?

b. What letters or numbers represent supporting sentences of the main ideas?

c. What letters or numbers represent examples of these supporting ideas?

d. What letters or numbers give more information about the examples?

e. Find the paragraph in Reading One that describes fears about the information highway. How does the outline reflect this paragraph?

Outlines

An **outline** helps you organize your notes or ideas before you begin to write. It helps you see the order in which you will talk about the main ideas, and it guides you in selecting details and examples to support those ideas. An outline shows you where to add more details, give more examples, or change the order of the main points. Preparing and following an outline is a useful pre-writing activity.

- -

The Structure of an Outline

An outline is usually written in the following way:

    I. Main idea (can also be written as a topic sentence)

(indent) **A.** Supporting detail **1** (always relates to the topic sentence)

    (indent) **1.** example (exemplifies the supporting detail)

        2. example

            a. further example (exemplifies the example)

            b. further example

      B. Supporting detail **2** (supports the topic sentence)

        1. example (exemplifies the supporting detail)

            a. further example (exemplifies the example)

        2. example

            a. further example (exemplifies the example)

            b. further example

It is not necessary to write your ideas in complete sentences, although some people like to write the main idea as a topic sentence. Some outlines are quite simple: They list only the main ideas (I, II) and a few supporting details (A, B). Some outlines are more detailed: They include many ideas (I, II, II, IV), details (A, B, C, D), examples (1, 2, 3, 4), and further explanations (a, b, c, d).

2 *Read the last paragraph and chart of "Thoreau's Home," and complete the outline with appropriate details.*

I. The house is efficient in size and economical.

    A. Size and description

        1. ten feet wide by fifteen feet long

        2. _____

        3. garret and closet

        4. _____

        5. two trap doors

        6. _____

        7. brick fireplace

    B. Economical construction

        1. work done himself

        2. total cost $28.12\frac{1}{2}$

3 *Read the following paragraph and write it in outline form.*

    Bill Gates and Henry David Thoreau represent very different philosophies and approaches to life. On the one hand, Bill Gates embraces technology as a necessary and essential tool for the advancement of humankind. For example, he believes that technology has enhanced our lives and enabled people to live longer and better lives. Thoreau, on the other hand, believed that technology could actually stop the advancement of humankind. He believed that technology takes us away from living truthfully. In other words, technology stops us from enjoying the simple pleasures such as reading a book or walking in the woods.

4 *Write a complete three-paragraph essay following the outline below. Be sure to include a topic sentence, supporting sentences, supporting details, and concluding statement. (See Unit 1, pages 21 and 22, and Unit 2, pages 47 and 48, for review.)*

I. There are many wonderful things technology has done for us.

    A. Sciences

        1. better health care

        2. healthier food preservation

    B. Communication

        1. worldwide

        2. nationwide

    C. Comforts

        1. television

        2. computers

II. There are also many negative sides to technology.
　　A. Acid rain from cars and industry
　　　　1. affects 45 percent of lakes in Sweden
　　　　2. costs millions of dollars to repair damage
　　B. Interpersonal relations
　　　　1. loss of face-to-face contact
　　　　2. traditional writing skills decline as e-mail becomes more common

III. We need to produce "smart technology" that makes our lives better without damaging the environment.
　　A. Research groups
　　　　1. produce useful research and smart technology
　　　　2. maintain funding for innovative technology
　　B. Educate our citizens
　　　　1. start in elementary schools
　　　　2. encourage young people to think about the difference between wasteful and dangerous technology and smart technology

7 ON YOUR OWN

A. WRITING TOPICS

Write about one of the following topics. First make an outline. Try to use the vocabulary, grammar, and ideas you learned in this unit.

1. Thoreau wrote, "Our life is frittered away by detail. An honest man has hardly need to count more than his ten fingers, or in extreme cases he may add his ten toes, and lump the rest. Simplicity, simplicity, simplicity!" Thoreau felt that we need only a simple life without modern comforts and technology to appreciate the world around us. Do you agree or disagree? Explain your answer.

2. Imagine you have to eliminate five technological devices from your life. What would they be? What, if anything, would you replace them with? How would your life be different?

3. Technology is necessary to make people live longer and better. It would be impossible to live without technology. Do you agree or disagree? Explain your answer.

4. When is technology a luxury? Does the definition of a luxury change over time? When is technology a necessity? In other words, are some things that would have been thought of as luxuries ten, twenty, or one hundred years ago, now considered necessities of life? Explain your answer.

B. FIELDWORK

PREPARATION

Think about the role technology has had in your own life. What technological devices and machines do you have now that did not exist when you were younger? Has technology changed the quality of your life? Complete the following chart. When you are finished, share it with a partner. An example has been done for you.

WHAT I USED AS A CHILD OR YOUNG PERSON	WHAT HAS REPLACED IT	HOW IT HAS CHANGED THE QUALITY OF MY LIFE
books, library	Internet	I'm able to get information faster and more easily. Saves a lot of time!

RESEARCH ACTIVITY

You will interview an older person (for example, a teacher from another generation) about the changes he or she has seen in technology during his or her lifetime. Follow these four steps.

1. Decide where you will go and who you will talk to.

2. Prepare a list of questions you would like to ask. For example:

- In your opinion, what is the most significant technological advance in your lifetime? Why do you think so?

- What technological advance has affected you most personally? How has it changed your life?

Add at least three more questions.

- _____

- _____

- _____

3. Conduct the interview.

4. Write a report based on your interview. Present it to the class.

ANSWER KEY

UNIT 1 ◆
UNTRUTH AND CONSEQUENCES

1B. SHARING INFORMATION

1. a
2. b
3. Suggested answer: People are only interested in shocking or bad news.
4. Suggested answer: The news we receive is controlled by news directors.

2B. VOCABULARY FOR COMPREHENSION

Suggested answers:

Vocabulary Words	Print Media	Television	People in the News
Reporters	✓	✓	
Affiliates		✓	
Anchors		✓	
Celebrities	✓	✓	✓
Columnists	✓		
Correspondents	✓	✓	
Editors	✓	✓	
Heroes			✓
High-profile personalities		✓	✓
Journalists	✓		
Magazines	✓		
Movie stars			✓
Networks		✓	
Senators			✓
Tabloids	✓		

3B. READING FOR MAIN IDEAS

1. a   3. b
2. a   4. b

3C. READING FOR DETAILS

1. case of the retired minister
2. politicians
3. Gennifer Flowers
4. Oliver Sipple, Rosa Lopez

3D. READING BETWEEN THE LINES

1. disagrees
2. disagrees
3. disagrees
4. disagrees
5. agrees
6. agrees

4A. EXPANDING THE TOPIC

Suggested answers to follow-up questions (page 12)

After the bombing

1. He cannot work.
2. He cannot visit friends.
3. He doesn't go out. He can't walk the dog without being followed.
4. Reporters have taken all privacy from him.

5A. EXPLORING LANGUAGE: Idioms

1. a   6. b
2. b   7. c
3. c   8. b
4. a   9. a
5. b   10. b

5B. WORKING WITH WORDS

1. c. Shelby Coffey
2. a. Gennifer Flowers
3. f. Richard Jewell or e. Rosa Lopez
4. d. Peter Jennings
5. b. reporter of the minister's story
6. e. Rosa Lopez

6A. GRAMMAR: Passive Voice

❶ a. The common grammar structure in passive sentences is *be* + past participle (*by* + agent). This structure is different from the structure of the active voice.
   b. the minister, Rosa Lopez, Richard Jewell
   c. a hitchhiker, cameras and reporters, people
   d. the minister, Rosa Lopez, Richard Jewel. The words in the subject position in the passive sentences do not perform the action.

❷ 2. was broadcast, or was broadcasted
   3. was justified
   4. did not return
   5. were found

6. decided
7. was read
8. pointed
9. was deflected
10. were questioned
11. fled

❸ 2. was interviewed by the FBI
3. was shot
4. was convicted by the media
5. was married
6. was written by Peter Jennings
7. was found guilty

6B. STYLE: Topic Sentences

❶ a. News is everywhere.
b. News is everywhere.
It serves many different functions.
c. All sentences relate to the ideas in the topic sentence.

❷ 1. c   3. b
2. b   4. c

❸ Suggested answers
2. The way we receive the news has changed over the years.
3. The public has the right to know when a public figure, such as the president, is unfaithful.
4. Reading, like exercise, requires discipline and hard work.

UNIT 2 ◆
CRIME AND PUNISHMENT

2B. VOCABULARY FOR COMPREHENSION

1. a   6. b
2. b   7. b
3. b   8. a
4. c   9. c
5. a   10. a

3B. READING FOR MAIN IDEAS

a. 4   e. 5
b. 3   f. 2
c. 7   g. 1
d. 6

3C. READING FOR DETAILS

Type of Program	Arguments in Favor	Arguments Against
Teen Court	1. A way to teach teens before they become serious criminals 2. Reduces the number of cases in a very full legal system 3. It has proven to be successful	1. Few first-time offenders are likely to become serious criminals 2. There is no proof that it changes teens' behavior 3. Some teens admit to a crime they did not commit in order to stay out of adult court
Teen Curfews	1. Crime rates have fallen 2. Most large cities have them 3. Keeps kids safe	1. It's wrong to punish all teens 2. Curfews get in the way of after-school jobs 3. Curfews violate the right to peaceful assembly
Parental Laws	1. Forces parents to become involved 2. Crime rate has dropped 3. Minor offenders don't feel free to move on to more serious crimes	1. Too much government interference 2. You shouldn't be punished for someone else's crimes 3. It's unconstitutional

5A. EXPLORING LANGUAGE

1. a   6. a
2. a   7. a
3. b   8. b
4. b   9. a
5. a   10. a

5B. WORKING WITH WORDS

1. parent class/teen punishment by traditional courts
2. lashing/death penalties
3. murder/misdemeanors
4. spray graffiti/punishments for parents
5. jail time/teen court punishments
6. rioting/crimes of theft
7. stealing/corporal punishments

6A. GRAMMAR: Gerunds and Infinitives

❶ 1. decreasing (crime)
2. walking
3. breaking
4. Gerunds are formed by adding *ing* to the base form of the verb.
5. to be
6. offenders; to perform
7. to try

8. to obey
9. The infinitive is formed by using *to* and the base form of the verb.

2 **b.** 3. having
c. 5. to resist
d. 4. to perform
e. 4. to perform
f. 2. shoplifting
g. 6. to obey
h. 4. to live
i. 3. running
j. 4. to establish

3 Suggested answers
2. The teenager's parents failed to supervise him.
3. The boy admitted shoplifting.
4. It was wrong to punish the boy.
5. The judge sentenced the parents to participate in a course on effective parenting.
6. The teen was afraid of going to jail.
7. A community can choose many ways to protect its citizens.
8. The parent was supposed to hear that her son had been involved in a crime.
9. The teen apologized for stealing the car.
10. The teenager denied writing the graffiti on the wall.

6B. STYLE: The Three-Part Paragraph

1 1. teen curfew in our town
2. the many problems
3. sentences 2–5
4. sentences 6–7

2 1. b   3. b
2. c   4. a

3 2. Furthermore, in other countries these laws seem to work.
3. Juvenile crime was not an issue when I was growing up.
4. We are all citizens of planet Earth and must learn to get along.

4 Answers will vary.

UNIT 3 ◆ DYING FOR THEIR BELIEFS

2B. VOCABULARY FOR COMPREHENSION

Legal System Vocabulary	Medical Vocabulary
commit a crime	heal
convict	shed weight
go to court	suffer
judge	ailment
stand trial	ambulance
accuser	autopsy
attorney	consequence
consequence	diabetes
felony	physician
manslaughter	practitioner
practitioner	stomachache
prosecutor	listless
	sunken eyes

3B. READING FOR MAIN IDEAS

Suggested answers.
1. diabetes.
2. she had gone to the doctor.
3. they did not seek conventional medical help.
4. they believe the Hermansons did not hurt their daughter.
5. parents' freedom of religion and a child's right to grow up healthy.

3C. READING FOR DETAILS

1. T   4. T
2. F   5. T
3. F   6. F

3D. READING BETWEEN THE LINES

1. c   6. a
2. d, e   7. b
3. c   8. d, e
4. f   9. d
5. d, e   10. b

4A. EXPANDING THE TOPIC

Suggested answers to follow-up questions (page 65)
1. A very serious form of arthritis.
2. He wanted to fight the disease.
3. If negative emotions bring negative changes to the body, positive emotions should bring positive changes. Laughter has a positive therapeutic value.

4. Watching funny movies and reading funny books.
5. He was able to overcome his disease.

4B. LINKING READINGS ONE AND TWO
Suggested answers
1. *Similarities:* Both Norman Cousins's laugh therapy and Christian Scientists' therapy through prayer believe the mind plays an essential part in healing. They both believe that conventional medicine is not the only answer. *Differences:* Norman Cousins believes that both conventional therapy and laugh therapy work well together. In contrast, the Christian Scientists believe that using prayer is sufficient. They sometimes refuse conventional therapy.
2. Answers will vary.

5A. EXPLORING LANGUAGE
2. D   7. D
3. S   8. S
4. D   9. S
5. D   10. S
6. S   11. D

5B. WORKING WITH WORDS: Analogies
2. a   5. b
3. c   6. c
4. c   7. b

6A. GRAMMAR: Past Unreal Conditionals
1 a. T/F
   b. T/T
   c. T/F
2 2. F/F   6. F/T
   3. T/T   7. F/T
   4. T/T   8. F/F
   5. T/T
3 Possible answers
   2. If James C. Wilson had gone to a homeopathic doctor, he might not have had problems.
   3. If Cousins hadn't read extensively about alternative medicine, he might not have turned to alternative treatments.
   4. Cousins might not have gotten better if he hadn't tried laugh therapy.

5. If Futch had been a Christian Scientist, he wouldn't have given his daughter drugs.
6. If the teacher hadn't noticed that something was wrong, she wouldn't have called Amy's parents.
7. If Cousins had liked his doctor's treatment plan, he wouldn't have developed his own laugh therapy treatment.

6B. STYLE: Opinion Essays
1 Suggested answers
   a. The Hermansons should not have been convicted.
   b. Her background demonstrates that she is a knowledgeable and intelligent person.
   c. She uses her own medical experience and the medical treatment of her own children.
   d. Her conclusion is that treatment should be left to the individual; it is a constitutional right. Children die under conventional medical treatment, too, and no one brings those parents to court.

2 Answers will vary.

UNIT 4 ◆
THE CALM AFTER THE STORM

2B. VOCABULARY FOR COMPREHENSION
2. patience   7. straight
3. hope   8. divert
4. thick   9. inevitable
5. dark   10. search
6. glowing   11. blink

3B. READING FOR MAIN IDEAS
After Dark

Physical State	Emotional State
so dark, can't see the palm of his hand	terrorized
cold, wet	felt more alone in the dark
still not hungry or thirsty	desperate
feels his body in a realm that belongs to sea creatures	

Early the Following Morning

Physical State	Emotional State
has had no sleep	still hoping to see a plane
cold was more intense	still desperate
body glowed with afternoon sun embedded under his skin	
knee hurts	
water is penetrating his bones	

3C. READING FOR DETAILS

Suggested answers
1. He was afraid he wouldn't see a rescue plane.
2. He felt more alone and he was afraid of the sea creatures.
3. He learned to sit in (the basket of) the life raft, not on the gunwale.
4. He would be closer to the sea creatures.
5. He constantly looked at his watch.
6. Because time passed really slowly.
7. His main concern was spotting a ship.

3D. READING BETWEEN THE LINES

Answers will vary.

4A. EXPANDING THE TOPIC

Possible answers to follow-up questions (page 85)
1. Some of the damages were: telephone and telegraph systems disrupted; water mains burst; collapsed and smashed buildings
2. There were no crowds, no shouting or yelling, no hysteria, no disorder.

4B. LINKING READINGS ONE AND TWO

Possible answers
1. Man is helpless against nature.
2. The atmosphere becomes quiet and time seems to move slowly.
3. People's reactions seem to change from one of shock and panic to one of resignation and acceptance of what has happened.
4. The people have nothing left. Suddenly, their lives have changed completely with one act of nature. They have lost control of their lives. There is a calm acceptance of doom.

5A. EXPLORING LANGUAGE

Suggested answers
loneliness: immense, infinite, endless

sea: immense, icy, infinite, red, stubborn, tranquil, vast, endless, dark, abandoned, dense
city: immense, doomed, glowing, icy, tranquil, stubborn, vast, endless, dark, abandoned
patience: immense, infinite, stubborn, tranquil, vast, endless
wind: icy, strong, stubborn, tranquil
sky: glowing, immense, red, infinite, vast, endless, dark

5B. WORKING WITH WORDS: Synonyms

2. stowed
3. hold out
4. stuff
5. fling
6. cunning
7. contrivances
8. doomed
9. panic-stricken
10. hemmed in

6A. GRAMMAR: Identifying Adjective Clauses

1 a. (A woman) who wept, (a man) who was excited, (a person) who was panic-stricken
   b. That you can't stop checking (it)
   c. (The afternoon) when I searched the horizon for airplanes
   d. Who, that, when/nouns or noun phrases

2
2. where	7. which
3. which	8. that
4. in which	9. who
5. when	10. where
6. that	

3 Suggested answers
   2. I lived in the town which was destroyed by a tornado.
   3. Forest fires kill many animals that live in national parks.
   4. A hurricane is a tropical storm which has winds of at least 73 miles per hour.
   5. We found the mountain climber who had gotten lost during the storm.
   6. My flight was canceled because of the storm that dropped 32 inches of snow on the city.
   7. The avalanche which trapped the climbers occurred at night.

8. I spoke with a man who survived 38 days alone on a life raft.
9. The house which the flood destroyed had been in Mary's family for over 200 years.
10. The reporter who wrote a story about Hurricane Andrew was hit by lightning.
11. The afternoon when the forest fire broke out was sunny and hot.

6A. STYLE: Descriptive Writing

1 1. b   3. a
    2. b   4. a

2 Answers will vary.

3 Answers will vary.

UNIT 5 ◆
FROM TRASH TO TREASURE

2B. VOCABULARY FOR COMPREHENSION

a. 10   f. 3
b. 4   g. 1
c. 8   h. 5
d. 2   i. 6
e. 7   j. 9

3A. INTRODUCING THE TOPIC

The pun is the word *worm*. The common expression is *a warm welcome*, not *a worm welcome*. The pun suggests a link become composting and worms; it suggests that the St. Paul couple may have given worms a warm welcome.

3B. READING FOR MAIN IDEAS

a. 5   d. 4 or 2
b. 3   e. 1
c. 2

3C. READING FOR DETAILS

1. "I ordered worms during the winter."/Worms don't travel well in winter. She should have ordered them at a different time of year.
2. "I put them in a cardboard shoebox."/There should be a screen at the bottom for drainage.
3. "I filled the box with dry newspaper."/They prefer moist bins.

4. "I would give them . . . chicken . . . orange peels."/Meat scraps shouldn't be added because they create odors. She should have added eggshells to balance the acid in the orange peels.
5. "I set my apartment . . . for 80 degrees."/She should have kept the apartment between 65–77 degrees.
6. "After six months . . . I decided to change their bedding."/The worms should be sorted and restarted in fresh bedding every four months.

3D. READING BETWEEN THE LINES

1. b   3. b   5. a, b, c
2. b, c 4. c

4B. LINKING READINGS ONE AND TWO

Suggested answers

Impact on Society	Vermi-composting	Earthship Homes	Other Programs
Benefits to the individual	Provides compost for garden. Reduces waste in home.	They can be less expensive than conventional homes. Owner can participate in building.	Answers will vary.
Benefits to the environment	It provides compost and lessens waste in public land-fills.	They reuse otherwise useless tires. There are fewer trees cut down than with conventional home building.	Answers will vary.
Ease of care or upkeep	It's easy to maintain. It's clean and quiet.	It's easy and economical.	Answers will vary.
Cost	It's very cheap.	They are cheaper to build and heat than conventional homes.	Answers will vary.

5A. EXPLORING LANGUAGE

2. a. recycle
   b. recyclable
   c. recycling
   d. recycled

3. **a.** initiated
   b. initiation
4. **a.** compost
   b. composting
5. **a.** reproduce
   b. reproductive
6. **a.** store
   b. storage
7. **a.** participation
   b. participate
8. **a.** fertilization
   b. fertile
   c. fertility

5B. WORKING WITH WORDS

1. recycling
2. initiated
3. landfill
4. innovative
5. compost
6. recyclable
7. participation
8. reproduce
9. innovations

6A. GRAMMAR: Adversity and Obligation in the Past

1 b

2 2. Emily shouldn't have fed her worms just orange and grapefruit peels. She should have added eggshells to their diet.
3. Juan Carlos could have used old tires to build his earthship. He should not have built it with new tires.
4. He shouldn't have thrown all those compostable materials away. He ought to have composted them.
5. Mr. Mergenthal shouldn't have ordered them late in the year (in the winter). He might have taken better care of them.
6. He shouldn't have faced all the windows north. He ought to have faced the windows south.

3 Answers will vary.

6B. STYLE: Cause and Effect

1 **a. Cause Clauses**
- Because the earth and rubber from the tires trap heat
- The worms don't like the light
- Since Mr. Mergenthal's worms weren't thriving
- The homes are totally self-sufficient
- As a result of these homes being made with old automobile tires

b. Effect Clauses
- Heating is never required
- So they go to the middle of the pile
- Mary Mergenthal placed a classified ad in the newspaper to ask for advice
- They are very affordable
- They are very affordable

c. because, so, since, consequently, as a result

2 as a result, because, because, since

Cause	Effect
1. Houses are very expensive.	Many people have to invest all their savings.
2. They are made with old automobile tires.	Earthship homes are affordable.
3. They are well insulated.	They don't create high heating or cooling bills.
4. Owners can participate in the construction.	The cost is controlled.

3 2. C/E The ozone layer is becoming depleted; therefore, there are more cases of skin cancer each year.
3. C/E The world's rainforests are rapidly shrinking; consequently, there will be fewer valuable medicines available.
4. E/C Climate changes from global warming are making weather patterns more extreme; as a result, there are more heat waves and cold snaps.
5. E/C Because people have been throwing hazardous waste in landfills for years, drinking water near many landfills has become contaminated.
6. C/E People have been cutting down large areas of forests; for this reason, many animal species have become endangered.

7. C/E   Since Julian didn't use fertilizer in his garden, his plants didn't grow very well.

④ Answers will vary.

UNIT 6 ◆
GIVE AND LEARN

2A. BACKGROUND

2. f and a   4. e and a
3. d and a   5. b and a

2B. VOCABULARY FOR COMPREHENSION

❶

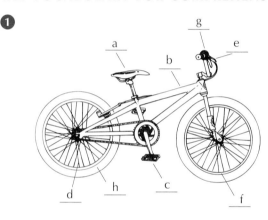

❷ 2. modest   8. hate
3. allow   9. take
4. misery   10. lessen
5. uncertain   11. complete
6. order   12. saddened
7. sell

3B. READING FOR MAIN IDEAS

Suggested answers follow.
1. a young boy who likes to work on bikes and give them away.
2. he donates his time and energy to other people.
3. giving him bikes to fix up and money to buy them.
4. it makes him feel good.

3C. READING FOR DETAILS

Suggested answers.

Benefits	Examples
Gives a sense of . . .	After he built the first bikes for the Kilbarchin boys, he felt very good knowing that they loved the bikes.
Opens people's eyes . . .	He built bikes for all kinds of people in need: women in women's shelter, people with AIDS, and people in a housing project.
One successful . . .	He continued to build bikes after the Kilbarchin project.
Helps you find out . . .	He found out he could take on a big project and complete it. He found out he was good at rebuilding bikes.

3D. READING BETWEEN THE LINES

1. b   5. b
2. c   6. a
3. a   7. a
4. c   8. b

4A. EXPANDING THE TOPIC

Suggested answers for the follow-up chart (page 136)

For Mandatory Volunteering	Against Mandatory Volunteering
1. Constructive way to spend time.	1. Volunteering is a personal choice.
2. A way to support your interests.	2. It's an extracurricular activity (personal choice).
3. Gets kids involved in the community.	3. Many students already volunteer.
4. Some people would not know how great an experience volunteering is unless it were required.	4. Students may become resentful and never volunteer again.
	5. Many students don't have time.
	6. It's an oxymoron.

4B. LINKING READINGS ONE AND TWO
Answers will vary.

5A. EXPLORING LANGUAGE
Answers will vary.

5B. WORKING WITH WORDS: Phrase Verbs

    1. a   6. c
    2. b   7. c
    3. c   8. b
❶ 4. a   9. c
    5. c   10. b

6A. GRAMMAR: Tag Questions

1 a. the statement and the tag
b. isn't he, does he, didn't they
c. The verb is negative. The verb is positive.

2
1. l
2. f
3. d
4. h
5. j
6. a
7. b
8. e
9. c
10. k
11. g
12. i

3
2. is he
3. haven't they
4. isn't it
5. should they
6.
7. won't they
8.
9. were they
10.

6A. STYLE: Punctuation

1 a. the third sentence
b. the first sentence
c. the second sentence
d. semicolon, colon, dash

2
2. a. The dash sets off extra information.
3. b. The colon illustrates or gives further information about a noun phrase.
4. a. The dash introduces parenthetical information.
5. b. The colon introduces a quotation.
6. b. The semicolon connects two closely related independent clauses.

3
2. — (dash)
3. : (colon)
4. — (dash)

UNIT 7 ◆
HOMING IN ON EDUCATION

2A. BACKGROUND

Suggested answers
1. quality of education, freedom from peer pressure, freedom from harassment and bullying from other children.
2. of inadequate preparation for college, inadequate assessment, emotional development

3. Answers will vary.

2B. VOCABULARY FOR COMPREHENSION

a. 11
b. 4
c. 7
d. 10
e. 5
f. 9
g. 2
h. 6
i. 8
j. 3
k. 1

3B. READING FOR MAIN IDEAS

1. MI
2. SD
3. MI
4. MI
5. SD
6. SD
7. MI
8. SD

3C. READING FOR DETAILS

1. a, b
2. b, c
3. a, b
4. a, c
5. a, b

3D. READING BETWEEN THE LINES

Answers will vary. Possible answers.

Issues	Traditional School	Home School
peer pressure and bullying	Lots of peer pressure and bullying.	Students don't have to worry about this because they study at home.
socialization skills	Children socialize with lots of other children at school—socialization skills are not an issue.	Could be a problem—children may have limited opportunities to socialize with other children.
teaching methods/materials	Teacher decides on methods and materials. Teacher teaches.	Students and parents decide together on methods and materials—allows more freedom.
role of teachers, role of parents	Teachers are the authority and are in control. Parents have small role at school.	Parents are the teachers. Parents are directly involved.
self-discipline and motivation	Students do not have to be as self-disciplined as home schoolers. Motivation comes from students' interest in teacher's materials and methods.	Motivation comes from the student. Students must be very self-disciplined.
student interest in learning	Limited to what the teacher provides and what the student is interested in.	Students can make the learning as interesting as he/she wants because the student is directly involved.

4A. EXPANDING THE TOPIC
Suggested answers to follow-up chart

	Teaching at Home Hits New High with Internet	**The Fun They Had**
1.	The teacher can be parents, community people, special tutors, . . .	The teacher is a computer.
2.	At home, in a community center, all around.	At home.
3.	The parents and students.	The computer and inspector.
4.	Local authorities and parents.	Parents, computer, and inspector.
5.	At community centers and clubs, after and during school hours.	With neighbors, after school time, during breaks.
6.	They like it a lot.	They don't like it.

4B. LINKING READINGS ONE AND TWO
Answers will vary.

5A. EXPLORING VOCABULARY
Answers will vary.

5B. WORKING WITH WORDS: American and British Spelling

British Spelling	American Spelling
specialise	specialize
institutionalised	institutionalized
behaviour	behavior
honour	honor
cancelled	canceled
connexion	connection
learnt	learned
neighbour	neighbor
mediaeval	medieval
spelt	spelled
memorise	memorize
equalling	equaling
smelt	smelled

6A. GRAMMAR: Direct and Indirect Speech
① a. Direct speech has commas and quotation marks.
b. The verb tense and pronouns change in indirect speech. *That* is added.

② 2. a   5. b
3. b   6. a
4. c   7. b

③ 2. The inspector told Margie's mother (that) he thought the geography sector had been a little too difficult.
3. He added (that) he'd slowed it up to a ten-year level.
4. Tommy said that was the old kind of school that they had had hundreds and hundreds of years before.
5. Margie told Tommy (that) her mother said a teacher had to be adjusted to fit the mind of each boy and girl it taught.
6. Tommy told Margie (that) she could read the book with him again the next day.

6B. STYLE: Concessions
① 1. Home schooling
2. Inadequately prepared parents and weak curricula
3. By acknowledging the side of traditional schools, and then presenting his own opinion
4. The opinion of traditional schools

② Suggested answers
2. Though critics maintain there is no way to assess home schoolers, supporters of home schooling say that they are following a standard curriculum.
3. Although critics question whether home schoolers are being taught the basics, home schoolers are gaining in numbers every year.
4. Critics worry that traditional school students do not take school seriously in spite of the fact that many successful students graduate from traditional schools every year.
5. Home schooling is apparently very successful despite the fact that many people still believe in the benefits of traditional schooling.

③ Answers will vary.

UNIT 8 ◆ WE'VE COME A LONG WAY

1B. SHARING INFORMATION
② 1. 1961, Soviet Union
2. 1963, Soviet Union
3. 1969, United States of America
4. 1975
5. MIR
6. Answers will vary.

2A. BACKGROUND
Answers will vary.

2B. VOCABULARY FOR COMPREHENSION

2. a	**7.** c
3. c	**8.** a
4. b	**9.** b
5. a	**10.** c
6. b	**11.** b

3B. READING FOR MAIN IDEAS
5
6
2
4
3
1

3C. READING FOR DETAILS

1. c	**4.** a	**7.** c
2. b	**5.** c	**8.** a
3. b	**6.** c	**9.** b

3D. READING BETWEEN THE LINES
Answers will vary.

4A. EXPANDING THE TOPIC
Suggested answers to follow-up questions (page 192)
1. It was their link to the outside world. It brought news and supplies.
2. Books, fresh food, and candy

4B. LINKING READINGS ONE AND TWO
Suggested answers

	Yuri Gagarin's Mission	Shannon Lucid's Mission
Objective or goal of the mission	Enter into orbit	Scientific experiments
Length of the mission	89 minutes	6 months (Shannon Lucid) Since 1986 (Mir)
Number of people on the mission	One	Three
Nationality of the people involved	Soviet	American and Russian
Physical conditions of the spaceship	Very small	Larger living spaces with kitchen, sleeping quarters, and bath

5A. EXPLORING LANGUAGE: Paraphrasing
2. different—an impromptu lunch is not planned; a scheduled lunch is planned
3. similar
4. similar
5. similar
6. different—outer space and outside are different
7. different—in sentence **a** the Jello is excellent, in sentence **b** the idea is excellent
8. different—donned means put on, the opposite of took off

5B. WORKING WITH WORDS: Phrasal Verbs

2. c	**6.** b
3. a	**7.** c
4. a	**8.** a
5. c	

6A. GRAMMAR: Phrasal Verbs

❶ **a.** called off, dropped out, thought back on
b. <u>Call</u> means shout or cry; <u>call off</u> means cancel
c. <u>Drop</u> means to fall or let fall; <u>drop out</u> means to quit
d. <u>Think</u> means to believe or reason; <u>think back on</u> means to remember

❷ **1. b.** invented
   c. regained consciousness
2. a. participate
   b. disassemble
   c. dominate
3. a. continue
   b. leave
   c. review
4. a. loose speed
   b. be dominated by
   c. break
5. a. not work
   b. departed
   c. removed

❸ **1.** departed—took off
   approached—came up to
   participate—take part in
   break—fall apart

2. invented—came up with
dominated—took over
participating—taking part in
continue—go on

6B. STYLE: Chronological Order—Expressing Time

❶ a. "The crew of Mir had quite a smelly surprise when they opened *Progress*," "Gagarin felt wonderful while he was in space," and "during the time they are in space, crew members do valuable scientific research."

b. "As soon as Shepard heard about Gagarin's successful space flight, he became depressed."

c. One event takes place before or after another.

❷ 2. After Yuri (had) completed special courses and entered the Air Force, he became a fighter pilot.

3. As soon as Lucid discovered there was a refrigerator on board, she asked for Jello.

4. The three astronauts opened the hatch after *Progress* (had) docked on Mir.

5. Before Lucid arrived with different food, the cosmonauts had never eaten Jello.

6. As soon as the astronauts started to open the hatch to *Progress*, they smelled the food.

7. During the time the Russians and Americans were enemies, the space programs began.

8. Until the cold war (had) ended, there was not a lot of cooperation in space exploration.

❸ 2. b   5. b
3. a   6. a
4. b

UNIT 9 ◆
THE GRASS IS ALWAYS GREENER

2B. VOCABULARY FOR COMPREHENSION

1. a   6. b
2. a   7. b
3. b   8. b
4. b   9. a
5. b

3B. READING FOR MAIN IDEAS

Suggested answers
1. F. Lucy was uncomfortable with the newness. She wanted to go back to where she came from.
2. F. She was disappointed by the reality, ordinariness, dirtiness of New York. Everything was new: the elevator, the food, the climate.
3. T.
4. F. Lucy felt she lived in a "not so nice" situation and wanted to go somewhere else. She was generally sad and discontent with life.
5. T.
6. F. Her dreams turned into the disappointment of reality. She suffered from homesickness.

3C. READING FOR DETAILS

Suggested answers
1. The weather was not warm and sunny; it was cold and grey.
2. She didn't travel by boat; she traveled by plane.
3. She didn't think the sights were beautiful; she thought they looked ordinary, dirty, and worn down.
4. She didn't have a refrigerator in Antigua.
5. The sun was not bright; it was pale yellow.
6. The dress was not right; it was not warm enough.
7. The weather was not warm; it was cold.
8. She didn't eat pink mullet and green figs; she only thought about eating them.

3D. READING BETWEEN THE LINES

Suggested answers
1. Things she thought about to make her happy.
2. New things can make you confused and feel out of place.
3. Because she's confused by or doesn't understand all the new things.
4. Because in her own country, she knew what to expect and what was expected of her.
5. She can't run away from her feelings or your problems.

4A. EXPANDING THE TOPIC

Answers to follow-up questions (page 218) will vary.

4B. LINKING READINGS ONE AND TWO
Suggested answers

Theme	Example from "Poor Visitor"	Example from "Nostalgia"
1. weather	Everything is cold and gray. The sun isn't warm.	He's dying of the cold.
2. food	She always ate her grandmother's cooking.	He longs for a dish of chicken and rice and a good cup of coffee.
3. search for a better life	Lucy was unhappy in her native land and thought she could improve her life in America.	He came to establish his store in New York.
4. homesickness	She misses her family.	He misses his country.
5. New York is not what they expected	Everything looks ordinary, dirty, and worn down.	What he sees around him is a sad panorama.

5A. EXPLORING VOCABULARY: Compound Words

Compound Word	First Word	Second Word	Your Example (Possible answers)
2. undergarment	under	garment	underground
3. homesickness	home	sickness	homework
4. daydream	day	dream	daylight
5. overcast	over	cast	downcast
6. outgrown	out	grown	overgrown
7. grandmother	grand	mother	grandfather

5B. WORKING WITH WORDS: Sentence Completion

1. outgrown
2. overcast
3. grandmother
4. daydream
5. lifeboat
6. homesickness
7. undergarment

6A. GRAMMAR: Past Perfect

❶ **a.** She imagined what New York looked like first.
   b. No, she put on her summer dress first.
   c. Her longing to go there happened first.
   d. The verb tenses and the time words (by the time, when, before).

❷ 2. 2/1   6. 1/2
   3. 1/2   7. 1/2
   4. 2/1   8. 1/2
   5. 1/2

❸ Answers will vary.

6B. STYLE: Comparisons and Contrasts

❶ 1. In the same way introduces things that are similar. While, in contrast, and whereas introduce things that are different.
   2. The topics are: weather, living conditions, food, and problems.

❷ Suggested answers
   2. Dávila dislikes harsh winter with its bare trees in the same way Lucy dislikes the pale winter sun.
   3. Lucy misses her grandmother's home cooking. Similarly, Dávila misses his country's native food.
   4. Dávila opened his own store in New York; on the other hand, Lucy worked for a family as a nanny.
   5. Lucy is a young woman; in contrast, Dávila is an older man.
   6. While "Poor Visitor" was written in the last half of the twentieth century, "Nostalgia" was written in the first half of the twentieth century.
   7. Dávila misses his culture whereas Lucy misses her family.
   8. Jamaica Kincaid was born in Antigua; however, Dávila was born in Puerto Rico.

❸ Answers will vary.

UNIT 10 ◆ TAKE IT OR LEAVE IT

2B. VOCABULARY FOR COMPREHENSION

1. ostentatious
2. unobtrusive
3. visual recognition
4. remote control
5. monitor
6. database
7. information highway

8. console
9. network
10. interface
11. image browsing

3B. READING FOR MAIN IDEAS

1. a
2. b
3. b

3C. READING FOR DETAILS

I. Began thinking about home in the late 1980s
  A. Style preferences
    1. craftsmanship
    2. not ostentatious
  B. Must accommodate sophisticated and changing technology
    1. not obtrusive
    2. functions as servant, not master

II. Selected the perfect property
  A. Location
    1. shore of Lake Washington
    2. easy commuting distance
  B. Living space—average size.
    1. living room
      a. size = 14 × 28 feet
      b. areas for watching television or listening to music
    2. other cozy spaces for one or two people
    3. large reception hall
      a. accommodates one hundred

III. Electronic pin controls the home environment
  A. Tells the home who and where you are
  B. House uses pin information to meet your needs
    1. light follows you
    2. music follows you
    3. movie or news or phone call follows you

IV. Other readily and easily available technology
  A. Hand-held remotes and consoles in each room
    1. controls tell monitors:
      a. to become visible
      b. what to display
  B. Visual displays
    1. large choice
      a. thousands of pictures
      b. recordings
      c. movies
      d. television programs

e. many options for selecting information
    2. house can control visual displays
      a. materialize when you enter and vanish when you leave rooms
      b. house can change programming depending on who is in the room

V. Home has a state-of-the-art database
  A. First homeowner to have it
  B. Database has more than 1 million still images
    1. includes photographs
    2. includes art reproductions
  C. Guests can call up anything they like
    1. portraits of presidents
    2. pictures of sunsets
    3. skiing in the Andes, etc.

VI. Future availability of quality images
  A. On the information highway
  B. In homes in the future

VII. Fears about the information highway
  A. Reduce the time people spend socializing
    1. homes will become too cozy and self-contained
    2. people will become isolated
  B. Not in agreement
    1. people are social animals
    2. highway only provides more entertainment and communication options
      a. personal
      b. professional
      c. employment
    3. people will decide to spend as much time out of their homes

VIII. Benefits of the information highway
  A. Makes it easier to:
    1. maintain distant relationships
    2. find new companions
  B. Makes life more interesting
    1. people will meet in person
    2. meet people with common interests

IX. Conclusion: Experimenting and the future
  A. Bill Gates enjoys experimenting and may decide to
    1. conceal monitors
    2. throw away pins
  B. Hopes
    1. may like everything
    2. wonder how he got along without it

3D. READING BETWEEN THE LINES

Suggested answers
1. hand-held remotes and discreet consoles
2. cozy spaces for one or two people
3. automatic lighting
4. personalized music and a large database of images
5. you can keep up with friends and form new relationships
6. Bill Gates is flexible about changing his plans if something doesn't work out or if something needs to be modified

5A. EXPLORING LANGUAGE: Word Forms

Noun	Verb	Adjective
behavior	behave	X
brightness	brighten	bright
communication	communicate	communicable
convention	X	conventional
entertainment	entertain	entertaining
friendship	befriend	friendly
information	inform	informative
material	materialize	material
ostentation	X	ostentatious
television	televise	televised
vision	visualize	visual/visible

5B. WORKING WITH WORDS

1. b. entertain
   c. entertainment
   d. visions
   e. visual
   f. entertaining

2. a. communicate
   b. communication
   c. information
   d. informative
   e. inform

3. a. friendships
   b. friendly
   c. materialize
   d. materials
   e. material

6A. GRAMMAR: Future Progressive

1. a. future events
   b. the fact that events are ongoing

2 2. he'll be meeting
3. he'll be trying
4. he'll be dictating
5. talks
6. he'll be eating
7. will be testing
8. he'll be
9. eats
10. he'll be talking
11. he'll be having
12. he'll be sleeping
13. won't be waiting

3 2. In February, Allison won't be visiting Walt Whitman's home in New York. She'll be going on a winter camping excursion.
3. In March, Allison will be building a model of the cabin at Walden Pond.
4. In April, Allison won't be walking the beaches of Cape Cod. She'll be building the cabin.
5. In May, Allison won't be building the cabin. She'll be living in it.
6. In June, Allison won't be living in the model of Walden Pond cabin. She'll be walking the beaches of Cape Cod and writing about her experiences.
7. In July, Allison will be traveling by boat on the Concord River.
8. In August, Allison won't be studying transcendentalist philosophy. She'll be taking the railroad from Concord to Maine.
9. In September, Allison won't be taking the railroad from Concord, Massachusetts. She'll be living in the backwoods of Maine.
10. In October, Allison won't be living in the backwoods of Maine. She'll be traveling by boat on the Merrimack River.
11. In November, Allison won't be traveling by boat on the Merrimack River. She'll be studying transcendentalist philosophy.
12. In December, Allison will be writing about her experiences.

6B. STYLE: Outlining

1 a. fears about the information highway, benefits of the information highway
b. A, B
c. 1, 2
d. a, b, c
e. The outline presents all the information in the paragraph in the same order.

❷ 2. eight-feet posts
4. large window on each side
6. one door at each end

❸ Suggested outline

I. Bill Gates's and Henry David Thoreau's philosophies on technology
   A. Bill Gates: Technology is necessary
      1. essential for advancement of mankind
         a. enhances our lives
         b. enables us to live longer and better lives
   B. Henry David Thoreau: Technology is unnecessary
      1. stops advancement of mankind
         a. takes us away from living truthfully
         b. stops us from enjoying the simple pleasures in life

❹ Answers will vary.